THE ART OF LIFE

GILLIAN E. HANSCOMBE

THE ART OF LIFE

Dorothy Richardson and the Development of Feminist Consciousness

All Rights Reserved. No part of this publication may be reproduced in any form or by any means without the prior permission of the publishers.

Library of Congress Cataloging in Publication Data

Hanscombe, Gillian E.
The art of life.

Bibliography: p.
1. Richardson, Dorothy Miller, 1873–1957.
Pilgrimage. 2. Richardson, Dorothy Miller, 1873–1957
—Political and social views. 3. Feminism and
literature. I. Title.
PR6035.I34Z72 1983 823′.912 82-22589
ISBN 0-8214-0739-2
ISBN 0-8214-0740-6 (pbk.)

Originally published by Peter Owen Limited, London.
First American Edition published 1983.
Printed in the United States of America.
All rights reserved.

First published 1982
© Gillian E. Hanscombe 1982

For my sister
Kristine

CONTENTS

Within me . . . the *third* child, the longed-for son, the two natures, equally matched, mingle and fight? It is their struggle that keeps me adrift, so variously interested and strongly attracted, now here, now there? Which will win? . . . Feeling so identified with both, she could not imagine either of them set aside. Then her life *would* be the battlefield of her two natures.

Dorothy Miller Richardson
Revolving Lights

I wouldn't have a man's – *consciousness*, for anything.

The Tunnel

ACKNOWLEDGEMENTS

There are many people without whose valuable assistance and encouragement this book could not have been completed. I am particularly indebted to Mrs Sheena Odle, executrix of the estate of Dorothy Miller Richardson, for making available material collected by her mother-in-law, Rose Isserlis Odle, for permission to quote copyright material, and for her time and interest. I am indebted also to Mrs Elizabeth Turner, Dorothy Richardson's niece, for her reminiscences of Dorothy Richardson and Alan Odle and for allowing me to examine materials in her possession. I am grateful to Virago Press for granting permission to quote extracts from *Pilgrimage.* Special thanks are due to D.K. for making available materials in his possession and for his perceptive comments on Dorothy Richardson, Alan Odle and his mother Veronica Grad. I should like to thank the Beinecke Rare Book and Manuscript Library in Yale University for permission to reproduce letters from Veronica Grad to Rose Odle in the Appendix, and Miss Marjorie Wynn, research librarian in charge of the Richardson papers held there. Her personal interest and efficiency have been considerably greater than could reasonably have been expected. Dr Gloria Glikin Fromm offered extremely helpful discussion of some essential points during my research for the doctoral thesis upon which this book is based. I am particularly appreciative of the warmth, intelligence and high professional skills given by Dan Franklin, my editor at Peter Owen Ltd. Finally, it is a pleasure to express my gratitude to Mrs Dorothy Bednarowska, Fellow and Tutor of St Anne's College, University of Oxford, whose patience, guidance and academic acumen during the five years I spent at Oxford working on Dorothy Richardson were given with the utmost generosity.

G.H.

PREFACE

Dorothy Richardson's *Pilgrimage* is a long sequence-novel in thirteen volumes whose nature insists that it is read thematically. It would be impossible in a book of this length to deal adequately with the range of inference and connotation it evokes, even if that were the purpose of this study. An elucidation, furthermore, which undertakes to describe the artistic consequences of Dorothy Richardson's particular vision at once takes the researcher outside the bounds of *Pilgrimage* to her personal correspondence and other writings and further inside the terms of reference which the fiction implies, so that the usual parameters which divide art and life are questioned. It has been impossible, therefore, for reasons of space, to treat each volume with equal attention. There is relatively little critical analysis offered of some of the middle volumes, whereas more attention is given to the opening three and three of the closing ones, since the particular feminist vision that sustained Richardson is suggested at the beginning of her story and enacted towards the end. For this reason those volumes must assume priority within the context of this discussion. In tracing other areas of interest, for example the relationship between Richardson and H.G. Wells (as enacted by Miriam and Wilson in *Pilgrimage*), closer attention to the detail of the middle volumes would be more appropriate.

The first eleven chapter-volumes of *Pilgrimage* were published between 1915 and 1935 : *Pointed Roofs* (1915), *Backwater* (1916), *Honeycomb* (1917), *The Tunnel* (1919), *Interim* (1919), *Deadlock* (1921), *Revolving Lights* (1923), *The Trap* (1925), *Oberland* (1927) and *Dawn's Left Hand* (1931) by Duckworth, and *Clear Horizon* (1935) by J.M. Dent and The Cresset Press. The next volume, *Dimple Hill,* was first published in the Dent Collected Edition of 1938, and the final volume, *March Moonlight,* in the Dent Collected Edition of 1967.

The 1967 Collected Edition of *Pilgrimage* has been cited throughout. There are several reasons for preferring this edition as the most authoritative text. First, and most obviously, it is complete, since neither *Dimple Hill* nor *March Moonlight* was ever issued separately. Secondly, Richardson always insisted that each novel was a 'chapter' of the whole and that all the volumes should appear and be read as one sequence. Thirdly, manuscript versions, except in three instances, have not survived.

In February 1949, desperate to help a relative in America, Richardson wrote to an American friend disclosing her attempt to sell the manuscript of *Pointed Roofs*: 'At the same time, I am trying, through Knopf, to discover a possible purchaser of the only *Pilgrimage* ms I ever kept: that of *Pointed Roofs.*' [1] This manuscript is now held by the Beinecke Rare Book and Manuscript Library in Yale University. A part of the manuscript of *Dimple Hill* is held by the Humanities Research Centre in the University of Texas at Austin. In her biography, *Dorothy Richardson,*[2] Fromm makes reference to a surviving manuscript of *Dawn's Left Hand,* which is now in the McFarlin Library, University of Tulsa, Oklahoma.

Richardson herself, as she makes clear in a letter to S.S. Koteliansky, was not satisfied with the Duckworth first editions of the first ten volumes of *Pilgrimage*:

> And here, for you, is *Pilgrimage*, which has, so to speak, never been published. Ten chapter-volumes have found their way into print, into an execrable lay-out & disfigured by hosts of undiscovered printer's errors & a punctuation that is the result of corrections, intermittent, by an orthodox 'reader', & corrections of those corrections, also intermittent, by the author. . . . I believe, all told, that a decent, corrected edition – in the form of two, or three, of the short volumes bound together – would pay its way. . . . A real edition by a real publisher would greatly comfort me & might make it possible for me to finish the book.[3]

Her terms for an authoritative edition of *Pilgrimage* she laid out as follows:

> But really my *Pilgrimage* business is very simple: The rights are available for any reputable publisher who will:
> 1) pay Duckworth, (a) £57.19.3, which is the amount of my mortgage still not paid off (b) £242 -, for stock, plates & moulds.
> 2) issue a definitive, corrected edition, unlimited, of *Pilgrimage* in four volumes, beginning either at once or almost immediately after the publication of the new volume, now half written.
> 3) pay £30 advance royalties on the new volume.[4]

Further, there is Richardson's assessment of single-volume publication:

> Of late years, & this is, incidentally, an important factor, there have been, uniformly, rather more sales of *Pointed Roofs* than of the subsequent volumes, clearly indicating that a proportion of new readers

> falls away after reading this small crude chapter. I am not alone in believing that these, if they had read the first three volumes in one cover, would have gone on to the rest.
>
> For this reason, & for many others, I still believe that the plan I outlined to Mr Koteliansky, & that Duckworths would long ago have followed, had not the early volumes been mistakenly set up in varying types, is sound. Namely the publication, at intervals of a few months, of sets of volumes at 7/6d each, up to & including *Clear Horizon* - - - -* the number of persons who write to me suggesting and pleading for a compact edition of the scattered chapters must represent a crowd.[5]

Dent, who did finally publish the Collected Edition, took over the agreements between Richardson and Duckworth after *Dawn's Left Hand. Clear Horizon*, the next volume, was the only one to be issued separately by Dent. Duckworth's *Interim* stock was taken over by Dent and issued with an attached flap. Manuscripts are normally returned to authors and there is no trace of any Richardson manuscripts in the Dent archives. The Duckworth first editions, in addition to using varying types, have double quotation marks, whereas the Dent editions use single quotation marks. This was presumably a matter of house style.

In the matter of foreign translations, Richardson seems to have been equally unfortunate. It was her consistent opinion that both her publishers failed to take an intelligent initiative in creating a European readership for *Pilgrimage*.[6] *Pointed Roofs*, always the most popular chapter-volume of the sequence, was published in French in 1965, after Richardson's death. A proposed Spanish translation was rejected by the Spanish censor. The only other published translation is a Japanese edition of *Pointed Roofs*.

G.H.

* In this and subsequent extracts from Richardson's writings, dashes (- - - -) indicate an omission. The prose style of *Pilgrimage* is characterized by a fragmentation and modification of the syntax of English sentences and by an idiosyncratic punctuation, including the use of repeated stops to indicate gaps in the flow of consciousness. It is also a technique Richardson occasionally uses in her other writings. To avoid confusion, therefore, the normal academic conventions appropriate to quotation are modified in this book: in quotations from Richardson's texts, three dashes (- - -) indicate omissions from the portion of the text being quoted, where the omission belongs within a sentence. Similarly, four dashes (- - - -) indicate an omission that includes two or more part-sentences or a new paragraph. Sequences of stops (. . .) and (. . . .) appearing in quotations are always Richardson's own.

NOTES AND REFERENCES

1 DR to Bernice Elliott, 27 February, 1949.

2 Gloria G. Fromm, *Dorothy Richardson: A Biography*, University of Illinois Press, 1977. (Gloria G. Fromm published previously under the name Gloria Glikin. Articles under both names are listed under Fromm in the Bibliography.)

3 DR to S. S. Koteliansky, 11 December, 1933.

4 DR to S. S. Koteliansky, 8 August, [1934].

5 DR to Richard Church, 14 April, 1936.

6 'Duckworth, by repeatedly asking too much, missed chance after chance of French & German translations – foolish to expect anything from trans. beyond publicity – so there is only a strange little *Pointed Roofs* in Japanese, all preface & footnotes & Glossary, very pretty to look at.' DR to Peggy Kirkaldy, 14 February, 1943.

BIOGRAPHICAL NOTE

Dorothy Miller Richardson was born in Abingdon, Berkshire, on 17 May, 1873, the third of four daughters. Her father, Charles Richardson, came from a prosperous family of grocers, but longed to give up 'trade' and to be a gentleman. He sold the business and lived off the proceeds for some years but eventually was made a bankrupt in 1893. Her mother, whose maiden name was Mary Taylor, came from East Coker in Somerset, from a family whose name was listed among the gentry in local directories.

When she was five years old, Dorothy Richardson was sent for a year to a small private school where she learned to read and spell; apparently nothing else interested her. The next year, owing to her mother's ill health and her father's financial straits, the family moved to the south coast, near Worthing. When she was ten, her father's investments improved and he moved his family up to London. Her life at this stage included croquet, tennis, boating, skating, dances and music: apart from musical evenings at home, she was introduced to the classics, to Wagner and Chopin, and to Gilbert and Sullivan. She was taught for a year by a governess, of whom she later wrote that she, 'if she could, would have formed us to the almost outmoded pattern of female education: the minimum of knowledge and a smattering of various "accomplishments" - - - - for me - - - she was torment unmitigated'. After this, she was sent to Southborough House, whose headmistress was a disciple of Ruskin and where the pupils were encouraged to think for themselves. Here Richardson studied history, French, German and literature, the last presenting her with 'the fascination of words, of their sturdy roots, their growth and transformation, and the strange drama of the pouring in from every quarter of the globe of alien words assimilated and modified to the rhythm of our own speech'. She declined geography and instead studied logic and psychology; about logic she 'felt, with the growth of power to detect faulty reasoning, something akin to the emotion later accompanying my acquisition of a latch-key'. Psychology, by contrast, aroused an 'uneasy scepticism'. She remembered this part of her education with gratitude. At this point, her father, through disastrous speculation, lost the greater part of his resources, which forced Richardson to seek employment as a governess. This first appointment in a German school later provided the material for *Pointed Roofs.*

After six months Richardson returned to England : two sisters were engaged to be married, the third had a position as a governess and her mother was near to a nervous collapse. In order to be near her mother, she took a post at the Misses Ayre's school in Finsbury Park, North London. Her impressions and experiences here provided the material for her second volume, *Backwater.* In 1893, Charles Richardson was finally declared bankrupt : the house and possessions were sold and the family moved to a house in Chiswick, generously provided for them by John Arthur Batchelor, who became the husband of the eldest daughter, Kate. By 1895, Richardson had moved from Finsbury Park to a post in the country as governess to two children, her experience of which is recorded in *Honeycomb.* On 29 November, 1895, while on holiday at Hastings with her daughter, Mary Richardson committed suicide by cutting her throat with a kitchen knife. After this, Richardson needed to break away : '- - - longing to escape from the world of women, I gladly accepted a post - - - - a secretarial job, offering me the freedom I so desired'. She lived in a Bloomsbury attic on a salary of £1 per week. London became her great adventure. During these years she 'explored the world outside the enclosures of social life', which included writers (in particular, H.G. Wells, with whom she had a long friendship and a brief affair), religious and political groups, and, through books and lectures, science and philosophy. At this time she found the philosophers 'more deeply exciting than the novelists'. These interests and activities provided the contextual material for her subsequent volumes. From working as a secretary, she gradually branched out into translation and freelance journalism. As a result of a series of sketches contributed to *The Saturday Review,* a reviewer urged her to try writing a novel. She later wrote that the suggestion 'both shocked and puzzled me. The material that moved me to write would not fit the framework of any novel I had experienced. I believed myself to be - - - intolerant of the romantic and the realist novel alike. Each - - - left out certain essentials and dramatized life misleadingly. Horizontally- - - - Always - - - one was aware of the author and applauding, or deploring, his manipulations'.

In 1917, at the age of forty-four, she married Alan Odle, an unknown artist sixteen years younger than herself. The marriage, in spite of misgivings, was a happy one, providing her with 'a new world, the missing link between those already explored'. She died in 1957 at the age of eighty-four.

Introduction

It is often tacitly assumed that where the words 'women', 'female' and, latterly, 'feminist' and 'feminism', appear in literary criticism, the ensuing discussion is likely to be an instance of special pleading, or a polemic, or a sub-literary manifesto. Such assumptions are implicit, and it is necessary, therefore, to make them as explicit as possible, so that the writing under discussion may be evaluated fairly within an appropriate context.

The problems women writers have had with their names, for example, are one index of the problems they have had with their literary identities. When they marry, they give up their own names; if a name is a sign of identity, then women have had less chance to be confident in their identities than have men. Male writers who have achieved, or who are expected to achieve, a degree of eminence, are referred to by critics and reviewers simply by surname. Only in cases where two or more writers share the same surname are they distinguised by initials or by a first name. For women writers, by contrast, there has been no such simple convention. Until the twentieth century many women writers, aware that their work would be judged by different, and, we must infer, inappropriate, criteria, if their sex were known, chose to publish under male pseudonyms : the Brontës and George Eliot are obvious examples. Others published under, or were referred to by, their marital status names, as were Mrs Humphrey Ward and Mrs Henry Wood. In the early years of this century, still others used their full names, without title, as did Dorothy Richardson. Katherine Mansfield disguised her names, but not her sex. Contemporary reviews between 1915 and 1940 refer variously to Dorothy Richardson and Miss Richardson, Virginia Woolf and Mrs Woolf, Katherine

Mansfield, Miss Mansfield and Mrs Middleton Murry. At the present time, convention still has it that we refer to James, Conrad and Joyce, but also to Dorothy Richardson, Virginia Woolf and Katherine Mansfield. Beneath the apparent triviality of this convention lies a confusion between the 'respect' accorded to femininity by social custom and the seriousness with which women may be considered as writers – a confusion between social role and artistic vocation which does not arise in the evaluation of male writers.

Even more subtly dismissive than the use of proper nouns are the common nouns ascribed to women writers. The description of Elizabeth Barrett Browning and Christina Rossetti as 'poetesses' ensures a semi-conscious pre-judgement that they are necessarily more flippant or incompetent or 'sentimental', less serious or powerful, in their work, than are their male counterparts. The word 'authoress', similarly, still connotes the inferior genre and inferior readership of 'women's fiction', a sphere of activity that invites universal intellectual contempt. 'Yet', note Miller and Swift in *Words and Women*, 'H.W. Fowler, the lexicographer and expert on English usage, rebuked women writers who would not accept the designation *authoress* as he thought they should. "Their view", he said (obviously without consulting them), "is that the female author is to raise herself to the level of the male author by asserting her right to his name". But who is to say that it is his name and not hers?' [1] Miller and Swift go on to argue that once grammatical gender has been superseded there is no reason to differentiate on the basis of sex between two qualified people, unless, of course, there is an unconscious assumption that sex is part of the qualification. This means, by implication, that the distinction between male author and authoress is not a distinction between male and female but between the standard and a deviation. In the performing arts, the words 'actress', 'musician', 'singer', 'ballerina', 'diva', and so on, do not carry derogatory associations precisely because women's roles in those arts, since the Restoration, have become accepted as complementary to men's roles. Further, the words 'artist', 'painter', and 'composer' do not have a feminine form probably because the women who have entered these spheres have been too few to be thought to constitute a group. The same might be said to apply to the academic titles 'professor' and 'doctor'. The traditions of Western philosophy since Plato and of Western psychology in the modern period, attest the importance in our culture of a synonymity between nomenclature and identity across the whole range of our experience, from the classification of species to the psychosocial descriptions of human beings. The confusion of usages between Miss Richardson, Mrs Woolf and Katherine Mansfield, between poetess and poet, authoress and author, together with the more neutral words 'writer' and 'novelist', are an indication of the semi-conscious confusion of attitudes towards the status and claims of women artists and their works. The term 'woman writer' itself suggests duality and therefore conflict, whereas the term 'man writer' would be a tautology.

It could reasonably be considered too wide-ranging to suggest, in a literary study, something of the cultural norms within which women writers in the present century have worked. Nevertheless, it is one contention of this study that unless some of these norms are perceived and their enormous conditioning potential is appreciated, the works written by women have little chance of achieving a fair reading. Unlike the specific norms developed within racial minority sub-cultures, politically repressed groups or the pop culture generated by the urban masses, the traditions, values and preoccupations of women have little cohesion and even less self-consciousness. This is due in part to women not being a minority group and not being forced to live only with one another in slums or ghettos. They are slightly over half the human population and they retain slightly over half the residue of human experience. It is due in much greater measure to the complex process of social role-learning through which every woman in our society must pass. This is not to say that men, too, are not socialized to conform to male role stereotypes, but the significant difference lies in the assumption that the male role is inclusive of artistic vocation, whereas the female role is exclusive of it. Artistic aspiration in women, therefore, necessarily induces conflict.

Almost since the inception of the novel as an acceptable literary genre, women have gradually become more able to interpret, to imagine and to structure their experience in novels, in a way in which they have not done in any other art form, except for the performance arts – acting, singing and dancing – which specifically require women. They have not, generally speaking, achieved eminence as dramatists, painters, architects or composers of music. This may be explained, in part, by their exclusion, for so long, from academies and other institutions responsible for teaching the crafts necessary to the practice of these arts. But such an explanation is too gross a measure to account for the relative failure of female poets, for example. Much of the explanation certainly must lie in the subtleties of the development of 'feminine' personality and its proper goals. The novel is illuminating from this perspective, since, being historically the youngest of our arts, it has the least tradition of its own, and is therefore more susceptible than the older arts to infusion from unlikely sources, including the world-views of women. Further, its nature is such that it can be pursued in the fits and starts of domestic life and its concerns have been such that they approximated closely to the socially legitimized spheres of influence and experience accommodated by women. It has been in the novel that women have begun to present world-views different in major respects from those of their male contemporaries, so that by the middle of our own century the attribution 'masculine' as a term of praise and 'feminine' as a term of derogation, are no longer as simply acceptable as they once were.

One issue is basic to all the others : are there, or are there not, essential differences between women and men as artists? If we assert that there are not, and if we refer only to traditional aesthetic criteria, the fact that male achievement in the arts is superior to female achievement, both in quality and in quantity, entails the conclusion that women are inherently less capable as artists than are men. If, on the other hand, we assert that there are differences, further questions arise : what kinds of differences are they? are they significant? are they appropriate to the forming of aesthetic judgements? [2] Attempts to answer these questions lead to the problem of role-conflict, evidence of which is found in the experiences of women writers, in their recorded introspections and in the way they write. The conflict is always presented as a response to two alternative perspectives of reality : the actual and the phenomenal, or the objectively perceived and the subjectively perceived. Changes in women's actual situation have taken place slowly during the last century and a half. The high points of legislative reform stretch from the Married Women's Property Act, to the gaining of the franchise, to the Sex Discrimination Act and the gradual implementation of equal pay. Changes in women's phenomenal perspective have been far more indistinct, but, especially with regard to writers, far more pertinent. How women perceive their role, their possibilities, their tasks and their talents, has recently become an important focus for feminist political theory, but it has for a longer period been of critical concern to women writers. This is one of the reasons why the application of 'pure' aesthetic criteria results in a distorted reading of their works. The establishing of a feminist aesthetic would presuppose that due weight be given to the place of role-conflict in a woman's world-view and to the ways in which this conflict shapes what she writes. Changes in actual circumstances, moreover, have not always been considered relevant by women writers; the gaining of the franchise, for instance, did not free Richardson or Woolf as creative writers, nor did they feel it to be one of their central concerns. Women are often accused of political naïveté, or, equally, of a lack of 'social conscience', but since the phenomenal has been more the concern of twentieth-century writers than the actual, it is consistent to find Woolf prepared to testify as an expert witness[3] in the Radclyffe Hall obscenity trial and yet to find her absent from the activities of the Women's Social and Political Union and post-1919 feminist gatherings. For women artists, on the whole, actual conflicts are perceived to be irrelevant, even though it may seem to us, from hindsight, that they were very relevant indeed. Further, in the liberal humanist tradition of literary criticism, a preoccupation with actual conflict is usually considered deleterious in that it may lead to didacticism and subjective involvement. Woolf, for instance, jealous for a place in that tradition, zealously strove to write 'pure' fiction, and Richardson is considered the less able novelist partly because of her persistent refusal to accept the authority of that tradition, as well as for her feminist complaint.

Such a judgement initiates a basic critical problem : if Richardson's novels are to be considered strictly 'as novels', they must be so considered according to the same canons of taste and judgement as are the novels in the mainstream of English fiction. If, on the other hand, they are to be considered as 'female' novels, what canons can be used? Do 'female' novels form a corpus antithetical to 'male' novels? Are 'female' novels a variant of or a deviation from the norm? Is the order of reality created in novels dependent on the sex of their writers and of their characters? Are the male characters in books by women less 'masculine' than the male characters in books by men, and, if so, does this mean that the female characters created by men are less 'feminine' than those created by women? Can the words 'masculine' and 'feminine' even be used in this way? If these questions are the right ones to ask, and if the answers to them are affirmative, it must be apparent that the experience of women cannot be identified with that of men within a totality called 'human' experience, and, further that the artistic projection of experience would preserve, albeit unconsciously, something of the same differential. Since it is generally evident that art does not precede experience, a subsuming of male and female experiences into a totality called human experience is a mere hypothesis. At the phenomenal level, women do not share men's 'broad view' any more than they have shared men's actual lot, as, for example, soldiers of fortune, holders of wealth or political power, innovators and inheritors of the traditions of learning. Particular women, certainly, have gained access to some areas of men's affairs, just as particular men have abnegated them, but to assume that women writers have always been able to do so seems very sweeping. Precisely this asymmetry of experience and the phenomenal conflict it engenders, drove Richardson to challenge the conventions of the realist novel and directed Woolf towards her theory of the androgynous vision. By the early twentieth century the traditional styles themselves, rather than their 'subjects', were felt by women to be inadequate and inappropriate. Both Richardson's polemicism and Woolf's aestheticism are positive symptoms of this crucial dissatisfaction. It is mistaken to excuse these attitudes to style as subjective overcompensations or as abberations of correct technique. If it is the case that women writers felt alienated from the tradition which, as artists, they were moved to extend, and if it is the case that they diagnosed their alienation as a symptom of their femininity, then it must certainly be the case that this same alienation became a central factor in both the preoccupations and the manner of their writing. Richardson is an especially interesting figure in this regard, since she was, as can be seen both in her fiction and in her letters and articles, firmly convinced that a woman's life and a woman's art inhabit a different order of reality from those of men. Such a conviction may clearly now be called 'feminist', asserting, as it does, an alternative polarity in human experience and understanding. Richardson herself would have rejected the term 'feminist', since, in her own time, it described those who were engaged in the struggle for suffrage and other forms of social and political equality. For her, women were neither equal to, nor inferior to, nor superior to, men; they were different from men in every respect, but most importantly for her, in their very consciousness.

Feminism, therefore, in the works of the female modernists, Richardson and Woolf in particular, is generated from and sustained by a self-conscious sense of female psychology and of the female mind, a self-consciousness new in English literature. It exemplifies, as do Lawrence's novels, which give an opposing perspective, an awareness of alienation between the sexes and it protests against such a condition. It provides for women writers a focus of positive identification which can replace what they feel they unjustly lack : intellectual training, access to the world of public affairs and continuity within the tradition of the English novel. Richardson's feminism is not the stuff of practical polemics nor does it wish to insinuate political solutions. Nevertheless, it shares with these and other feminist trends a basic intellectual position, which is the belief that feeling and thought are by no means always simply 'human' but, more often than not, either male or female. Whether such a belief is a mere act of faith or is a theory with supporting evidence would indeed be difficult to determine, in as much as the material for such a determination would be experience itself – experience already circumscribed by convention and circumstance. The ultimate truth or untruth of the belief, however, is perhaps of considerably less relevance than the power it can be seen to exert in the writing of women, and on Richardson in particular.

At the present stage of social research, it is assumed by some sociologists that there is such a partition in human consciousness and that its causes and effects may be elicited by careful investigation. Much of this work is owed to the charismatic effect of Freud's theories of personality formation, which has been so extensive that it can hardly be exaggerated. Although, for the most part, writers and intellectuals have disagreed with Freud's pronouncements, they have been forced to modify their systems of ethics and social behaviour, together with their views of Nature, in the light of Freud's revolutionary thesis that the characteristics of the human adult issue from his or her unconscious life. It is true that for centuries a similar concept has been familiar to artists and aesthetic philosophers, culminating in the theories of the Imagination held by the Romantics. Before Freud, however, the sources of inexplicable attributes and achievements were thought to be outside the mental life of the individual. Since Freud, the demythologizing of human creativity has made it possible to explore the divergent achievements of men and women without recourse to the dogmatic determinism of theories of Nature. Female children, in other words , are not born into the world with a blueprint for 'feminine' personality : 'femininity' is something they acquire as a result of the social conditioning of their unconscious drives.

The significant features of Freud's description of the development of the feminine personality are penis-envy and the castration complex which must resolve into heterosexual love and the desire for babies. This resolution is a complicated affair because it entails the rejection of the mother as the primary love object. The development of masculine personality is much simpler in so far as the male's heterosexual drive must transfer from the mother to some other female. The crucial factor, which puzzled Freud all his life, is that infants of both sexes begin the same way, with the mother as the primary love object. The extent to which some of this original love must remain at the core of every individual's social learning, Freud explained in terms of the greater degree of bisexuality in women than in men and equally in terms of the relative weakness of the superego in women compared with men. This latter observation is consistent with the attribution to women, in our culture, of more 'natural' instincts, more emotionality and irrationality, than men are deemed to possess. By contrast, men are thought to be more logical, less sentimental, and to have a more refined sense of moral judgement. It is obvious that the internalizing of such a feminine model in the case of women aspiring to any of the male arenas of excellence, such as literature, would result in a self-image that would be very difficult to reconcile with the demands of art as they have been understood: technical competence, confidence, discipline, ambition and tough-mindedness. Most of the traits required of good literature, as of its creators, are in direct opposition to the traits required of the good wife and mother, or the good nun, so that a woman aspiring to be a serious writer will either question her own femininity, have it questioned for her, or both. Women who persist in spite of the force of their conditioning face two alternatives: the disintegration of the ego, which results in insanity,[4] or the neutralizing and denial of normative femininity, which is expressed in the recluse (Emily Brontë, Emily Dickinson), the feminist (Dorothy Richardson, Virginia Woolf), or the lesbian (Gertrude Stein, Vita Sackville-West). The number of women writers who, before the advent of efficient contraception, successfully submitted to the normative role and became wives and mothers is so small as to be significantly suggestive of the incompatibility of the two roles.

The practical and emotional sides of the wifely role converge in the concept of the wife as a 'helpmate' to her husband; she harmonizes the continuous flow of needs and events which constitutes the domestic arena, as well as providing emotional relief and support for her husband's endeavours. A male artist 'naturally' calls upon the support of his wife, mistress, mother, sisters and daughters. A woman artist, by contrast, is unable to assume the authority-dependence nexus of domestic life, because it is the prerogative of the man. She is potentially isolated twice over: first, from the domain of affairs because of her social role, and, secondly, from emotional support and encouragement, because of her domestic role.[5] Many women writers have continued to provide support for their men and at the same time turned to other women to support them: Katherine Mansfield is a striking case of this phenomenon.

Apart from the work being done in the social sciences, the fiction of almost all the early-twentieth-century novelists shows a preoccupation with this theme, D.H. Lawerence's novels offering an obvious example. For the woman writer of this period, and especially for Richardson, the pressure to modify gender-typical attitudes and the need to integrate the role of artist with the role of woman are specific problems to be resolved, both in the practice of art and in the conduct of living. Richardson's merging of these two demands on her personality, her merging of art and life, and the resulting autobiographical fiction she created, become, in this context, of absorbing and particular interest.

Richardson's gradual formulation of her problem, the problem of being a woman, took two parallel lines of development. The first consists in how she lived her life, the second in how she wrote her fiction. Each may properly be called experimental.[6] Her life was unusual for her repeated attempts variously to escape, overcome, modify or repudiate the traditional way of living she perceived to be expected of her by society – the way of love and marriage. Her writing is unusual in the intensity of its challenge to the structural devices in their traditional usages, and to the modes of apperception, of the novel as she knew it. What is especially remarkable and interesting is the way in which these two 'experiments', in living and writing, clashed and coalesced, until the usually clear demarcation between them becomes, in her case, blurred and unhelpful. In one sense, that is, *Pilgrimage* is not fiction because the events recorded by its narrative and the characters it introduces, are direct replications of Richardson's own life experiences. On the other hand, it is not autobiography, since we are given no explicit chronology, no objective accounts of people and events and no assurance that the authorial voice and the persona's voice are always to be identified as synonymous. Richardson herself always insisted, perhaps ingenuously, that *Pilgrimage* was fiction and that she had chosen herself as its subject precisely because that was the subject about which she could be most authoritative.[7] Any writer, however, could make the same claim; if that is all there is to be said, then the phenomenon of *Pilgrimage* can be accounted for as failure of nerve (and imagination), coupled with a colossal egotism, which may well lead us to admire its testimony to sheer industry, but not its testimony to art. Authors, in any case, rarely have the last word on the nature of their own work and readers may justifiably take such pronouncements of authors as a starting point, rather than as a conclusion. In Richardson's case, too, her own statement is a good starting point; if her work is genuine fiction, however experimental, to what extent can we measure it according to traditional critical criteria? Is a woman's book different from a man's book just because Richardson says it is? *Pilgrimage* is clearly 'different' from the novels preceding it, but can its difference be adequately explained by reference to the fact that its author is a woman?

The attempt to answer this question leads to three main areas of enquiry: an understanding of what Richardson meant by 'the feminine', which entails examining all her writings; an understanding of what she meant by 'the novel', which means examining her judgements of other novels, found in reviews, in personal correspondence and in *Pilgrimage* itself; and an understanding of what she meant by claiming that attempts to categorize life and art are false to the nature of experience,[8] which entails examining the particular manipulations she performed, in her personal life and in *Pilgrimage*, in order to demonstrate her claim. Enquiries of this kind immediately provoke methodological problems.

In the first instance, it proved impossible for this study to proceed in what seemed the most natural way, that is, by comparing and contrasting Richardson's letters, journalism and fiction in their chronological sequence, with reference to the context of her life experiences. Such a method would have biased the direction of the study towards literary biography and indeed it is the method followed in Fromm's recent and very thorough account.[9] The material did not yield a development of literary or feminist theory, so much as a continuous reiteration of what for Richardson were fundamental and almost self-evident precepts. A linear development which would be consistent with an explication following natural chronology is absent from Richardson's work, or at least its presence is far more psychological than it is intellectual. The feminist stimulus to her fiction is contextual rather than developmental. The whole corpus of her writing is derived from her central role conflict between the demands made upon her as a woman, first by life, and secondly, by art. And since that thematic core is so crucial to an understanding of *Pilgrimage*, it has been necessary to dispense with a critical narrative based on the natural chronology of her writings, as well as to dispense with a narrative based on the chronology of her life.

Secondly, the very technique of *Pilgrimage*, together with Richardson's convictions about the nature of experiential time, of memory, of literature, of the negative value of analytical rationalism, and of the differential psychology of women, all affirm her own repudiation of natural chronology as an adequate framework for discourse. It is, of course, always a matter of academic judgement whether, or to what extent, the structure of a careful elucidation should follow the implicit structure of the material itself, or should impose an alternative structure upon it. Examples of the latter would include Marxist criticism, in which an ideological structure external to the material, can, by providing an alternative reading, illuminate unconscious assumptions shared by both authors and readers; or, again, linguistic criticism, which can demonstrate, by concentrating on the application of a theory of general language structures to particular language instances, the viability of the theory itself. In Richardson's case, however, the degree of her insistence on particularity and the high level of self-consciousness with which she does insist, render her work inapposite to be considered representative in these ways. This does not, of itself, mean that she has less value as a literary figure: Blake's work, for example, has proved more elusive than that of his contemporaries to elucidations which do not pay great attention to his personal universe.

Thirdly, the principal concern of this study is an examination of *Pilgrimage* as a unique and definitive example of autobiographical fiction. And the structure of *Pilgrimage* is thematic, not chronological. Richardson often said herself that a reader should be able to read the pages of a novel in any order[10] and *Pilgrimage* certainly fulfils that requirement, sometimes overwhelmingly so. The thematic structure is always implicit and is given no explicit support from the conventional devices of narrative, characterization, chronology or the delineation of milieux. Although the prose exhibits thematic coherence, the lack of explicit reference makes enormous demands on the reader. Richardson does not question, for example, the reader's ability to recall at will any one detail of Miriam's total range of experience. Miriam, indeed, does have a past which she can recall; she does grow older; she does have a memory. And not only is the reader's memory taxed in this way; so too, is his or her knowledge. Richardson assumes a familiarity with Miriam's reading, with the clubs and societies she attends, with the places she remarks upon, indeed with all the significations of her contemporary world. But although Richardson expects the reader to identify with Miriam's consciousness and to see things as Miriam does, she seems singularly unwilling to admit, by providing contextual explication, that Miriam knows things that the reader cannot possibly know.

The extent to which *Pilgrimage* is 'autobiography', or, as Richardson would claim, 'life', is the extent to which the people, places, events and ideas can be documented outside the bounds of the work itself.[11] The extent to which it is 'fiction', on the other hand, is the extent to which the interrelation of themes implicit *within* the prose provides a context for the otherwise disparate passages which confront the reader. If, therefore, the material is circular rather than linear in its configuration, then its central point, from which all attempts at discovery radiate and to which they return, is Richardson's conviction of the 'otherness' of a woman's consciousness. There is, in other words, a central point rather than a starting point; there is expansion and dissolution, but not development; and there is reiteration, but not a deductively reasoned conclusion. In this way, Richardson tried to forge in art what she could not fight in life : the subjection of the self to the external imposition of linear time and to all its consequences – in macrocosm, the structures of society which have been imposed by history and the structures of intellectual investigation and of literature imposed by tradition; and in microcosm, the structures of personality and of human relationships imposed by learning and by expectation. Only human consciousness, Richardson claimed,[12] could be freed from the tyranny of linear time and only female consciousness, being less committed than male consciousness to the demands of an external world which had been shaped by men, could apprehend this 'reality' more or less directly. Both her life and her work testify to this unwavering conviction but, inevitably, it was in her work that she could make her own rules. Our judgement of her work, then, must take careful account of her convictions, personal though they are, if we are to understand in what ways 'life itself', which she sought so passionately to 'realise',[13] as she called it, becomes 'art', as we would call it.[14]

On the other hand, it is necessary not to slip too far into an uncritical adoption of Richardson's own canons; that would mean, at the least offensive but also the least helpful level of elucidation, a mere description and synopsis of the progress of *Pilgrimage*, and at the other polarity, a dogmatic affirmation of the generalizing potential of her views.[15] Such a stance would erode any possible literary status for *Pilgrimage* by excusing its faults on ideological grounds and treating it as a persuasive, if unsuitably long, piece of polemic. It is true that Richardson's writing discloses a peculiar integration of life experience and artistic realization, but it is also true that the integration is uneasy. Further, it seems clear that the external motivations for the integration would have been pertinent to any female writer of the time : lack of access to, and experience of, intellectual tradition; the role conflict implicit in the choice between independence and marriage; the inferior social status of women; and so on. Certainly her world-view generated her technique, but the world-view must be seen in this light, must be seen as explanatory, rather than as 'true', which is what she would have claimed it to be. This kind of link between world-view and technique is indeed symptomatic of her fellow-experimentalists, Mansfield and Woolf :

> The fiction of Dorothy Richardson, Katherine Mansfield, and Virginia Woolf created a deliberate female aesthetic, which transformed the feminine code of self-sacrifice into an annihilation of the narrative self, and applied the cultural analysis of the feminists to words, sentences, and structures of language in the novel. Their version of modernism was a determined response to the material culture of male Edwardian novelists like Arnold Bennett and H. G. Wells, but, like D. H. Lawrence, the female aestheticists saw the world as mystically and totally polarized by sex.[16]

The requisite balance to the necessary prominence accorded to Richardson's views must come, therefore, from an examination of how her experimental technique modified the elements of her life, which she chose as her subject matter, not by changing their configuration in space and time, but by changing their relational context, so that what to her was their 'real meaning' became accessible, and what to us must be their artistic integrity becomes comprehensible.

Her perception of the feminine self is her starting point; her conviction of the importance of that perception is her motivating drive, as a writer, and is, also, the sustaining power which keeps Miriam intent on her pilgrimage towards self-realization. But the role conflict at the centre of that perception, the choice between individuation and relationship, between independence and marriage, between 'art' and 'life', embodies an ambivalence which Richardson tried always to resolve and it is towards this resolution that Richardson as the author of *Pilgrimage* is really directed. Unwilling though she might have been to ally herself with the writers of 'women's fiction' and hostile though she certainly was to 'male' novels, marriage and motherhood remain central metaphors in *Pilgrimage*, metaphors which carry both personal and cultural energy. In *Pilgrimage* Miriam considers marriage as a viable solution to her problems with self-definition, but then rejects it. In life, Richardson had already married when she was affirming Miriam's rejection of marriage. Indeed, it is significant that she could not bring herself to portray Miriam at the point of accepting marriage as she herself had done. Yet this apparent contradiction is made comprehensible when we become aware of the psychological circumstances of her own marriage, in which she compromised the terms of her conflict by agreeing to a marriage in which she could play a maternal role. Alan Odle, an original but little-known artist, was fifteen years younger than herself. In fact, as she declined to put her correct age on her marriage certificate, it is doubtful whether he ever knew how old she was. He was a man in such poor health that the armed forces refused to accept him for military service. Had Richardson thought he might live a normal life-span, she probably would not have married him :

> If at the time I had had the remotest inkling of the possibility of his surviving me, I would never have consented to marry him.[17]

And to another friend she wrote :

> But if anyone had told me 25 yrs. ago that we'd live, both of us, to see our silver wedding, I might have hesitated even more than I did.[18]

When Alan did predecease her, her response was immense relief :

> . . . there fell from my heart a burden oppressing it for years past, the dreadful possibility of leaving him to face life alone.[19]

Alan Odle was, in Richardson's eyes, unworldly to such a point of near-helplessness that he might never have survived alone. According to every source to date, he was extremely undemanding of her personal autonomy, accepting her companionship and solicitude as might a child. The maternal role, it seems clear, gave Richardson her only access to a relatively stress-free relationship with a man,[20] precisely because it did not provoke any serious threat to the integrity of her consciousness. But as they grew older together, the thought of what might happen to Alan after her death preyed on her mind and she often conveyed this anxiety to her friends. Peggy Kirkaldy, a friend to both of them, offered to take Alan into her home if Dorothy should die first; to which offer Dorothy responded with a gratitude that can also be characterized as 'maternal'. Her reply, in a letter from Padstow in Cornwall, dated 12 February, 1943, is worth quoting in full, revealing as it does the quality of her concern :

> Peggy my dear, you have lifted from my heart its worst load. Sympathy real, I knew you would give, for I know the rare power of your sympathetic imagination. But I did not envisage you rising up, with a flaming sword in your hand, between my helpless darling & all I saw confronting him. Surely even you, with all your bigness of heart, will see the picture, if you look at it from outside, as *almost* incredible, bless you.
>
> And, for ought [*sic*] you knew, the poor lamb would not be only helpless but penniless! Well, that is not quite the case. A tiny income will be his, about £150 a year. Thus: Bryher, who has been endlessly good to us, when she started, in memory of Sir John Ellerman, a trust-fund for the benefit of artists & authors & nominated me as one of the beneficiaries, made over to me, by deed, the capital sum producing my annuity, absolutely, & this of course goes to Alan under my will. The trustees are Butts & Co, who are also my executors. Since I had my Civil Pension in '39, reckoned retrospectively to cover '38, I have scraped & saved all I could in the hope of covering rainy periods. Our bank account has been transformed into a 'Joint & Several', so that A. can draw on it & am learning him, whenever a few certificates can be bought, to write a cheque. It takes him nearly as long as a small drawing. The annuity, of course, is fully taxed at source & I have done my best to explain the rebate business, the tax vouchers from Coutts to be carefully cherished & sent in with income-tax returns & the resultant treasury cheque to be banked & held to spread over the following year to make up income. My Civil List pension is tax free, so there will be nothing to claim from the last of that. In a note-book labelled 'Data for Alan' I have set down all this lore, including the way to fill up income-tax

returns. But the poor lamb cannot do compound addition & although it was a relief to get these data set down, it is nothing to the relief of communicating them to you, &, when the time comes, he shall know to whom he can turn for advice. Perhaps sooner if opportunity offers. At present he knows only that my heart is shaky & I must go warily.

Worry drains away from me as I write. Even the prospect of his being landed down here alone – he can't pack & is lost in railway stations – with everything to attend to, is less daunting than it was. I'm leaving what instructions I can, in case the war is still on. If not, I see you perhaps able to arrive & find a bed. (At present all are packed). I see you bundle all my things into a vee-hickle & deposit them with my little friend Miss Ellery of the Sunshine Café in Padstow to distribute amongst the Padstow poor.

A. ready to post. This must be continued in my next. You had the Horizons? B. sent us the Colossus book. First class Pagan animism.

Much love, & bless & bless & bless you

Dorothy

That Richardson began writing *Pilgrimage* before she agreed to marry foreshadows her real eventual position, that is, that the only solution to her personal alienation as an imperfectly socialized woman in a man's world, was to become a writer, but a writer who could manipulate relationships so that they would affirm her world-view in life, as well as in art. In this way, life and art would not be merely contiguous, but continuous. That is why it is of special interest to the reader of *Pilgrimage* to know how exactly the important characters Wilson, Shatov and Amabel in the fiction accord with their real-life models, Wells, Grad and Veronica, and, more importantly, how in life Richardson manipulated her relationships with those people and then showed, in *Pilgrimage*, the meaning of those manipulations for her own liberation as a writer. Therefore, in this study, particular attention is paid to the replication in *Pilgrimage* of Richardson's involvements with these people as agents of vicarious action from which the writer must desist in order to observe. Further, motherhood as a metaphor for creativity, in the context of *Pilgrimage,* takes on a peculiar piquancy, since it is not simply the allegorical parallel of mother and child, author and novel, which Richardson wishes us to accept, but the experiential equivalence of her own motherhood with Amabel's, with Veronica's, of the child resulting from the marriage of two people who first loved her and who then married each other because she wished it. The enormity of this particular solution of female role conflict is something Richardson may well have been unaware of, but its implications for the reader of *Pilgrimage* become clear when documents from 'life' are examined alongside the account given in 'art'. And the baby Miriam holds in her arms at the end of *March Moonlight* becomes more than the conventional symbol of new life; the image is invested, by all that has gone before, with the possibility that female creative energy may issue, not only separately in the production of babies on the one hand, and books on the other, but also simultaneously in the production of both, by the manipulation of art to produce life. The influence at work here is mysticism, not aestheticism. Late in her life she could still affirm the same view, in a letter to Bernice Elliott: 'The sole possible translation of a belief is a life.' [21] Richardson's implicit, but unique and daring treatment of the meanings of motherhood is a connecting thread in the complex thematic fabric of *Pilgrimage.*

What Richardson is doing in *Pilgrimage* is not a straightforward attempt to record the journey towards identity; it is an attempt to record the gestalt of her life. When she says, both explicitly and implicitly, that she wishes to show what a woman's consciousness is like, she means that though the events of her life occurred sequentially, they were not perceived sequentially. Richardson's inner life, like Miriam's, appears to have violated the chronology of events and to have consisted, also like Miriam's, in a collection of foreshadowings and portents, together with the juxtaposition of memories which bear a thematic relationship with one another, each of all these being as 'real' as any point of experience in the outer world. Wells, by contrast, in his *Experiment in Autobiography,* based his account of the development of his own mind on strictly scientific premises. He believed that external reality could be, indeed was, perceived directly, and that the perceptions thus gained were not distorted or modified by the filter of his own consciousness. Richardson would have judged Wells' alternative view as a necessary corollary of masculinity, since her own view of reality, like all her other views, she ascribed finally to her femininity. In an article for *Vanity Fair* called 'Women and the Future' [22] she claims that the truly 'womanly woman' is a person who 'lives . . . in the deep current of eternity . . . one with life, . . . she thinks flowingly, with her feelings. . . .' Even in this most abstract concept of identity, the differential between women and men is still seen to be a potent force, potent enough to shape the very contours of consciousness itself.

The argument of this book, therefore, is that the psychological role conflict between 'personhood' and 'womanhood' suffered by Richardson gave rise to her bi-polar world-view, in which female consciousness is contradistinguished in nearly every particular from male consciousness. This perception of the distinctiveness of female consciousness in turn gave rise to the evolution of an experimental technique of fiction, and because Richardson held constantly to the validity of her perception and because, also, we can see how the perception shaped her technique, we may justifiably call it 'feminist'. The technique itself is known to literary criticism as 'stream of consciousness' style, an appelation Richardson despised [23] but which has been for so long an accepted umbrella term under which Joyce, Woolf and other experimentalists have been grouped, that it would seem pedantic now to deny its appropriateness to Richardson, who was, after all, its original practitioner in English.[24] The force of Richardson's feminist convictions was so great that she was led to challenge all the accepted stylistic conventions of the novel and to believe that the use and very fabric of language itself was an objectification of the dominance and, to her, inappropriateness of the male mode of perception. How men say things and how Miriam must defend against what they say, becomes an important focus in *Pilgrimage* of the alienation between men and women. Miriam's arguments with Wilson, the writer, for whom scientific rationalism is an intellectual tool equally at the disposal of scientists, politicians and artists, effectively dramatizes this conflict.

But if Miriam cannot identify with men as a group because of the demands of her womanhood, nor can she identify with women as a group because of the demands of her personhood. Her intellectual needs are satisfied by men, but her romantic needs are not; in the end, all her romantic attachments to men break down because they threaten to violate the authenticity of her consciousness and she learns that for her, marriage based on romantic attachment is not a viable solution to her problem. From women, on the other hand, she cannot get the intellectual stimulation she craves, although her romantic needs can be fulfilled by women precisely because, since they share its configuration, they do not threaten the integrity of her consciousness. However, even close proximity to a woman is no final solution because the creative potential of such a relationship is unclear. First of all, some role must be found for men and a context must be found for relationships with men. Secondly, some way must be found in which relationships with women can be productive. But against all such involvements, Miriam's need for psychological isolation persists: isolation may be lonely, but it is not loneliness she finds painful [25] and, further, only isolation can give her the silence she demands in order to forge afresh the instruments of language which she needs for her own purposes. Because she is a woman, however, who 'thinks flowingly, with her feelings', relationships cannot be simply abandoned but must, instead, be modified. She is led, consequently, to bring together the man and the woman who have been of most romantic importance to her, in a symbolic union of the masculine and the feminine, as well as an actual union of male and female which is capable of fruition. In this extraordinary way, Richardson affirms, certainly to herself and potentially for readers of *Pilgrimage,* the supreme validity of her own consciousness as an index of reality, by the manipulation of living people as her material.

The implications for literature which may be drawn from Richardson's stance are both startling and trivial: startling with reference to the general problem, facing all women with artistic aspirations, of the resolution of feminine role conflict which is dramatized in *Pilgrimage*; and trivial, with reference to the uncompromising individualism of Richardson's personal universe. The balance between these two areas is, in a sense, the balance between Richardson's achievement as a writer of fiction which, being art, necessarily generalizes, and her achievement as a writer of autobiography which, being an account of a life, necessarily personalizes. In *Pilgrimage,* the interdependence of the one with the other is compelling, offering, by any standard, a significant contribution to our understanding of the demands of art and of the processes inherent to its generation.

The representation of how consciousness recognizes reality is not Richardson's sole aim; its corollary is the fact that this process is distinctly female; that is, that the representation of a woman's consciousness is, for Richardson, a subject which has not previously received any significant treatment in the history of the English novel. Her prescription for female art – of which *Pilgrimage* is itself an enactment – entails the manipulation of reality in as conscious and assiduous a manner as the fictional subject-matter is manipulated. The female artist must accept and affirm her own egoism, assigning to it the highest degree of virtue and eschewing all other systems of ethics. She must separate, with the utmost scrupulousness, the component parts of her social personality – her sexuality, her emotionality, her professional persona, her intellectuality and her maternalism – but at the same time she must keep whole and coherent her synthetic, all-inclusive consciousness, which characterizes herself to herself in secrecy and isolation. She must guard her psychological autonomy with the utmost rigour, disdaining to endorse any structures of thought or of institution which are incompatible with her personal, intuitive perception of truth. She must consider real only what is real for her. She must accept total responsibility for her own life and none at all for any other life, even another life intimately connected to her own. She must accept, finally, when she has created her life and produced her art, that her vision may be judged an eccentric exercise in the annals of egotism.

Dorothy Miller Richardson's *Pilgrimage* is testimony of this vision. For this reason, if for no other, it must stand in the first rank of those works which have brought to consciousness the particular dilemmas of the twentieth century.

NOTES AND REFERENCES

1 Casey Miller and Kate Swift, *Words and Women: New Language in New Times*, Gollancz, 1977, pp. 45-6.

2 The standard feminist answer to this question is affirmative. See, for example, H. R. Hays, *The Dangerous Sex: The Myth of Feminine Evil*, Methuen, 1966, p. 287.

3 See Vera Brittain, *Radclyffe Hall: A Case of Obscenity?*, Femina Books, 1968, pp. 90-1. The trial took place in 1928.

4 See A. Alvarez on the Plath – Hughes marriage in *The Savage God: A Study of Suicide* [1971], Penguin, 1974; and Phyllis Chesler on the Zelda – F. Scott Fitzgerald marriage in *Women and Madness* [1972], Allen Lane, 1974.

5 George Lewes and Leonard Woolf stand out as exceptions; they were, however, both writers themselves, so they understood something of what was needed in the way of support. Furthermore, both these relationships were childless, making it more possible for the women to pursue their vocations.

6 Artists, Richardson claimed, are 'life's irregulars'. See Preface to F. Ribadeau Dumas, *These Moderns: Some Parisian Close-Ups*, trans. Frederic Whyte, Humphrey Toulmin, 1932, pp. 5-10.

7 This is affirmed on the basis of numerous statements to the effect made by Richardson to Louise Morgan and Mrs Beresford in conversation

and to many others in correspondence. See Fromm, *Dorothy Richardson*, op. cit., pp. 66, 405.

8 DR to Henry Savage, February 1947: 'An obtuse being, in some regards, was the good Goethe or he would never have placed in opposition, truth and fiction, since by "truth" he will certainly mean the data of experience, facts rather than "truth", appearing piecemeal, chronologically and, so to say, horizontally, and often apparently unrelated.'

9 Fromm, *Dorothy Richardson*, op. cit.

10 This is a view often stated in her reviews as well as a view Miriam arrives at before she begins to write herself. See, for example, Richardson's review of two novels, *Eyeless in Gaza* by Aldous Huxley and *Break of Day* by Tristram Beresford, in *Life and Letters Today*, Winter 1936-7, pp. 188-9: '. . . following my usual habit of beginning the reading of a book either in the middle or at the end . . .'

11 This is a common characteristic of fiction of this period, and particularly of women's fiction.

12 DR to Henry Savage, 1948: 'To me, D.H.L[awrence]. does make his presentations of experience *current*, as is all experience if presented as a result of a sufficient intensity of concentration. No experience, whether one's own or that of others realised with any full degree of imaginative sympathy, is past. "Time", i.e. clock time and cosmic time is atomised, unreal. The central dimension in which we have our being is indivisible, infinitely expandable and bearing no relation to measured time. Does detachment bring, as you suggest, indifference? Is it not rather the very condition of real attachment?'

13 Richardson wrote in her manuscripts the letters I.R. – which stood for 'Imperfectly Realized' – against passages which seemed to her mere listing or recording.

14 Biographical information, that is, informs the fictional text. Richardson's own critical stance she formulated as follows: 'But though intimate knowledge of a writer's way of life may be essential to a just appreciation of his work, it is nevertheless secondary to that work.' Preface to *These Moderns*, op. cit.

15 For a discussion of this point see Elaine Showalter, *A Literature of Their Own: British Women Novelists from Brontë to Lessing* [1977], Virago, 1978, p. 258.

16 Ibid., p. 33.

17 DR to Henry Savage, 31 May, 1947.

18 DR to Peggy Kirkaldy, 25 September, 1941.

19 DR to Peggy Kirkaldy, [February] 1948.

20 See Veronica Grad to Rose Odle, Appendix [to this book], Letter 9: 'Dorothy mothered & took care of him'.

21 DR to Bernice Elliott, 1951.

22 'Women and the Future: A Trembling of the Veil before the Eternal

Mystery of "La Giaconda" [*sic*]', *Vanity Fair*, 22, April 1924, pp. 39-40.

23 See Richardson to Shiv Kumar: 'In deploring the comparison of consciousness with a stream and suggesting that fountain would be a more appropriate metaphor, I do not recognise the latter as a suitable label for the work appearing early in the century. This, I feel, was a natural development from the move away from "Romance" to "Realism" (the latter being a critical reaction to the former). It dealt directly with reality. Hence the absence of either "plot", "climax" or "conclusion". All the writers concerned would agree with Goethe that drama is for the stage.' DR to Shiv Kumar, 10 August, 1952.

24 *A Portrait of the Artist as a Young Man* was published in 1916; *Jacob's Room* in 1922. *Pilgrimage – Pointed Roofs* was published in 1915.

25 Even in old age, and as a widow, Richardson held to this view. In 1952 she wrote to a young friend, Pauline Marrian, 'Certain of your personal feelings distress me, the more deeply because at one time I occasionally experienced one of them, falling headlong into a pit of "loneliness". Easy it is to say that this pit is imaginary. But I think you will know what I mean. When one is within it, one is apt to exaggerate the quality of human "belongings", particularly, whether in the case of "love" or of "friendship", or of the two combined. These relationships are perpetually on the move, like all else, & unless at their centre there is some common faith they cannot endure save as conventions or conveniences. The idolators of such things, describing them from outside, fill our literature with falsities. Solitude is neither loneliness nor lovelessness.' DR to Pauline Marrian, 25 July, 1952.

1 · 'A Woman's Sentence'

I

Dorothy Richardson regarded traditional language use as a predominantly male mode of expression, maintaining that men and women used two different languages. Part of what Richardson insists upon is what Ros Coward points to, referring to the work of Lacan: the potency in language use of 'the presence of the unconscious in language with its use of multiple meanings, puns and so on. It constantly brings in across language the modes of signification which the language of male-dominated rationalist discourse refuses'.[1] In her Foreword to the 1938 Collected Edition of *Pilgrimage* Richardson specifically describes the stimulus to her own experimental technique as the polarity between male tradition and female consciousness:

> Since all these [realist] novelists happened to be men, the present writer, proposing at this moment to write a novel and looking round for a contemporary pattern, was faced with the choice between following one of her regiments and attempting to produce a feminine equivalent of the current masculine realism.[2]

This is Richardson's stand: the succeeding argument of the Foreword, couched in complex rhetorical sentences in the passive voice, is a sardonically flavoured repudiation of critics who would deny her this stimulus by imputing her experimentation to the influence of fashion or to an overshadowing by Proust or James.[3] 'Feminine prose', she concludes (and as Dickens and Joyce both realized), 'should properly be unpunctuated, moving from point to point without formal obstructions.' Both the isolation of Miriam's experience and her feeling that language is ill-suited to convey its essence are symptoms of her conviction that hers is an authentic female vision and that men are constitutionally incapable of understanding it. Like all Richardson's pronouncements this was not originally a philosophic position but an experiential one, deriving initially, it would seem, from her relationship with her father, then developing as a result of her socialization and finally taking intellectual contours during her rebellion against it.

Her literary aspirations coalesced with her feminism in the aim of producing the 'feminine equivalent of the current masculine realism',[4] an aim sufficiently realized in her fiction for Woolf to discern its stylistic uniqueness in precisely those terms :

> She has invented. . . a sentence. . . of a more elastic fibre than the old, capable of stretching to the extreme, of suspending the frailest particles, of enveloping the vaguest shapes. . . . It is a woman's sentence, but only in the sense that it is used to describe a woman's mind by a writer who is neither proud nor afraid of anything she may discover in the psychology of her sex. . . .[5]

This new kind of sentence, fragmented across the conventions of English syntax and punctuation, was the technical unit which provided the basis for her feminine vision. At the same time, there are features of her work which belong to traditional practice; her use of a governess persona follows in the wake of the Brontës, and her abandonment of the distinction between impressionism and realism in the wake of Henry James. Like Dickens, she peoples her work with a host of subsidiary characters. Like Hardy, her sense of place is animated almost to the degree of anthropomorphism. Whatever may appear Victorian in her sentiments, however, is countered by her very un-Victorian abnegation of a moral analysis of the dynamics of society.

Between 1902 and 1938 Richardson wrote and published numerous sketches, reviews and occasional journalism, as well as all the volumes of *Pilgrimage* except *March Moonlight*. The wide scope of these activities, apart from suggesting the pressures of near-penury, indicates some ambivalence, even confusion, in her development as a writer. In the manuscript fragment, 'Literary Essays',[6] she dates the beginning of her development from 'some thirty? articles sent in and accepted, all but one during 1908-1913' as middles for the *Saturday Review*. She was urged by Arthur Baumann (of the *Review*) to attempt a novel, but was discouraged, initially, by Wells. For her it was, to begin with, a 'distasteful idea'. The *Dental Record* articles, for instance, show, in some measure, the extent of her ambivalence; they derive directly from her experiences as a dental secretary in a Harley Street practice, so that she treats current events in the domain of dentistry with a professional seriousness, while at the same time using the columns of the *Record* as a forum for more partisan views on diet, general hygiene and, more importantly, the conditions and opportunities relevant to women's employment. The *Crank* articles reveal two further interests : the nature of book reviewing and the relevance of socialism as a practical philosophy. Her views on both these subjects are more passionate than they are informed, a characteristic no doubt enhanced by the brevity of the articles. The *Saturday Review* sketches reveal yet another preoccupation, this time with the intensity of sensuous response and with the immediacy of experience. Richardson clearly practised journalism with one eye on her pocket, since her financial circumstances never permitted her to write only when and what she chose. To E.B.C. Jones, for example, she complained : 'No time for Miriam nor do I know when I shall have. I've short things for three mags. Run by friends neither of which pay a living wage. And just keep alive. A line now and again of Miriam.' [7]

The pressure on her time was almost comical in its relentlessness :

> A nice little French book, by a Swiss, translated & now in proof, was to have been done in two months, was just begun when H. G. asked me to read his autobiography: 200,000 words to correct, comment upon & generally trim up. Page proofs to read, with the author away in Russia, & his helper to help in the business of seeing the two volumes through the press. When all was complete, one month was left for my translation, which somehow was done to time, the last word being typed at 5.20 on the promised day & Alan, at 5.55., racing down the Strand with the ms – me panting far behind with my eye on the clock of St. Mary-le-Strand. He broke in as they were closing.[8]

The note of self-pity is not difficult to detect, yet Richardson is capable also of a wry humour, knowing that however justifiably resentful she may feel, it is nonetheless gratitude that she is expected to display :

> I also wait to hear from a publisher whether I may translate for him a French book and from another publisher whether I may translate for him a German book. And Heaven knows as well as I do that I don't want to do either and yet must be grateful if I may.[9]

It is left to the fiction to map how all her divergent concerns relate to each other. And the relation between them issues from the motivating stimulus which generates *Pilgrimage*; the search for identity and the search for style, which are alternately separated and co-mingled in Richardson's depiction of female consciousness.

The experimental process took a long time. She planned several novels but all 'founded on an "idea"' which was 'somehow too easy, utterly distasteful & boring'.[10] Ideas, she felt, were so mutable, and she had 'a growing desire to express the immutable'. She wrote several short stories, 'each backed by an idea, and reading as if written by a man'. Here, explicitly, is the psychological formulation of her creative dilemma; traditional narrative proceeds from an 'idea', which is the characterizing mark of masculine intelligence. It is her feminism which impels the search for a way of presenting 'the mass lying unexpressed'. Bunyan and the mystics had expressed it, but novels had not. Novels 'exclude the essential'. The 'essential', the 'unexpressed mass', she calls 'first-hand life'. In 1909, she records, she wrote 'a mass of material each part expanding in the mind unmanageably, choked by the necessities of narrative. Close narrative too technical, dependent on a whole questionable set of agreements & assumptions between reader and writer.'[11] By 1911, she had conceded that novels were 'founded on experience' but they were 'written for the reader, as if by the reader, things explained showmanwise'. Another manuscript fragment, headed *Sussex Period*[12] (the period recounted in *Dimple Hill*), dates the beginning of the resolution of the problem. The note is written in the third person and might be taken to refer equally to Richardson and to Miriam. It is headed 'Discovery of style' and marks her awareness that what is written is inseparably contingent upon the way it is written:

> Loses track of the arguments by the effect upon her of style. Reading, feeling only the [responsive beat of her blood her nerves *deleted*] glowing of her nerves & the beat of her blood or whole being.
>
> Investigating the climax of the [sentence *deleted*] communication held up until all else even modifications are set down.[13]

The deleted 'sentence', here, is a vital clue to the process she is trying to analyse; the syntactical unit becomes subordinated to the pressure to include everything pertinent to what is being described. Eventually, by the time Richardson comes to write *Pilgrimage*, she accepts psychological veracity as a more authentic measure of artistic direction than technical conformity, so that she tries to shape her prose according to the former. This results in the characteristic breaks in syntax, in elisions and omissions, which are designed to articulate the process of Miriam's awareness. For example :

> A *German*, not a Russian ethnologist, and therefore without prejudice, had declared that the Russians were the strongest kinetic force in Europe. He proved himself disinterested by saying that the English came next. The English were 'simple and fundamentally sound.' Not intelligent; but healthy in will, which the Russians were not. Then why were the Russians more forceful? What was kinetic force? And . . mystery . . . the Russians themselves knew what they were like. 'There is in Russia, except in the governing and bourgeois classes, almost no hypocrisy.' What was kinetic. . . . And religion was an 'actual force' in Russia! 'What is ki—' [14]

The passage begins with a conventionally formed sentence, the purpose of which is to provide context, although since even external context must be filtered through Miriam's mind, the insertion 'therefore without prejudice' already introduces a value judgement, so that the reader is meant to take the German seriously for the reason Miriam does. This view of the German is reinforced in the following sentence – 'He proved himself disinterested' – and the perception has shifted from being stated in a dependent clause to a main clause. Next we are given direct quotation, which moves the context even more closely towards Miriam in the act of receiving information. Then comes the bridge between the external context and Miriam's internal reflections, and the bridge is technically composed of the two styles : the internal prefigured in the phrase 'not intelligent', which is made to stand alone, and the external, which is given a conventional co-ordinating clause. After that we move directly into Miriam's reflecting consciousness by means of her two silent questions. And since they are silent, what follows are loose associations, focusing on 'mystery' and what the Russians think they are like. The associations are not sequentially connected, so that the missing links are indicated by a series of points. Miriam's reflections are then punctuated by another properly formed sentence which comes from outside her. But her associations flow on; she wonders what 'kinetic' means. Yet still the external world obtrudes, with a further idea, this time about religion being an 'actual force', before she has been able to assimilate the first. The pressure forces her now to bring the question in her mind out into the external world : 'What is ki—'. But she is cut off before she can complete it.

The interactions between inner consciousness and external reality are conveyed in this way by the manipulation of the sentence as the structural unit of language. What Richardson wants is an open-ended mode that has neither structural, ideological, nor psychological parameters, so that she can feel able to suggest the nature of experience itself, which is necessarily open-ended in the real world. Traditional novels fail to do this because they 'shut one up with humanity, tragically or comically. Amen. Certain.'[15] Philosophers fail because they depend upon 'some single interpretation of life'. Poetry is 'somehow always only half-true'. An open-ended presentation must be 'experience without reference', all parameters being falsifications : 'Drama, even the drama of the objective description of a cabbage, was falsification, a deliberate enclosure when nothing is enclosed'.[16]

Traditional aesthetic conventions order the representation of reality into discrete sections and adduce techniques accordingly, without assuming a synonymity between art and and life. Richardson, however, denies this parallelism by seeking to establish a mode which will present the texture of life itself. 'All "art",' she wrote, 'is in some way false, conveying the surface, not penetrating beneath.' [17] What is 'beneath' or 'inside' is her true subject-matter, so that the pilgrimage undertaken by Miriam is not confined to the search for identity; it is also the search for style.

II

The opening of *Pointed Roofs* demonstrates Richardson's commitment to the realization of 'life itself'. Unlike autobiography it does not begin at the beginning, nor does it provide any explanatory preamble :

> Miriam left the gaslit hall and went slowly upstairs. The March twilight lay upon the landings, but the staircase was almost dark. The top landing was quite dark and silent. There was no one about. It would be quiet in her room. She could sit by the fire and be quiet and think things over until Eve and Harriett came back with the parcels. She would have time to think about the journey and decide what she was going to say to the Fräulein.[18]

From this we learn only that Miriam is to undertake a journey; we are not told anything else about her, nor do we learn who Eve, Harriett and the Fräulein are. On the other hand, the incident is clearly placed and seen unambiguously through Miriam's eyes alone. Attention to details of physical place is a consistent feature in *Pilgrimage,* used not merely as an aesthetic device but also as a structural one, since the narration does not rely for its cohesion on the dramatic disposition of plot and character characteristic of the nineteenth-century novel. Since the writer does not permit perceptions other than Miriam's, details of time and place must provide a framework for the reader's awareness of the external world as the only possible counterbalancing reality to Miriam's consciousness. This is a principal reason why the sequence is not surrealistic; we are never in any doubt that the external world 'really' exists for Miriam, but we are aware, also, that its existence can only be realized through the filter of personal consciousness.

The information that Miriam is to undertake a journey is followed by two features of the life she is leaving – schooldays and domestic leisure. The continuity of the past in the present through the nature of memory and association is now a commonplace in the literature of the twentieth century, having its roots as much in psychoanalysis as in the work of Henry James. It is easy to underestimate how original such a style was in 1915. The centrality of Miriam's consciousness, rather than the expectations of the reader, is the sole springboard for the associations selected, so that the structure of the work must depend entirely on the credibility of that consciousness; further, the degree to which a fiction of this kind will be convincing or not will depend on the degree to which authorial comment can be abnegated.

In Richardson's work, the technical implication is that the reader should identify Miriam's voice with that of the author, since no other consciousness is brought into play, as in the novels of James, nor is distance created between persona and author by providing a precision of time, place and circumstance, and a logic of reflection, as in the later novels of Woolf; Richardson maps Miriam : Woolf oversees Clarissa Dalloway. Because of the near-synonymity between Richardson and Miriam, judgements passed upon Miriam will generate from the reader's critical self-consciousness rather than from his capacity for fantasy. At the opening of the first chapter, then, Miriam, anxious about departing, is forced by her own associations to contemplate what she is leaving : 'The sense of all she was leaving stirred uncontrollably as she stood looking down into the well-known garden.'[19] The garden, symbol of refuge, innocence and the coming of knowledge, recurs throughout *Pilgrimage* as the original location of the isolated and perceiving consciousness. The associations continue: a piano-organ's tune makes her think of her schooldays; the fire makes her think of summer; the summer makes her remember 'a white twinkling figure' who came to tea every Sunday afternoon:

> Why didn't he say: 'Don't go,' or 'When are you coming back?' Eve said he looked perfectly miserable.[20]

The reader is not told who the gentleman is. That is not important. What is important is Miriam's hurt at his seeming indifference, so that hurt resolves into

> There was nothing to look forward to now but governessing and old age. Perhaps Miss Gilkes was right. . . . Get rid of men and muddles and have things just ordinary and be happy.[21]

The seeming banality of this advice is deceptive; for a young woman whose future might well be no more than 'governessing and old age' a retreat from intellection and observation into having things 'just ordinary' might possibly secure contentment and social acceptance, both of which are no mean alternatives to isolation. But the prose carries its own implicit judgement; the imprecision of 'men and muddles' and the sentimentality of having things 'just ordinary' prevent the option from receiving serious consideration. The reader is reminded that the reflection has grown out of hurt, so that it takes on the tone of an angry response rather than a neutral judgement. The anger is caused by the gentleman's failure to show initiative and Miriam's awareness that her female role prohibits her from soliciting it. By contrast, the next section shows her to be perfectly capable of soliciting reassurance from her sister:

> 'You'll feel better to-morrow.'
> 'D'you think I shall?'
> 'Yes – you're so strong,' said Eve, flushing and examining her nails.
> 'How d'you mean?'
> 'Oh – all sorts of ways.'
> 'What way?'
> 'Oh – well – you arranging all this – I mean answering the adver-

tisement and settling it all.'

'Oh, well, you know you backed me up.'

'Oh, yes, but other things. . . .'

'What?'

'Oh, I was thinking about you having no religion.'

'Oh.'

'You must have such splendid principles to keep you straight,' said Eve, and cleared her throat. 'I mean, you must have such a lot in you.'

'Me?'

'Yes, of course.'

'I don't know where it comes in. What have I done?'

'Oh, well, it isn't so much what you've done – you have such a good time. . . . Everybody admires you and all that. . . you know what I mean – you're so clever. . . . You're always in the right.'

'That's just what everybody hates!'[22]

Here the jerkiness of the dialogue underlines the taut embarrassment of the situation, but Miriam's need for reassurance is so strong that she persists in spite of Eve's reticence. Nor does she deny that she is always in the right; on the contrary, she knows that it is a trait people hate. It is also clear that Miriam appears confident and happy, although she does not feel so. The awkwardness of the exchange continues:

'It'll be ghastly,' continued Miriam, 'not having any one to pour out to – I've told you such a lot these last few days.'

'Yes, hasn't it been funny? I seem to know you all at once so much better.'

'Well – don't you think I'm perfectly hateful?'

'No. I admire you more than ever. I think you're simply splendid.'

'Then you simply don't know me.'[23]

The use of cliché here glosses over the inchoate sympathy between the two. Eve finds Miriam's confidences 'funny' – unusual and perplexing – and the conventionally emphatic adverbs – 'perfectly' and 'simply' – serve to compound the sentimentality to a degree of intensity which is too much for Eve, who weeps and hugs Miriam. The reader is already aware that there is something ruthless about Miriam's desire for truth which is not alleviated by thinking her naïve or insensitive.

In the next section Miriam awakes from a dream about her prospective position in Germany in which she has been rejected by the staff, who 'looked at her with loathing'. She reminds herself of her motivation for going; she is aware that she can only escape a future of 'governessing and old age' through education. But the price to be paid is to take her place in the world of women. Germany will not be romantic and exotic; it will consist of 'those women' who will 'smile those hateful women's smiles'. What is provoking about these smiles is the reason for them, which Miriam understands only too well. They are 'self-satisfied smiles as if everybody were agreed about everything. She loathed women. They always smiled.' [24]

Miriam makes a contrast with the world of men, represented by her father:

> Pater knew how hateful all the world of women were and despised them.
>
> He never included her with them; or only sometimes when she pretended, or he didn't understand. . . .[25]

The conflict between these worlds is a central theme throughout *Pilgrimage*. Women are hateful because they are unquestioning and accepting: men are, by implication, positive, interesting, powerful, satisfying. But Miriam has a woman's consciousness and a woman's role to play, so that part of the meaning of *Pilgrimage* is the act of writing it – that is, only the self-conscious woman can comprehend the world of men and thereby enter it. It is important to give due weight to this conflict or the explicit feminism which pervades the text might appear to be mere propaganda – to be, that is, not generated by the tone and direction of the writing and therefore to be structurally extraneous.

There follows an exchange with Harriett, characterized by the same awkwardness of dialogue used for the exchange with Eve, this time coloured by the use of a private slang – 'Ike spect it's easy enough' – and which again reveals Miriam's need for reassurance. She tells her sister that 'it's no good bothering when you're plain', which brings the response that no one in the household does think Miriam plain. Again Miriam seems surprised:

> 'I'm pretty – they like me – they *like* me. Why didn't I know?' She did not look into the mirror. 'They all like me, *me*.' [26]

The reader, however, is not as surprised as Miriam. There is an ingenuousness in her response which is irritating and which raises the critical question of Richardson's control. Since the reader is asked to accept an identification between persona and author, it seems improbable that Miriam's self-image should be so out of phase with how others perceive her, except if it is the case that Richardson is introducing a degree of detachment between herself and Miriam which enables her to present Miriam's immaturity as an authentic condition of her consciousness at this stage. That this is so must be argued from the quality of the dialogue; the fumbling for words and the reversion to slang demonstrate that, at this point, Miriam suffers a kind of emotional incompetence, an ineptitude, in direct confrontations of this sort. Her need for truth is a need for others to say the truth, a need for reassurance. What is satisfactory about the dialogue with Harriett is its presentation of Miriam's immaturity. What is unsatisfactory about it is the lack of energy and confidence in the writing; a prose texture composed of the cliché associations of slang and the inarticulate feelings suggested by the grammatical fragmentations is too thin to bear the degree of significance which the author intends. This is always a problem with attempts at verisimilitude, but it must be maintained that ingenuous writing is not justified by the author's intending to demonstrate the ingenuousness of a fictitious character. It is important to notice this here, since the same kind of dialogue appears at various stages, throughout *Pilgrimage,* significantly with reference to Miriam's dealings with women, and forms an interesting contrast with the more confident and therefore convincing style of dialogue characteristic of Miriam's dealings with men.

After the exchange, then, Miriam repeats to herself that she is pretty, but carefully avoids looking into the mirror, not daring the possibility of undermining this new source of confidence. She then dresses for breakfast, donning an old red stockinette jersey and a blue skirt, which she refers to as 'darling old things', in preference to her heavy best dress which is hanging ready for the journey. Throughout *Pilgrimage* Miriam is very concerned about clothing and very careful to observe its details, which is another indication of her insecurity. As she goes in to breakfast, she realizes that she has never thought of the feelings the others may have about her going away. Again, throughout *Pilgrimage,* although she can recognize and rationalize them, she finds it almost impossible sympathetically to perceive and understand other people's feelings.

Several things are clear about this opening : that Miriam is thought of as clever and independent to be going away, whereas her own motivation is the chance of learning; that she suffers from a female anxiety about her attractiveness and needs to be reassured that she is pretty; that her sense of identity is threatened, on the one hand, by the world of women, and on the other, by her father's not including her in it; that her experience of relationship is modified by a self-conscious detachment. Structurally, these themes are implicit and discernible only through the juxtaposition of incident and reflection. Technically, the prose weaves from dialogue to memory to reflection to dream without the framework of formal narrative, sequential chronology or authorial comment. From the beginning, the text demands of the reader a sympathetic identification with Miriam comparable to the author's own, since the organization of Miriam's world depends entirely upon Miriam's perceptions of it. This demand for identification issues partly from the absolute lack of any other consciousness and partly from the nature of Miriam's own; she seems not to want to feel into the world outside, but to stand apart from it, wondering, defining, conjecturing. She is more a philosopher than a poet. But since the text demands the status of fiction and since we are aware of the fusion between Richardson and Miriam, we are left in the paradoxical position of confronting an egocentric reality in the absence of explicit authorial direction, a position which led Woolf privately to complain :

> I suppose the danger is the damned egotistical self; which ruins Joyce and Richardson to my mind: is one pliant and rich enough to provide a wall for the book from oneself without its becoming, as in Joyce and Richardson, narrowing and restricting?[27]

For Richardson, the 'egotistical self' is the focus of experiential reality and the novelist's art therefore consists in rendering it faithfully and credibly. Ironically, she too objected to Joyce's 'egotistical self' which seemed to her over-displayed in *Finnegans Wake*, saying that she held herself off

> from any attempt to state what emotion tranquilly recollected could have produced this tremendous effusion and concentrating rather upon the goods & bads of this particular example of the novels [*sic*] integration into poetry-with-the-author's signature across every sentence - - - - For me much of the book is deliberate 'patter', the shoutings of an erudite, polyglot cheapjack, & the suspiciously explicit guide to the

reader, sandwiched in somewhere about the 100th page, gives away a great deal of the game. But not all.[28]

Woolf's frustration with Richardson's work, on the other hand, apart from its stemming from a natural antipathy to the work of other contemporary novelists, does pinpoint the reader's dilemma. *Pilgrimage* makes little concession to artifice, thus demanding of the reader the exercise of critical intelligence in response. In novels with a structured narrative, for example, the plot functions as a public mode, directing readers to acquiesce in the logic of the sequence of events and in the precision of locations in space and time. In later novels, by James or Conrad, for example, the passage between the world of inner reflection and the world of outer happenings is carefully manipulated by the author, by the use of action and interaction, by the play of comment, interpretation, contrast and consequence. In *Pilgrimage*, however, the author intends deliberately not to manipulate the reader's response according to any framework extrinsic to Miriam's consciousness. Therefore, in order to judge the credibility of that consciousness, the reader's own 'egotistical self' is aroused, since the only framework of reference allowed by the text is 'reality' itself. Because readers all have their own notions of what reality is, Miriam's credibility cannot depend absolutely on her own frontiers of consciousness. Because, too, the text provides a minimal framework for collective response, the reader's individual self-consciousness must provide that counter-balance to Miriam's sense of reality to which the author appeals. What is meant by 'public mode' is an author's manipulation of material sufficient to enable the reader's response, at crucial points, to be generalizable and therefore to be expressed as 'we'. Novelists before Richardson, on the whole, appealed in this way to a consensus of judgement. Richardson was aware of these uses of artifice and chose deliberately not to employ them. That is why, paradoxically, a work which faithfully intends to erase the presence of the author in fact insists on it: we identify author with persona because explicit distinctions between them are not made. By contrast, both traditional narrative novels and conventionally realist novels allow the reader more flexibility of response and judgement precisely because the actions and reflections of characters will occur with reference to conventions which are understood, if not shared, by the reader.

The role conflict characteristic of feminism has already been established in these opening sections, a conflict between Miriam's female role and Miriam's human mind. It is this conflict which provides the dramatic context for Miriam's pilgrimage towards fulfilment in the outer world and towards identity in the inner world. These two selves are paralleled by the partition in the outer world between the separate spheres of influence and expectation dominated respectively by men and women. Miriam's reflections are variously directed by her feelings of isolation, resentment, rage, scorn and frustration, because she perceives herself to be shut out from the larger world of affairs which is dominated by men. On the other hand, she cannot be entirely given up to these destructive impulses; her humanity responds to aesthetic and sensuous pleasures with feelings of astonishment and curiosity. Her quest for enlightenment becomes identified with a need to understand and resolve the partition in herself, which she perceives, platonically, as a reflection of the partition in the outer world. It is precisely this conflict which impairs her relationships with other people, giving the text the peculiar detachment of suppressed passion.

III

By the end of *Honeycomb*, the third chapter-volume of *Pilgrimage*, Richardson is using her expanded, fragmentary sentence with considerable skill, creating not only an impressionistic sketch of the place where Miriam and her mother are on holiday, but also conveying the pain and the nightmare quality of her mother's suicide. In the middle volumes of *Pilgrimage*, the unit of the sentence becomes vastly more complicated; the declarative sentences characteristic of *Pointed Roofs* become more flexible, accommodating Miriam's increasing complication of abstract thought and encompassing, too, subtler fusions between descriptions of the external world and inner reflections. In this way, Richardson's 'woman's sentence' as the correlative of Miriam's consciousness is consolidated, matching, with the expansion of its range, the gradual development of her perceptual power. In *Deadlock*, for example, Richardson records one of Miriam's important insights into the balance she is already seeking between life and literature :

> She felt eager to jest. Ranged with her friends she saw their view of her own perpetually halting scrupulousness and marvelled at their

> patient loyalty. She shared the exasperated intolerance of people who disliked her. . . . It could be disarmed . . . by fresh, surprising handling. . . . Because, she asked herself scornfully as she opened the door to go downstairs, she had corrected Mr Lahitte's unspeakable lecture? No. Sitting over there, forgetting, she had let go . . . and found something. And waking again had seen distant things in their right proportions. But leaving go, not going through life clenched, would mean losing oneself, passing through, not driving in, ceasing to affect and be affected. But the forgetfulness was itself a more real life, if it made life disappear and then show only as a manageable space and at last only as an indifferent distance. A game to be played or even not played. It meant putting life and people second; only entering life to come back again, *always*. This new joy of going into life, the new beauty, on everything, was the certainty of coming back.[29]

'Ranged with her friends she saw - - -' has an ambiguous status in reality, since it is not clear whether Miriam is imaginatively projecting herself into the company of her friends, or whether she is actually among them. And the ambiguity itself allows Miriam the possibility to observe this situation from outside, both to identify her friends' view of her and to respond to it by 'marvelling' at their 'loyalty'. The next sentence brings another, complementary image; this time of people who are not her friends, but who dislike her. These too, by means of her observer's stance, Miriam can identify with, by sharing their 'exasperated intolerance'. At this point the syntax fragments, suggesting that even though Miriam can observe equally impartially those who like and dislike her, her composure can still be unsettled by negative affect. Her immediate response to this unspoken threat, however, is to rush quickly to her own defence by asserting that 'exasperation' can be 'disarmed'. But here the syntax breaks again, this time under the pressure of momentary uncertainty: disarmed by what? Miriam rushes on, answering her own doubt with 'by fresh, surprising handling', a generalization without detail or example, whose abstraction leads also to fragmentation. Impatient with her own attempts to affirm this confidence, she looks for an immediate cause; is it merely, she wonders, the result of correcting 'Mr Lahitte's unspeakable lecture'? She is sure that it is not. Rather, she had 'let go'. Here comes the final ellipsis in this short passage; as Miriam remembers letting herself go, Richardson enacts the process by letting the sentence go. The capacity to allow these subtle shifts from affirmation to insecurity ensures the possibility of returning again to affirmation.

Thus the letting-go is able to precipitate the formulation that Miriam has 'found something'. The 'something' is then presented in unbroken syntax, but the more even rhythm of these unfragmented sentences is disturbed now in a different way; Miriam's effort to probe the nature of her discovery is essentially abstract. The manipulations of 'leaving go', 'passing through', 'not driving in', 'manageable space', 'indifferent distance' and so on, have an algebraic quality, the effect of which is to show that Miriam's observations of herself have become objective in an extreme way, under the pressure of her attempt consciously to master her affective environment. What this kind of writing suggests is that Richardson sees Miriam's gradual acquisition of insight and control as an act of consciousness rather than an act of will, that is, as intellectual rather than moral virtue.

The end of *The Trap* shows a further development of stylistic flexibility, utilizing the previous shifts from description to impressionism and from observation to abstraction and adding another element, the passing without comment between first- and third-person pronouns. It is not the first time this fusion has appeared in the prose, but by the end of *The Trap* Richardson is using it with firm technical agility. Like nearly all her best passages, the subject of this one is, characteristically, a representation of an important insight, in this case Miriam's realization of what her rejection of Selina Holland may mean :

> I am left in a corner with death. But it is I who am left, and not dead. Only out of my own element in which, if I were alone, even death would look quite different.
>
> And far away below evidence and the clear speech of events, even now something was answering. Suddenly like a blow bringing her sharply awake, it came: refusal. Surging up and out over everything, clearing the air, bringing a touch of coolness in the stifling air.
>
> Profanity. My everlasting profanity.
>
> She listened guiltily, glad of its imperiousness. Everything had been thought out. There was nothing appearing behind it. There was in the depths of her nothing but this single knowledge that she was going away from this corner where she had been dying by inches. No consideration of right or wrong. No feeling for persons; either Miss Holland or those people downstairs, or those of her own she had been able to help by this cheaper way of living.
>
> She sighed in pure sadness as she faced this deeper self. For it was

clear now for ever that to be good was not all in all to her. To endure, suffer long and be kind was not her aim. She had never been quite sure whether it was not the hidden secret of all her decisions, born in her, independent of thought. Now and then hearing commendation of endurances that did not bring bitterness, she had been tempted to feel that there must be, since she had endured much and not become bitter, in her own character the things called sweetness and fortitude.

It had always been a strange moment. Two impressions side by side. The certainty that conscious fortitude and sweetness could not persist in their own right, and the uncertainty of approving of these things in their unconscious simplicity; a dislike of being discovered in a state of helpless merit.

Greater than the sadness of not being good, more thrilling, was the joy of feeling ready to take responsibility for oneself.

I must create my life. Life is creation. Self and circumstances the raw material. But so many lives I can't create. And in going off to create my own I must leave behind uncreated lives. Lives set in motionless circumstances.[30]

The opening reflection is a commonplace; the end of any relationship is a prefiguring of death and Miriam is right to assert that the 'I' is always alive and therefore always an onlooker. Then, however, the static quality of this awareness of the ego gives way to the abstract and therefore inchoate swell of the id, that is, the emotion that inevitably accompanies reflection : below evidence and speech comes 'refusal'. The force erupts from 'below' speech, so that its impact is first, its formulation second. What the socialized consciousness cannot accept because it would mean the acceptance of intolerable guilt, the id can force in a way which the consciousness cannot deny, that is, with 'imperiousness'. The third-person 'she', the accusative 'her', together with the passive 'everything had been thought out', emphasize the objectivity of the observer, further rationalized in short declarations in which the subject has been completely elided : 'No consideration of right or wrong. No feeling for persons - - -'. Her consciousness can only sigh in 'pure sadness' in the face of the 'deeper self' of her unconscious individuality and this defeat of her socialization brings her a new insight : her pilgrimage is not a journey towards Pauline charity. Then follows a series of very abstract sentences in which Miriam rationalizes her search to make conscious her own motivations and to discover the alternative morality which has underpinned all her decisions. Her rejection of Pauline ethics is part-logical, part-psychological; if 'fortitude' and 'sweetness' are virtuous then they are qualities which ought to be striven for, but if they are, they become part of consciousness and lose their merit. On the other hand, if these qualities are achieved and remain unconscious, thus retaining their virtue, the personality is rendered 'helpless', vulnerable to discovery and therefore without mastery. That is Miriam's Rubicon and she crosses it with joy. 'To take responsibility for oneself' is a personal ethic whose psychological correlate is the need and the capacity to take control of one's circumstances. The discovery of this ethic more than compensates Miriam for the 'sadness' of 'not being good' and this liberation, as well as releasing Miriam from her observer's stance, releases the prose from abstraction. The syntax now moves immediately to the first-person 'I' in order to enact Miriam's new integration of consciousness and unconsciousness : 'I must create my life - - -'. This is to have profound meaning both for Miriam and for the lives of those closest to her, since her abnegation of all ethics to her personal sense of responsibility for creating her own life must result in a higher than usual degree of conscious calculation in the conduct of relationship.

Later, Miriam formalizes her insights, again in the first person, in the measured rhythms of regular sentences, conveying the affect that this new stance is already familiar to her consciousness :

> This is life. However far I go away, this will go on. To go away is only to get mental oblivion of it. Yet that is just what I am planning. Here in the midst of it is the hope that my lucky star, the star that keeps even my sympathies clear of being actively involved, will carry me through this, too, without bringing it into my hands.[31]

This kind of calculation, the planning to remain uninvolved, is chilling in its deliberated anti-humanism and while the reader may sympathize with Miriam's sense of hope and liberation, he or she may also tremble on behalf of those people around her who must suffer its consequences. Nevertheless, despite Richardson's lack of intelligent wit at this point, her formulation of what has always been the ethical stance of the artist, is devastating in its honesty. The implications of the image of creation are obvious; in order to create, some things must be destroyed, devoured, irrevocably changed. No uneasy truce with charity is possible in such a context and Miriam, determined upon self-discovery, does not offer one. The unconscious irony, which Richardson certainly does not admit, is that Miriam is accepting the very posture she has so vociferously opposed in Wilson and other writers, that is, the manipulation of the material of other people's lives, a behaviour which Miriam previously judged to be an intolerable arrogance. Similarly, in the domestic social context of the conventional world of women, Miriam's judgements on traditional feminine calculations have been harsh in the extreme and she has prided herself on her rejection of these behaviours. The increasing complexity of Richardson's style and the increasing dexterity with which she uses the unit of the sentence, enact more confidently the processes which enable Miriam's consciousness to develop.

Towards the end of *Dimple Hill* it becomes clear that Richardson's original instinct for declarative and descriptive statement has given way, under pressure of closer attention to psychological subtleties, to a technique in which the central concentration is the delineation of perceptual reality, that is, how the perceiving mind interacts with external stimuli :

> Rain chores softly down amongst lime leaves. Which bend to its touch. It whips the laurels and rebounds. Or slides swiftly off their varnished surfaces. Amongst beeches it makes a gentle rattling, a sound like the wind in the Dutch poplars. The hiss of strong rain on the full leafage of the wood. Its rich drip drip in the silent wood. The rising wind opening the tree-tops, sending down sudden sheets of light; like lightning.

> Awake deep down in the heart of tranquillity, drinking its freshness like water from a spring brimming up amongst dark green leaves in deep shadow heightening the colour of the leaves and the silver glint on the bubbling water. A sound, a little wailing voice far away across the marshes, dropping from note to note, five clear notes, and ceasing. This was the sound that brought me up from dreamless sleep? Again the little wailing sound, high and thin and threadlike and very far away.[32]

The verb 'chores' efficiently establishes the fusion in Miriam's mind of observation and affect. As 'chores' is transposed from its normal grammatical function of noun to the unusual application of verb, the association of regularity and familiarity connoted by its noun use becomes incorporated into Miriam's affective response, which animates the rain's activity by the connotation of intention proper to the grammatical function of a verb. The observation described and the affect imputed are thus brought together to render an impressionistic prose. Ellipsis has been discarded; the sentences are shorter and tighter and dismembered both of subject and of verb. The description of physical detail characteristic of Richardson's earlier style gives way here to traditional poetic techniques of onomatopoeia and assonance : the rain 'whips', 'slides' and 'hisses'; the word 'chores', in addition to its grammatical transposition, carries with its sound the associations of 'charge 'and 'pour'. The wind 'opens' the tree-tops. The timelessness of experience, so important to Richardson, is represented by the abnegation of tense altogether; the initial present tense disappears into the temporally unconnected participle in 'rising', 'opening' and 'sending'. The persona remains hidden, since both subject and verb are missing from the opening sentence of the second paragraph. The single clue to her presence is given in the participle 'awake' and her psychological activity is again outside time, being represented by the present participle 'drinking'. Her tranquillity, like her previous insights, comes from 'deep down'. Even the most direct sentence comes in the form of a question : 'This was the sound that brought me up from dreamless sleep?' The accusative 'me' is the first explicit signification of the persona's engagement with the setting presented and its appearance in the accusative case emphasizes the intention of objectivity. The sound which has disturbed her comes from 'very far away'; that she describes it as a 'wailing voice' leaves an ambiguity between whether or not it is a human sound :

> It has come out of the sea, is wandering along the distant, desolate shore. Nothing between us but the fields and the width of the marshes. There it is again, leaving the shore, roaming along the margin of the marsh, in and out amongst the sedges, plaintive.
>
> It has reached the grey willows huddled along the dykes. Shrill and querulous amongst their slender leaves.
>
> Many voices, approaching, borne on an undertone, shouting and moaning, dying away into lamentations. Reaching the hedgerows, filling them with a deep singing. The evergreen oak quivers under the threatening breath, harplike in all its burdened branches. Stillness.
>
> Tumult, wild from the sea, sweeping headlong, gigantic, seizing the house with a yell, shaking it, sending around it the roaring of fierce flames. Rattling the windows, bellowing down the chimney. Rejoicing in its prey.
>
> The wind, is the best lover.[33]

A sentence complete with subject and verb comes at the point of highest confidence : 'It has come out of the sea', which is sustained with further mention of the voice – it 'is wandering', 'there it is again', 'it has reached'. The growing strength of the voice corresponds with its increasing animism. The persona's 'me' is now transposed to 'us', which first emphasizes the animism of the voice and then confers relationship on the voice and the persona, who are separated only by fields and marshes. The voice comes closer to her, as if by intent, passing from the sea, along the marsh, through the willows, and then gathering the strength of 'many voices' from the hedgerows and the trees. By the time the voice reaches the house it has the power of passion, can create 'tumult', is 'wild' and 'gigantic' and is able to 'yell' and 'bellow'. It has conquered its 'prey'. The last line of the passage identifies the voice as the wind while at the same time focusing the image of its progress as that of a lover wooing a beloved. The persona willingly takes the part of the beloved, being both unfrightened by the lover's force and undismayed by the suggestion that she is a victim about to be devoured, which the word 'prey' connotes. The explicit value-judgement of the last line is reinforced by its simple sentence form and by the use of the present tense. The movement from far-off wailing to bellowing climax is carefully done and establishes the imaginative intimacy Richardson intends. But the love-image is, after all, an image; and the rhetorical mode, whilst deftly able to record each shift in affect, forces the subject to remain figurative. Miriam in isolation is able to respond to passion she imputes to the inanimate much more fully than Miriam in relationship is able to respond to feelings issuing from other human beings. She can fall 'prey' to the wind much more readily than she can allow herself even to be touched by another person. The challenge to her consciousness from the inanimate comes only from its inscrutability; it may be a challenge, that is, to the resources of perception and intuition, but it is not a challenge to the power of egoism. Only an equivalent consciousness can present that threat.

The refinement of Richardson's technique thus brings her, in the end, to the point where she can represent not only the stimuli which Miriam receives and her ability to remember and to connect, but also the delicate shifts of apperception which describe Miriam's reality as a merging of observation and imputation. When she is experiencing this kind of reality, Miriam can be bold, confident, aware, even expansive. It is in the far more threatening arena of personal encounter and confrontation that Miriam feels she must fight for control and not only fight, but win.

NOTES AND REFERENCES

1 Ros Coward, 'The Making of the Feminine', *Spare Rib*, 70, May 1978, pp. 43-6.

2 Foreword, *Pilgrimage*, Collected Edition, 4 vols., Dent, 1938, p. 9.

3 In her private correspondence, Richardson's more trenchant opinions of Proust and James are often evident. See, for example, her remarks about Proust to Shiv Kumar: 'Proust, needing a mouthful of madeleine cake to recall the past, is surely far below Bergson for whom memory's excursions were the direct result of concentration. Abel Chevalley, author of *Le Roman Anglais de nos jours*, expressed to me his surprise over the status of Proust in England and described Proust's mind as a melange of Darwin and Ruskin, and his style as an imitation of Henry James.' DR to Shiv Kumar, 10 August, 1952. And to Henry Savage she wrote of James: 'His style, fascinating at a first meeting for me can only be, very vulgarly, described as a non-stop waggling of the backside as he hands out, on a salver, sentence after sentence, that yet, if the words had no meaning, would weave its own spell. So what? One feels, reaching the end of the drama, in a resounding box, where no star shines and no bird sings. Not fair, I daresay, and indeed he was a "writer," consciously and systematically.' DR to Henry Savage, 26 August, 1948.

4 Foreword, *Pilgrimage*, op. cit.

5 Virginia Woolf, 'Romance and the Heart'. *The Nation and the Athenaeum* Literary Supplement, 19 May, 1923, p. 229.

6 'Literary Essays', autograph manuscript draft of an essay on her development as a writer.

7 DR to E. B. C. Jones [no date].

8 DR to John Cowper Powys, September 1934.

9 DR to John Austen, October 1930.

10 'Literary Essays', op. cit.

11 Ibid.

12 'Sussex Period', autograph manuscript draft of an essay on her artistic development and the feminist movement.

13 Ibid.

14 *Deadlock*, p. 45. Cf. DR to S. S. Koteliansky, 30 July, 1944: 'Ages ago, when I was very young, a German ethnologist with a job at the St. Petersburg Acad. of Science solemnly assured me that the Russians were the strongest kinetic force in Europe.'

15 'Sussex Period', op. cit.

16 Ibid.

17 Ibid.

18 *Pointed Roofs*, p. 15.

19 Loc. cit.
20 Ibid., p. 16.
21 Loc. cit.
22 Ibid., p. 19.
23 Ibid., p. 20.
24 Ibid., p. 21.
25 Ibid., p. 22.
26 Ibid., p. 24.
27 Virginia Woolf, *A Writer's Diary: Being Extracts from the Diary of Virginia Woolf,* ed. Leonard Woolf, Hogarth Press, 1953, p. 23.
28 DR to John Cowper Powys, 25 October, 1942.
29 *Deadlock,* pp. 135-6.
30 *The Trap,* pp. 507-8.
31 Ibid., p. 509.
32 *Dimple Hill,* pp. 538-9.
33 Ibid., p. 539.

2 · *Men*

I

Richardson's relationship with her father defines her initial contact with the world of men, which she has her persona, Miriam, record. Miriam identifies strongly with her father, who had

> sacrificed everything to the idea of being a 'person of leisure and cultivation.' Well, after all, it was true in a way. He was – and he had, she knew, always wanted her to be the same and she *was* going to finish her education . . . in Germany. . . .[1]

Miriam is aware that her father wants her to be 'the same' as himself, but she is also aware that she has more resources than he and that her independence must be total. 'It must be the end of taking money from him,' she reflects. 'She was grown up. She was the strong-minded one. She must manage.' [2] Since money is a stock symbol for independence, for Miriam it represents a concrete channel between the demands of the external world and the demands of her inner struggle. Her drive for independence stems from her identification with her father, who stands for 'leisure and cultivation'; and the drive becomes associated with escape from the world she has known – the world, that is, of unprofessional women and the destinies it predetermines. It becomes associated, too, with escape from the domain of her father's protection, and escape, obviously, from England. Miriam's inner monologue is clear on this point: 'She would rather stay abroad on any terms – away from England – English people - - - - Away out here, the sense of imminent catastrophe that had shadowed all her life so far had disappeared.' [3] This fusion of needs, the need on the one hand to escape England and the familiar, and the need on the other to escape the 'catastrophe' of the female lot, becomes explicit in her uncertainty and her ambivalence about her father's inability to direct her without serving his own ego :

> She would ask Pater before he went. . . . No, she would not. . . . If only he would answer a question simply, and not with a superior air as if he had invented the thing he was telling about.[4]

The sense of ambivalence leads directly to a generalization about her social relationships, because she cannot identify either with the world her father represents, or with the world of women, with any degree of commitment. And they are the only worlds within the scope of her experience to date : 'I don't like men and I loathe women. I am a misanthrope. So's Pater. He despises women and can't get on with men.' [5]

The difference between Miriam's response and that of her father is that she is aware of her ambivalence, whereas he is not. As with the rest of Richardson's representation of experience in *Pilgrimage*, as with the motivation for the technique she evolved, the precondition necessary to understanding is self-consciousness. Furthermore, Miriam realizes the consequences of her identification with her father, thinking

> he's failed us because he's different and if he weren't we should be like other people - - - - If Pater had kept to Grandpa's business they would be trade, too – well-off, now – all married. Perhaps as it was he had thought they would marry.[6]

Richardson's sister, Jessie Hale, supplied a sketch of their father which offers an interesting comparison with the representation of Miriam's father in *Pilgrimage*. To Rose Odle she wrote : 'Dorothy's father. . .was a stern tall man over 6 ft with a pointed beard. He however became an Episcopalian, which made things much easier for his four daughters.' [7] Richardson's father, that is, symbolized an opposition between industriousness and cultivation and, by failing to show how the second is supported by the first, restricted both the psychological and the practical possibilities of his daughters to find marriage partners. When two of her sisters marry, Miriam thinks with relief : 'Sarah and Harriett, rescued from poverty and fear. . .' [8] Richardson's explicit endorsement of her brother-in-law, represented in *Pilgrimage* as Gerald, owes much to this factor, since Gerald was not only willing to marry Richardson's penniless, cultivated sister, but was also willing to provide a home and financial support for their bankrupt father.

Miriam's ambivalence towards her father contains, naturally, both positive and negative aspects. The negative side is that her father's bequest entails her own anti-socialization: a questioning of the woman's role and a disaffection for conformity, for compromising one's interests on behalf of others, and for business. The positive side is a recognition of her father's good taste, that he is, in his way, a person of 'leisure and cultivation'. It is clearly the negative side, however, which will prove the more potent in the search to establish her own identity, since it is as a woman that she must find her place. The superior airs of men enrage her quite as much as the quiescent smiles of women:

> Listening to sermons was wrong . . . people ought to refuse to be preached at by these men - - - - those men's sermons were worse than women's smiles - - - - droning on and on and getting more and more pleased with himself and emphatic . . .[9]

There are several things to be noticed here. First, there is a rejection of the preacher as a symbol of authority, to which Miriam is expected to submit. But she does not say 'refuse to be preached at by these *people*'; the emphatic 'by these men' compounds the concept of authority with the masculine gender. It is Miriam's psychological inability and intellectual unwillingness to detach the office of authority from the gender of the person who holds it which fuels her anger to the point where she cannot actually listen, and where, it seems to her, the preacher is merely indulging his own ego, 'getting more and more pleased with himself'. Men's sermons are 'worse than women's smiles' precisely because they have putative authority. Secondly, Miriam pronounces a moral judgement on the congregation; listening to sermons is 'wrong'. The people who collude with a man indulging himself in public in this way when they could exercise their free choice of censure by staying away, excite her moral disgust; it is wrong and base to submit. This language is not a rational mode of protest against authority – it has the tone of moral and psychological warfare, in which the opposing sides are men and women.

When Miriam does find a man attractive, it is his physical self which draws her: 'The sense of the outline of his shoulders and his comforting black mannishness so near to her brought her almost to tears.' [10] This man is a Swiss pastor and a widower and he is not only interested in Miriam but perceptive about her, attributing the fact that she does not enjoy school life to her country background. He recognizes her ambitiousness and then responds with his own :

> 'A little land, well-tilled,
> A little wife, well-willed,
> Are great riches.' [11]

Miriam, to her intense indignation, knows exactly what he means : it

> filled her with fury to be regarded as one of a world of little tame things to be summoned by little men to be well-willed wives. She must make him see that she did not even recognize such a thing as 'a well-willed wife.' She felt her gaze growing fixed and moved to withdraw it and herself.[12]

Again, as with her reaction to the sermon, her 'fury' is aroused by the implicit authoritarianism she perceives in the bearing of men; she needs to dissociate herself from a group of tame things who can be 'summoned'. Her need to dissociate is indeed so strong that it forces an internal dissociation between her own consciousness and her social identity : she looks at herself, not from the outside, but the inside, feeling her gaze 'growing fixed' so that she must 'move' to 'withdraw it'. The pastor responds unconsciously to this withdrawal and comes closer, asking her why she wears glasses. He removes the glasses and looks into her eyes, ostensibly to examine them. But for Miriam, to be without her glasses is to be literally without half her vision. Fromm points out that in this passage in the manuscript of *Pointed Roofs* 'the handwriting takes on a radically different appearance', as if 'Dorothy must have removed her own glasses and finished writing the scene under the same handicap as her heroine.' [13] As in this incident, it is so often the case in *Pilgrimage* that the fury evoked by the unspoken request to submit, implicit in the social relationships between the sexes, results in such a strong identification between Richardson and her persona that the reader must accept Miriam's view and value judgement as Richardson's own.

The blurred image of Pastor Lahmann is an apt symbol of Miriam's confusion. As he comes closer to her, she is able to push him out of focus. He understands her withdrawal, and, having remarked on her eyes, moves on to her hair, saying how blonde she must have been as a child. In this ambiguous attitude they are interrupted by their employer:

> Miriam was pleased at the thought of being grouped with him in the eyes of Fräulein Pfaff - - - - Pastor Lahmann was standing in the middle of the room examining his nails. Fräulein, at the window, was twitching a curtain into place. She turned and drove Miriam from the room with speechless waiting eyes - - - - Pastor Lahmann had made her forget she was a governess. He had treated her as a girl. Fräulein's eyes had spoiled it. Fräulein was angry about it for some extraordinary reason.[14]

Miriam's naïveté here is almost incredible for one so forthright and clever; what Richardson wishes the reader to see, however, is that Miriam's refusal of the feminine role entails a 'blindness' to the ways of lovers. Fräulein Pfaff's censure is unexpected by Miriam, who 'was pleased at the thought of being grouped with him'. But it is not unexpected by the pastor, who 'stepped back' at the sound of her voice and who then stands in the middle of the room 'examining his nails'. Miriam's blindness to the sexual innuendoes of the situation is here cleverly contrasted with her immediate recognition of the meaning of the older woman's look. Her inability to understand Fräulein Pfaff's anger is ironic; although pleased that she has been treated 'as a girl', she forgets that the basis of that treatment filled her with 'fury'. It is clear to the reader, if not to Miriam, that the reason for the Fräulein's anger is no more 'extraordinary' than the reason for Miriam's own. Miriam never comes to understand the basis of her employer's subsequent enmity towards her. Later, when she resigns, she does not understand why she is not asked to stay on. Miriam's response to the pastor is symptomatic; despite the stereotypic nature of the encounter she feels the same unbending fury as she does in her public persona, for instance, when she is asked to submit to a sermon or lesson. Neither the intensity of her physical response, nor the intimacy of the conversation, modify her feeling of difference and her need to be accepted from a position outside the perimeters of the female role. She is left with the confusion and its resulting ambivalence that the pastor both pleased her and made her furious by treating her 'as a girl'.

This abortive attachment to Pastor Lahmann is a prototype of others, similarly abortive, which provide one of the connecting links between the succeeding volumes of *Pilgrimage.* Mr Parrow, in *Back-*

water, Mr Hancock, in *The Tunnel*, Dr Densley, in *The Trap*, and Richard Roscorla, in *Dimple Hill*, attract Miriam as she does them, but her feminism proscribes any commitment. It is the Russian Jewish emigré, Michael Shatov, a fellow lodger in Mrs Bailey's house, who becomes Miriam's most ardent challenger in her personal battle of the sexes. He is the first man seriously to threaten the self-imposed isolation of her consciousness. She is unable to shut him out as a mere man; he is able to give her something which she realizes must mean 'the irrevocable expansion of her consciousness'.[15] She conceptualizes this to be his Russian expansiveness, which extends the imaginative parameters of her Europe, consisting previously of France, Germany and Italy. To the reader, however, it is clear that Miriam is primarily attracted to Shatov as a man. Here is a significant example of Miriam's inability to integrate and identify her actual responses; romantic attachment and erotic arousal she is driven to identify in other terms. There is, here, a hidden irony which affirms Hypo Wilson's assessment of women's writing – that it is mainly about 'love-affairs and so forth'.[16] Since Miriam's unconscious responses attract her both to men and to women, her conscious sense of the separation of the sexes leaves her with an enigmatic sense of the ensuing fragmentation – a fragmentation which is constantly reinforced. This compounds with her frustration at being outside the intellectual tradition, which exudes from, and is controlled by, the animus of men. It is her fragmentation which fuels her zeal for unity and wholeness. Unlike Wagner and Lawrence, Richardson's imagination is not fired by the dividing of the sexes, but profoundly depressed by it. Separation, for her, does not promise the consummation of passion, but ominously forebodes the limbo of isolation. Wagner and Lawrence propose that the union of spirits, before the final dissolution, is achieved through the consummation of the flesh. Richardson, by contrast, is convinced of the Cartesian division between the spirit and the flesh, a position which follows predictably upon the role conflict suffered by those women who resist accepting their expected destinies as wives and mothers. Their femininity lodges in the body, its attributes and capacities, while their sense of identity becomes synonymous with the mind, the personality and individuality which are, by the definition of division, sexually neutralized. Richardson dramatizes this conflict in *Revolving Lights* during a conversation with Shatov, significantly about revolution. The conversation marks the end of their courtship:

'- - - The women know that humanity is two groups [says Miriam]. And they go into revolutions for the freedom from the pressure of this knowledge.'

'Revolution is by no means the sole way of having a complete sense of humanity. But what has all this to do with *us*?'

'It is not that women are heartless; that is an appearance. It is that they know that there are no *tragedies*. . . .'

'Listen, Mira. You have taught me much. I am also perhaps not so undiscriminating as are some men.'

'In family life, all your Jewish feelings would overtake you. You would slip into dressing-gown and slippers. You have said so yourself. But I am now quite convinced that I shall never marry.' She walked on.

He ran round in front of her bringing her to a standstill.

'You think you will never marry . . . with *this*' – his ungloved hands moved gently over the outlines of her shoulders. 'Ah – it is most – musical; you do not know.' She thrilled to the impersonal acclamation; yet another of his many defiant tributes to her forgotten material self; always lapsing from her mind, never coming to her aid when she was lost in envious admiration of women she could not like. Yet they contained an impossible idea; the idea of a man being consciously attracted and won by universal physiological facts, rather than by individuals themselves.[17]

Women want to live in a unified universe, Miriam explains. This desire will suffice to motivate them towards revolution. But for Shatov, unlike Miriam, the political and the personal are discontinuous; there are, he asserts, other roads to unity. Miriam restates her position in an echo of the intellectual tradition and her exclusion from it : women 'know that there are no *tragedies*'. One man cannot die for the people and thus expiate their common sin. For Miriam there cannot be heroes because there is no unified humanity to produce them.[18] Again Shatov reverts to the personal, by responding to her body. Miriam, however, does not take this to be a personal response, but a general one, even though she reacts particularly. Her body is 'forgotten', because it is her 'material self'. She interprets the erotic response of Shatov to be the same thing as the erotic response of the male in general – that is, that his response to her is a submission to laws of physiology, a submission which can have no relevance to her as an individual. The paradox is ironic; Shatov, clearly, intends his caress to be utterly personal and completely consistent with his response to her as an individual, whereas for Miriam it projects their relationship to the archetype of the depersonalized conjunction of male and female flesh. Her feminist quest, while concentrating all her energy, intensity and interest on the expression and delineation of the feminine principle, completely excises from her consciousness the very thing which identifies her femininity, that is, her body. Only her unconscious self is capable of response, of being 'thrilled'. The disjunction between the particular and general is figured in a disjunction between the mind and the body, but it is a condition of which Shatov is profoundly unaware. It is clear to the reader, if not to Miriam, that the result of this disjunction is effectively to erase the division of the sexes in the most direct way possible, that is, by neutralizing sexual arousal. Miriam is driven to such extreme measures by her feminist need for recognition as a person, and by her woman's need to be accepted as a whole being. To be an individual in a man's world is to refuse to be any man's woman, since it is in submission to that role that the ultimate threat lies – the threat of the annihilation of female consciousness. Indeed, in Fromm's opinion, the rejection of conventional role behaviour can almost be seen as a role reversal:

> . . . evident at once, after the initial surprising embrace, is Miriam's physical resistance, markedly unlike that of a shy girl. She is more like an unprepared and embarrassed boy, while Michael assumes the attitude of an imploring maiden. . . . When she attempts to right the balance of their relationship by acceding to the feminine role, the result is an uneasy consciousness that her own face has begun to reflect the smug and 'irritating smile' of the sort of sexually competitive woman she has always held in contempt. With the desire for experience of love continually counteracted she can neither part from him – and leave the 'biggest world there is' – nor fully respond.[19]

Shatov, in any case, is in love with Miriam, even naïvely in love. He is represented as having neither the experience nor the will to make the assault on Miriam's consciousness which she fears but which is clearly required if the impasse is to be resolved. Hypo Wilson, on the other hand, seems to promise a real alternative. Already in a second marriage, already somewhat notorious as a seducer of women and already having proved his liking for Miriam, he may offer a less threatening intimacy. He spends a great deal of time and effort trying to seduce her. When she arrives back from holidaying in *Oberland*, there is a letter waiting for her from Wilson: 'Welcome to your London, my dear. I'm more in love with you than ever.'[20]

Miriam is flattered by Wilson's attentions, but as in all her dealings with suitors, again she feels that his response is not particular to her :

> He was 'in love' in his way, once again. But behind the magic words was nothing for her individually, for anyone individually - - - Supposing a kindly Philistine with a fixed world and almost no imagination were in his place? Impossible. Breathlessly impossible. Philistines or intellectuals . . . is there no alternative? Nobody, nobody. She wanted nobody she already knew. But did she wish him away? Or even averted? Only for a while forgotten. And that he could be, since he was fixed, in his place, far away.[21]

What Miriam wants seems to be something nobody can give – nobody, that is, who is either a Philistine or an intellectual. No third category presents itself. She wants not only to be sought, to be found desirable, but to be understood, recognized, endorsed and then accepted. The generalized gesture she ascribes to Wilson, indeed to all her suitors, results, to her mind, from a projection of their own feelings onto some woman, any woman, so that insufficient account is taken of the feelings a woman has of her own volition. Miriam yearns for experiences outside the restriction of the conventional mode of relations between the sexes. Richardson was, indeed, fully aware of the narrow range of relationships available to Miriam and Miriam's drive to extend that range. She wrote of *Honeycomb*, for example : 'I look in Honeycomb – in memory for my copy has gone astray, & see her aesthetically revelling, attracted to a society divorcée, rejoicing in clandestine meetings with an elderly roué, pitying her sisters married to the suburbs & duty; determined for her own part to hold on at any cost to a life that "features" etchings & masses of roses.' [22]

Her treatment of Gerald, Miriam's brother-in-law, provides a significant exception to Miriam's general intolerance of men. Neither Gerald, nor Harriett, his wife and Miriam's sister, provokes Miriam's scorn nor elicits her feelings of alienation. Gerald's response to Harriett is perceived by Miriam to be particular :

> . . . The edge of Gerald's voice, kind to every one, would always be broken when he spoke to Harriett. She would always be this young absurd Harriett to him, always. He would go on fastening her boots for her, tenderly, and go happily about his hobbies. She would never hear him call her 'my dear.' That old-fashioned mock-polite insolence of men . . . paterfamilias.[23]

Miriam's image of Gerald is unthreatened by any hint of passion; he is kind, tender, safe and unserious, able to go 'happily about his hobbies'. Because he has been assimilated into her sister's life, he presents no challenge to Miriam's autonomy. Because, too, he identifies with Harriett's acceptance of her, he need not become a target for Miriam's resentments. Miriam does not see Gerald as a man, but as a brother, as an addition to the familial structure. None of Miriam's three sisters ever threatens her sense of identity; with them she feels safe, accepted and acceptable. Hence Gerald's addition to the group may extend it but need not change it. Harriett and Gerald, indeed, appear to the reader to embody the image of the conventional married couple which so consistently provokes Miriam's derision and it might seem odd, therefore, that Miriam not only does not scorn them but derives positive relief from their company. This apparent inconsistency is clarified, however, by Miriam's insistence that Harriett and Gerald are not a 'married couple' but will remain, indeed, her sister Harriett with her friend, Gerald:

> . . . all this wedding was nothing. . . . She was Harriett . . . not the Mrs Ducayne Bob Grenville had just been talking to - - - she must remember all the years of being together, years of nights side by side . . . night turning to day for both of them, at the same moment - - - - It was all right - - - - The air that encircled them was the air of their childhood.[24]

What Gerald cannot threaten, that is, even if he seemed to wish it, which is not the case, is the continuing reality of their childhood. Childhood experience is, for Miriam, not only the most intense, but, more importantly, the most authentic. Her first intense experience, remembered as her 'bee memory', generates and sustains her sense of identity; similarly, her earliest social relationships with her family remain inviolate to any incursion from the outside.

II

Hypo Wilson seems to offer an alternative. The fictional character, although an admirable portrait of H. G. Wells which he acknowledged himself, incorporates elements of the later Wells in order, it seems clear, to sharpen the challenge to Miriam's autonomy which the life relationship between Richardson and Wells presented.[25] The recognizably older Wells, who appears as the young writer Wilson, may issue in part from the continuing influence of his dominating personality, since Richardson continued to know him until his death. But more important is the source of their intellectual and emotional divergence, which also continued throughout their relationship. Wells, especially in his later fiction, disdained the personalizing of points of view, preferring to create polemical discourse, although, as Bergonzi suggests,[26] the didacticism of the later style is much less true of the early works. Even so, the early romances show the individual already pitted against an external order. Richardson's view, by contrast, is that the individual consciousness is the only index of reality. In many of Wells' early stories a gifted consciousness is brought into submission by external pressures, which may well be morally inferior but which are nevertheless stronger. Perhaps even more fundamental to Richardson's telescoping of the didactic Wells into her portrayal of the younger Hypo Wilson is that both the life relationship and the fictional relationship are sustained by a power struggle. The terms of this struggle shift from mechanism versus individualism, to masculinity versus femininity. Richardson would not have been immune to the theme, evident in the early stories, of the dangers embodied in the female.[27] Richardson invested a great deal in her struggle with Wells, more perhaps than was comfortable for her. From her point of view, it was a struggle she needed to win, since the connection she discerned in Wells' thinking between mechanism, didacticism, invention and a rejection of femininity threatened her, if she allowed it, with the annihilation of reality itself.

Richardson met Wells in 1896. Bergonzi suggests that between 1894 and 1897 Wells was at the height of his poetic powers.[28] But already by the late 'nineties he was becoming involved in sociological theory. He was, that is, during the early stages of his long friendship with Richardson, already moving towards the didactic position which so threatened her own world-view, itself still forming and yet without literary expression. Not only was he a published writer and she still an apprentice, but, too, the speed with which he could change his opinions must have been disconcerting in the extreme. Wells had begun to stop taking fiction seriously, in the aesthetic sense, just when Richardson was beginning to formulate her own divergent views, equally intemperate and absolutely contradictory to his. Between her first meeting with Wells and the publication of *Pointed Roofs* is a period of nearly twenty years; yet even given the length of this developmental phase, Wells still performed a catalytic function. Since *Pilgrimage* is committed as much to the adumbration of fine details of perception and awareness, it is not surprising that the catalytic function performed by Wilson should entail a telescoping of the real time in which Richardson knew Wells. The pressure of his catalytic potential is suggested even in his fictional name, Hypo being the 'fixing agent' in the development of a photograph.[29] The ironic pun on its other meaning, of 'below', 'under' or 'beneath', contains Richardson's judgement that his world-view is an inferior version of reality.

Wilson does, indeed, offer something different and important to Miriam. Within the limitations of his projections – Miriam claims, for instance, that for Wilson women are 'merely pleasant or unpleasant biological material' [30] – he is able to defy convention in ways Miriam has not yet managed. He offers her, implicitly, an affair which need not entail any erosion of their friendship. And Miriam knows she is going to accept the offer: 'now she was surrounded by people all of whom Eve would see as "living in sin". And was about to join their ranks.' [31] At this crucial point, Miriam is fully aware of the division within her personality – of her man's mind and her woman's body, a division forced upon her by her feminist drive for the recognition of her individuality and yet the very condition that prohibits her union with a man, a male individual, which she seeks. She feels as if she were two people; the Miriam who lives and talks, and the woman who waits. Significantly, it is the talking self, the mind, the personality, which is not associated with being a woman, so that it is clear to the reader that unconsciously Miriam has adopted the very position she most deplores in men – that is, the equation of the feminine with the appearance and sensations of the body: 'There was a woman, not this thinking self who talked with men in their own language, but one whose words could be spoken only from the heart's knowledge, waiting to be born in her.' [32] She does, as she has already premeditated, allow Wilson to seduce her. The love scene between them is awkward in the extreme. Wilson caresses her, but instead of responding, Miriam's mind is outside the situation, watching herself, seeing herself through her friend Amabel's eyes, her woman's body engaged, her man's mind aloof. She feels, too, the disparity in their responses; she identifies with Amabel's perception of her flesh as 'impersonally beautiful', whereas to him 'each detail was "pretty" and the whole an object of desire'. His body is not beautiful to her, but 'interesting'; it does not stir her when naked as it had often done when Wilson was just walking about. The experience, for Miriam, is exactly that – an experience, part of her education, not a mutual sharing or fulfilment: 'This mutual nakedness,' her inner monologue runs, 'was appeasing rather than stimulating. And austere, as if it were a first step in some arduous discipline.'[33] Because he becomes pathetic to her, she feels solicitude, a protective maternalism, which leads her to clasp him and comfort him, as if he were a baby, all the time rocking him 'unsatisfactorily to and fro'. This absurd, comical picture is not that of a frigid woman, but one untouched, unmoved, unapproached in her being, unawakened. Wilson the man is seen as a blind, ineffectual child, and, being a child, not culpable. Miriam, by implication and by her response, is seen to mother him, to cradle, comfort and soothe. Here, as elsewhere, her maternalism is the relational mode most comfortable for her in her dealings with men. She rescues the situation by suggesting that they go for coffee together to her favourite café. She knows that his ingenuity will provide him with a 'formula' for the evening which will preserve him from any sense of failure.[34]

Later, during a visit to Wilson's country house, he comes to her at night. Again she remains unmoved and is again keenly aware of 'their essential unrelatedness'. Her lack of involvement seems incongruous to her:

> - - - she awaited the welling of appropriate emotion. But the power she felt the presented facts ought to wield, and might possibly yet attain, failed to emerge from them. Within her was something that stood apart, unpossessed.[35]

In this encounter, the division in Miriam between her mind and her body is obvious enough, and it is in the mind that her aesthetic responses are lodged. Presumably the corollary would also follow, that is, that in an encounter which evoked her physical response, the mind would be somehow vacant and 'unpossessed'. And if a union of body and mind cannot be achieved within her own personality, it seems certain that it cannot occur in the context of relationship between the sexes. The one possibility for integration inheres in the reinforcement of her maternal instinct, which can at once neutralize the potency of the male, can accept his humanity as it expresses itself in need, and can allow her creative energy an object.[36] Miriam's alienation from men, beginning with her father and then, through successive relationships, changing, modifying, evolving but never actually resolving, is repeatedly focused upon the systems of thought predicated on language, from which a woman, by the nature of her consciousness, is excluded. Miriam's holiday friendship with Guerini, for example, set in the Swiss mountains in *Oberland*, illuminates at once her failure to respond to a man within the context of personal intimacy, together with her rebellion against the more generalized female role elicited by the social context of meetings and dinner parties. The common root cause of these rebellions and the symptom of each, is what Miriam sees as the masculinization of language. All afternoon, Miriam relates, the two had been 'in harmony', talking easily and 'standing about together in the snow'. Then they begin arguing; we are not told explicitly about what, but Richardson makes clear that it is the same old problem – the inability or unwillingness of a man to accept the validity of a woman's point of view. Is there no way, Miriam pleads, for the battle between the sexes to end? Why, she asks, is it 'so much a matter of life and death, for men as for women? Why did each always gather all its forces for the conflict?' [37] The answer seems clear enough, at least for the reader. If Miriam, indeed if women, persist in claiming an exclusiveness of consciousness which not only reduces men's rationalist world-views to the status of relativist theories, but also repudiates them for untruthfulness to experience, then certainly men's resentment of this rejection may provoke them to anger and it is ingenuous of Miriam to expect otherwise. She insists, however, that men should be able to adopt her own view. Men, she argues to Guerini, seem incapable of

> 'unthinking the suggestions coming to them from centuries of masculine attempts to represent women only in relation to the world as known to men.'
>
> It was then he was angry.
>
> 'How else shall they be represented?'
>
> 'They *can't* be represented by men. Because by every word they use men and women mean different things.'[38]

The 'centuries of masculine attempts' form a cultural tradition and the 'representation' of women is specifically characteristic of art in general and of literature in particular. Two things, Miriam complains, are masculine: on the one hand, the attempts, and on the other, the world-view which is the context women are given by men. This is the same point of disjunction which Miriam comes to in all her relationships with men and it is a point she can never satisfactorily resolve. And, from her vantage point, the reason for the lack of resolution is men's seeming refusal to understand what she is saying. Guerini is 'angry'; not, Richardson implies, because he needs or wishes to feel superior, or to be thought 'right', but because he cannot understand Miriam's charge. He responds with helpless bewilderment – 'How else shall they be represented?' Miriam's answer is devastating in its absoluteness – 'By every word they use men and women mean different things.' Since Guerini cannot follow her argument, the implications of this statement must be supplied by Miriam herself, and so the prose shifts from dialogue to interior monologue, thus emphasizing Miriam's alienation :

> And indeed the problem presently will be: how to save men from collapsing under their loss of prestige. Their awakening, when it comes, will make them pitiful. At present they are surrounded, out in the world, by women who are trying to be as much like them as possible. That will cease when commerce and politics are socialized.[39]

Miriam's reasoning here is hardly abstract, but is couched in an uneasy emotional fabric of contempt and compassion, anger and confidence. Men have given themselves such prestige that they move in a world of childish egoism; yet when they do finally face reality, their loss of prestige will make them 'pitiful', and therefore in need of support. Behind both these images lies the deeper image of the knowing woman – the material figure who can both deceive and succour, an image reinforced by the angry charge that women are colluding in men's unawareness of reality by 'trying to be as much like them as possible'. But *that* – Miriam concludes – mysteriously, confidently and illogically – will cease 'when commerce and politics are socialized'. The implication here, perhaps, is that when women have succeeded in gaining equal access to wealth and power, they will no longer ape men but will be able to allow their natural energies full range.

Miriam's reflections continue :

> 'Art,' 'literature,' systems of thought, religions, all the fine products of masculine leisure that are so lightly called 'immortal.' Who makes them immortal? A few men in each generation - - - -'[40]

Again the prose is edged with contempt. The cultural tradition issues from 'masculine leisure', which implies, by logical corollary, 'feminine work', an implication which is reinforced by the denial of the importance to the perpetrators of cultural achievements of 'any sacrifice of the lives about them to the production of these crumbling monuments'.[41] For Miriam, 'art' does not excuse the human sacrifices demanded by male artists – excuses are accepted only by the artists manqués, the critics, who share what to Miriam is the perverted value system of artists. Women, Richardson argued elsewhere,[42] can never accept this valuation of art because they can never free themselves from the demands of real work and real living, being always, willingly or not, because of the nature of their consciousness, openly responsive to the real world.

As if to dramatize this point, Miriam's reflections are broken off by the appearance of the child Daphne, who comes noisily from the real world and whose obtrusion both Richardson and Miriam are powerless to resist. 'Works of art' crumble into silence under the pressure of Daphne's three-dimensional presence. The remainder of the chapter, therefore, is devoted to an exchange between Miriam and Daphne, who are joined by two further men – Vereker and Eaden. Only a child, that is, can sometimes bridge the gap between the world of men and the world of Miriam – and, by implication, the authentic world of women. And that it is a child adds yet another strand to the implicit reinforcement of the complex thematic fabric which supports the plethora of disparate incidents making up the surface action of *Pilgrimage* : a thematic fabric which implies that the only possible resolution of female role conflict lies in the adoption of the maternal persona.

III

The failure resulting from Miriam's role conflict in personal relationships with men has its uncomfortable counterpart in her relative inability to accept the feminine role in social relationships. The dinner parties and social evenings she attends while she is employed by the Corries, for instance, are a constant source of irritation to her. After one such evening she decides that women must pretend to be interested in what men are saying in order to keep the conversation going. 'That was feminine worldliness,' she reflects, 'pretending to be interested so that pleasant things might go on - - - - Feminine worldliness then meant perpetual hard work and cheating and pretence at the door of a hidden garden, a lovely hidden garden. Masculine worldliness meant never being really there; always talking about things that had happened or making plans for things that might happen.'[43] Women, Miriam suggests, want pleasure, and are forced to cheat in order to get it. Men, on the other hand, want action. But the cheating women do not find it easy to cheat: it means 'perpetual hard work' on the threshold only of something real and important – 'a hidden garden'. The garden is an ancient symbol for innocent union and for cultivation. Women know that the garden is there, but their cheating prevents them from entering it. Men are equally prevented from entering it, because they are never 'really there'; they live, Miriam speculates, either in the past or in the future, but not in the present. In the social intercourse of women and men, then, a joint apprehension is never possible; they cannot enter the garden. It is interesting that Miriam is not suggesting here that men prevent women – or that women prevent men – from the engagement with reality she clearly desires, but that she sees each group as its own obstacle. The acquisition of 'worldliness' as a means to social ends is unwillingly acknowledged.

The destructive potential of this denial of 'reality' is embodied in figures like Mrs Corrie, who, in particular, repels Miriam:

> Dead because of something she had never known. Dead in ignorance and living bravely on - - - - Nearly all women were like that, living in a gloom where there were no thoughts - - - - - - . . . no room for ideas; except in smoking-rooms – and – laboratories. . . . . . . - - - - That is what men could never forgive; the superiority of women. . . . 'Perhaps I can't stand women because I'm a sort of horrid man.'[44]

It is clear here that although the degree of alienation from men is extreme, so too is the inability to identify with women, and at this point of speculation, Miriam is forced to question her own gender identity. If she were 'a sort of horrid man', would that explain her exclusion from the social role expected of her? Miriam's preoccupation with this inadequacy makes her hypersensitive to any claims by anyone else, especially a man, to understand or explain what she cannot. One such man is Bob, who explains women without difficulty:

> 'The vagaries of the Fair, dear girl,' he said presently, in a soft blurred tone.

> That's one of his phrases, thought Miriam – that's old-fashioned politeness; courtliness. Behind it he's got some sort of mannish thought ... 'the unaccountability of women' ... 'who can understand a woman? – she doesn't even understand herself' – thought he'd given up trying to make out. He's gone through life and got his own impressions; all utterly wrong . . . talking about women, with an air of wisdom - - - - How utterly detestable mannishness is; so mighty and strong and comforting when you have been mewed up with women all your life and then suddenly, in a second, far away, utterly imbecile and aggravating, with a superior self-satisfied smile because a woman says one thing one minute and another the next. Men ought to be horse-whipped - - - - [45]

Again Miriam's anger gives way to the underlying violence of her resentment, a violence which she is at great pains to control and inhibit by her constant effort to understand the reactions around her, thus to rationalize them and strip them of their absurdity. It is not just Bob's judgement that upsets Miriam, and even not the conclusions she suspects lie behind it. It is his confidence, his 'air of wisdom', which, despise it though she may, she cannot dislodge. Her anger is so great that it disturbs her rationality, accusing him of having got impressions which are 'all utterly wrong'. This total and rather ferocious rejection of his comment and all she thinks it implies, leads inevitably to the exposure within herself of her own ambivalence, the ambivalence which is constituted in the supposition that although she is a woman, she must be, at the same time, some sort of 'horrid man'. She finds the confidence of 'mannishness' seducing and detestable. The phrase 'mewed up' suggests the unpleasant and claustrophobic atmosphere of the women's world she has been habituated to, and the contrasting freedom and strength of the 'mannish' alternative. Yet that also is an unreliable impression, since it gives way 'in a second' to a perception of 'mannishness' as 'imbecile and aggravating'. The confidence she admires and envies seems suddenly to be mere commonplace, which she despises. This shift in perception dramatizes the very characteristic which she projects onto men as their reason for dismissing women's comments as 'vagaries' – that is, the way in which a woman is capable of saying 'one thing one minute and another the next'. Miriam herself has just done exactly that. The irony of her position, which she only half realizes, leads back to the only resolution of the impasse – a resolution which is physical, not psychological : active, not contemplative – that is, that men 'ought to be horse-whipped', presumably by women.

What Miriam understands, therefore, is that the only civilized mode of conduct in which the social intercourse of the two sexes can take place at all is that of an uneasy truce, in which men deny reality and women pretend not to notice it. And part of women's pretence, Miriam concludes, is the erasing of all intellectual needs :

> So there was nothing for women in marriage and children. Because they had no thoughts. Their husbands grew to hate them because they had no thoughts. But if a woman had thoughts a man would not be 'silly' about her for five years. And Mrs Corrie had her garden. She would always have that, when he was not there.[46]

This complaint has the tone of a wail against the complete unviability of the normative female role. 'Thoughts', or independent opinions, are incompatible with that female attractiveness which makes a man 'silly' about a woman. But that same lack, having first endeared her to the man, is then the cause of his hating her. The two terms are extreme : hatred carries a violence which is made the more dangerous by its intimate context of marriage, whereas silliness has the ironic double edge of stupidity and romantic idealization. With such incompatible contending forces there can be no clarity of direction and the only resolution for the woman is isolation : 'Mrs Corrie had her garden'. As a symbol of innocence and refuge, the garden recurs throughout the *Pilgrimage* sequence. It is the one place where women can possess themselves; and each recurrence recalls Miriam's initial 'real moment', when she became aware for the first time, in the garden of her childhood : aware first of herself and then, consequently, of the flowers and the bees, themselves the stock sexual symbols of childhood. It is always the case, however, that such awareness and self-possession never occur when Miriam is in male company, and such, she assumes, is the lot of women. Mrs Corrie's garden is the refuge necessary to compensate her for the emptiness of marriage, an emptiness caused by the demand on her womanhood to be free of 'thoughts'.

In the society of the dinner party and the drawing-room, Miriam is unable, because of her inability to quell her 'thoughts', to take her woman's place. She finds it impossible to sit silently with the other women and listen to the men talk. On the other hand, to join in means committing a *faux pas* and ending the conversation altogether. During one dinner party at the Corries', the men, who have been discussing Darwin, are interrupted :

'We're not descended from monkeys at all. It's not natural,' said Mrs Craven loudly, across the irritated voices of the men. Their faces were red. They filled the room with inaccurate phrases, pausing politely between each and keeping up a show of being guest and host. How nice of them. But this was how cultured people with incomes talked about Darwin.

'The great thing Darwin did,' said Miriam abruptly, 'was to point out the power of environment in evolving the different species – selecting.'

'That's it, that's it!' sang Mrs Corrie. 'Let's all select ourselves into the droin'-room.' 'Now I've offended the men and the women too,' thought Miriam.[47]

Miriam's sour reflection that people with incomes are not necessarily very intelligent has two moral sources; the first is that people in power *ought* to be intelligent, in order to justify their superiority, and the second is that lack of intelligence is not excused by the hypocrisy of polite manners. But the sharpness of this judgement is modified by her part-identification with the bourgeois; she does not relish the idea that she has offended the women as well as the men. The lightweight remarks of the other women set off Miriam's remark as outlandish and excluding. The sardonic tone of this passage is nicely balanced by the comic portrayal of people who are not aware that they can seem foolish to one of their own number.The social roles of guest and host forbid the men from engaging openly in the argument they are really conducting; and the intervention of the women silences them altogether. Again the only solution is disengagement and separation, the women, under pressure of more than custom, being obliged to withdraw.

At a later stage the reader is shown Miriam musing over a book written by 'an elderly woman of the world' whose judgement Miriam respects: 'In speech with a man a woman is at a disadvantage – because they speak different languages. She may understand his. Hers he will never speak nor understand.' [48] Both Miriam's experience and her intellect endorse this view: 'Men and women never meet. Inside the life relationship you can see them being strangers and hostile; one or the other or both, completely alone.' The essential character, the very language of female consciousness is, it seems to Miriam, incommunicable to men. The conviction of this difference is a milestone on Miriam's pilgrimage, because it provides a focus, with some semblance of objectivity, for what have hitherto appeared to be idiosyncrasies of her personal psychology. Despite her search for the common humanity of men and women and despite her struggle to rid herself of the trappings of the female role, she is forced to remain, together with her half of the race, isolated from the other half, so that her sense of the wholeness of life must reside in her experience of the solitary moments of insight which are themselves, ironically, incommunicable, except to someone who has shared the same experience. Richardson's commitment to the language is always compromised by this fundamental sense of the division of human consciousness. For this reason, Miriam feels alienated from other women, whose communications hardly ever seem to have the authenticity she seeks.[49] Women like Mrs Corrie have learned to have no 'thoughts'. Clever women, on the other hand, who aspire beyond that condition, seem forced to have only the kinds of 'thoughts' that men have. They too, it seems, are engaged in pretending, in hiding what they really think and feel. It is the sense of calculation Miriam can't stand, the taking of a fixed attitude. What the women say is not independent to them, but either falters or criticizes the men they are with, according to which is the cleverer. It is not possible, Richardson is constantly asserting, for a woman to reveal herself when she is in the company of men. And male consciousness, according to Miriam, is characterized by its devotion to deductive logic and to determinism. It is therefore natural for Miriam, who cannot fit happily into her appointed role, to find this impossible to accept:

> If, some day, every one lived in the clear light of science, 'waiting for the pronouncements of science in all the affairs of life', waiting for the pronouncements of those sensual dyspeptic men with families, who thought of women as existing only to produce more men. . . admirably fitted by nature's inexorable laws for her biological role . . . perhaps she agreed or pretended to think it all a great risk . . . - - - La femme, c'est peu galant de le dire, est la femelle de l'homme. The Frenchman at any rate *wanted* to say something else. But why want to be gallant . . . and why not say: man, it is not very graceful to say it, is the male of woman?[50]

It is difficult enough for Miriam to accept the difference in consciousness between men and women, but the superiority assumed by men is something she cannot understand, and that women should be explained and destined by their anatomy whereas men are able to supersede their biological role, she finds aggravating, illogical and incomprehensible. Science, apart from typifying for her an impersonal system of thought inimical for its rationalism, embodies also a disregard for the humanity of women, making womanhood, she suggests, subject to 'nature's inexorable laws'. If such must be the case, she argues, why not take the female as the human norm and the male as the counterposing deviation? Here Richardson may have been merely recording the preoccupations of her younger self; but it is clear from her non-fictional journalism that her own position was substantially the same. Her column in *The Dental Record,* for example, contains many discussions of the same point; her constant accusation is that men and male science have relegated the meaning of female existence to the reproductive function and further, to compound the offence, have shown that they do not understand the physical and psychological character of even that most 'natural' of functions :

> Dr Cadwallader heartily deprecates the 'tricks of the sob artist in depicting the fearful and unbearable pains of parturition,' and declares that the pains of labour are not so severe as they are made out to be - - - - We would like to hear the answer of a few matrons, bearing children under the artificial conditions of modern life, to his cheery statements as to the simplicity, naturalness and easily bearable inconveniences of the function. We take take leave to think that the response would be a very ominous silence.[51]

IV

It is clear that, in her personal and social relationships with men, Miriam finds the female role she is expected to play both inhibiting and constricting. It is also felt to be deadly, since it threatens, on the one hand, the integrity of her consciousness, which is for her the definition of her identity and, on the other hand, the possibility of social integration, so that isolation becomes necessary for the preservation of identity. But if the female role is constricting and inhibiting, can the male role be in any way preferable? Since men enjoy, Miriam contends, the best of the fruits of industry, action and of the spirit, does that greater richness of experience make them worthy and admirable? Not at all, Miriam ventures :

> That's men, she said, with a sudden flash of certainty, that's men as they are, when they are opposed, when they are real. All the rest is pretence.

> Her thoughts flashed forward to a final clear issue of opposition, with a husband. Just a cold blank hating forehead and neatly brushed hair above it. If a man doesn't understand or doesn't agree he's just a blank bony conceitedly thinking, absolutely condemning forehead, a face below, going on eating – and going off somewhere. Men are all hard angry bones; always thinking something, only one thing at a time and unless that is agreed to, they murder. My husband shan't kill me. . . . I'll shatter his conceited brow – *make* him see . . . two sides to every question . . . a million sides . . . no questions, only sides . . . always changing. Men argue, think they prove things - - - -[52]

This passage is extremely pertinent and revealing, first because of the nascent violence Miriam feels in response to the hatred she suggests is displayed towards women by men, and secondly because it focuses the difference between male and female minds. Men are only 'real', that is, revealed, Miriam argues, when they are opposed. And again her image of the opposition between men and women is the relationship of marriage. Just as men grow to 'hate' women who don't have any 'thoughts', so, too, they hate women who do not agree with them. Such a man, in his 'real' persona, is nothing more than a condemning forehead with a face underneath – and the face, like an animal's, goes on eating and then goes off somewhere. The body of a man becomes all hard angry bones and the mind an instrument which can neither stop thinking nor think of more than one thing at a time. Confronted by opposition, Miriam concludes, they murder. Here is a quite explicit statement of what Miriam sees as a clear threat to the integrity of a woman's consciousness. If she allows herself to be openly engaged in disagreement with a man, she can expect him to annihilate her. Miriam's own aggression is aroused by the prospect of this threat to her survival; he won't kill her, she argues, because she will first shatter his brow, the brow that defends the always thinking mind and which is itself composed of hard bones. The man in this image commits murder by disengaging – he goes away. Miriam, on the other hand, needs to *make* the man see. She engages even more – to the point, that is, where she will attack him. The reader must be aware, here, that what operates in Miriam's troubled involvements with men is not only the fear that she can be annihilated, but also the fear, only partly perceived by her, that she may have the desire and the capability to annihilate them. As if to dramatize this point, the prose begins to break up, leaving Miriam and the reader with the disconnected phrases which contradistinguish a woman's thinking style. If a man thinks only one thing at a time, a woman is aware of two sides to every question. The final denial that there are even any questions is a denial of rationalism itself. The attempt to argue and to 'prove things' is therefore illusory, irrelevant to the million-sided reality which women, Miriam implies, know to exist. Men see things in linear dimension, whereas women judge the logic that men presume to be innate, to be merely a mental construct. The issue Richardson puts to the reader here is whether this dichotomy is a false one, ensuing from Miriam's lack of intellectual training and her envy of it, or whether it has experiential validity, and, if it does, whether that demonstrates a significant gender difference or, more simply, an individual difference between Miriam and her male companions. Miriam clearly believes the former; and Richardson, by faithfully detailing her persona's speculations, allows the possibility that escape from egotism may lie in the generalizing of personal experience, so that isolation, bewilderment and inadequacy may be given a social and not merely a subjective explanation. This is an extraordinarily difficult technical problem, since the author allows access only to Miriam's inner life and not to that of any other character; the generalizing potential of Miriam's interpretations of personal experience depends, therefore, on reiteration and repetition within social contexts where shifts of affect or attitude are only slight. Richardson intends the reader to see Miriam's dilemma, and her explanations for it, to be typical, in many respects, rather than idiosyncratic, so that the opposition between men and women which arouses, at a deep level, aggression and violence, expresses a neuroticism induced by the culture, rather than a failure resulting from a merely personal inadequacy. This is why Richardson's technique so challenges the inherent logic of language itself; at the points where Miriam is most assertive of the differential between male and female consciousness, the rhythm of the sentence is ruptured and the reader is given explanatory phrases whose connections with each other are implied, not stated. The connections, therefore, may be either, or both, denotative (logical) or connotative (affective).

It is men's ability to think, to intellectualize, which, of all their characteristics, most often arouses Miriam's despair and indignation. And Miriam's response was clearly Richardson's own, expressed in numerous disparate pieces of journalism, such as her *Dental Record* column. In one such article, discussing an essay which had appeared in *Science Progress*, she argued for

> the desirability of substituting 'life' direct, first-hand energizing experience, for interest in life, thinking and writing about life - - - - Every day, every moment is in a new sense a new creation. Only he who lives and reconquers his freedom every day is truly alive and free - - - - the moment of realization is the moment of entry into life - - - - It is a characteristic vice of the intellect to see the past as a straight line stretching out behind humanity like a sort of indefinite tail. In actual experience it is more like an agglomeration, a vital process of crystallization grouped in and about the human consciousness, confirming and enriching individual experience, living unconsciously in individual nerve-cells (we apologize for this term if the nerves have no cells) and consciously in individual intelligence, thanks and thanks only to Records.[53]

Several things are interesting here. First, the use of a quasi-scientific phraseology: 'agglomeration', 'crystallization', 'nerve-cells' (including the coy reference to whether or not nerves have cells; if she had really thought it important, she could surely have found out before publishing the article). Secondly, the rejection of the linear view of history, important because it challenges the concepts of cause and effect in human affairs, and, too, because it implies a similarity between the nature of personal experience and the nature of collective continuity. Thirdly, the passage affirms that faith in life as energizing and that impatience with systems and constructs about life, which are pervasive in all the volumes of *Pilgrimage*. The moral impetus is unmistakable: a person must 'reconquer' his freedom every day if he is to be 'truly alive'. It is an intellectual vice to see the past as a linear progression. 'Realization', therefore, which Richardson regards as the qualification for entering life, is an act of will, of moral choice, as much as a process of consciousness. The concept of reconquering freedom is indeed a strange one, as if a person is required to battle not with dangers from outside himself, but with the threat to 'realization' inherent in his own freedom. The human factors which affirm life, then, are direct experience, moral will, the unconscious storing of experience and the conscious operation of intelligence. The factors, by contrast, which negate life are the activities of the intellect: thinking, writing, describing, analysing and rationalizing.

Despite Miriam's resentment towards men and all their works, she wants very much to have access to their world, from which she feels her upbringing and training have excluded her. During her period as a teacher at Banbury Park she reads a newspaper for the first time; the activity confronts her with her ignorance of general affairs. She does not know, for instance, what actual powers the sovereign has, or what is the constitutional relation between the sovereign and the Privy Council. Her feeling of ignorance makes her querulous and defensive. Here is the experiential gap which renders her schooling irrelevant to the pursuit of understanding the world around her. All she has to do, she tells herself, is to sit in an armchair and read all about everything. But it is men, the alien group, who sit in armchairs and gain knowledge, and it is the women who are denied. Similarly, when her dentist-employer, Mr Hancock, takes her to a lecture, she realizes what she could have been learning during all the previous years : 'Then all those years they might have been going sometimes to those lectures. Pater talking about them - - - and *never* saying that members could take friends or that there were special lectures for children . . .' [54] Mixed with Miriam's anticipation is her sense of betrayal; her father had deliberately excluded her from his intellectual pastimes by never (she emphasizes the 'never') disclosing that she could have accompanied him. The implication is that her father needed to be exclusive, presumably to maintain his authority and superiority. Later, as she does enlarge her intellectual horizons, she begins to reject the creations of intellect in which educated men place such faith, but her rejection is always tinged with ambivalence, since her responses are correlative to what she sees as men's rejection of women :

> There was nothing but man; man, coming from the ape, some men a little cleverer than others, men had discovered science, science was the only enlightenment, science would put everything right; scientific imagination, scientific invention. Man. Women were there, cleverly devised by nature to ensnare man for a moment and produce more men to bring scientific order out of primeval chaos - - - the business of the writer was imagination, not romantic imagination, but realism, fine realism, the truth about 'the savage', about all the past and the present - - -[55]

This rejection of science is also a rejection of the ideas propounded by Hypo Wilson, who believes that science can save the world. Again the argument is not couched in abstract philosophical terms, but in the terms of sexual polarity. Science, for Miriam, defines a man-made world in which the only part women are supposed to play is that of reproducing more men, in order eventually that man should triumph over nature. Clearly Miriam's ignorance of scientific thought and discovery accounts in part for her alienation; and clearly too her identification of science as an exclusive product of male consciousness accounts for a major part of her repudiation. Nevertheless, the ascendant progress of a scientific culture is of itself anathema to her temperament, since her beliefs about the nature of identity depend fundamentally on the experiencing of 'real moments' which cannot issue from a scientifically controlled environment. Nor, of course, does she accept that human feelings and sensations are equivalent to 'primeval chaos'. The ambivalence Miriam feels about men and their world is a constant source of frustration. On the one hand, there are the limitations of being female, on the other, the inadequacies of being male.

During a conversation with her friends Jan and Mag, she manages to focus her antipathy on the distinctive intellectual characteristics of men :

> 'You don't want to be a man, Jan.'
> 'Oh, I do, sometimes. They have the best of everything all round.'
> '*I* don't. I wouldn't be a man for anything. I wouldn't have a man's – *consciousness*, for anything.' [56]

Male consciousness, as far as Miriam is concerned, has been responsible for literature and science of a kind that misleads people about the true nature of things.

As well as feeling shut out from the discoveries of science, Miriam also feels that she is asked to suffer the indignity of being one of its specimens and to accept the fact that she has been found wanting. Apart from the humiliation this causes her, she finds it revolting and illogical that everything about her is explicable in terms of the reproductive part of her biology. Science, she accuses, has explained woman entirely in terms of her usefulness to man, so that science is not only a preserve of male privilege but an invention of male consciousness. It is important to see the implications of this position : as long as science is exclusive knowledge and is deemed to be true, its acquisition may be sought and its exponents admired and emulated. But if it is held to be just as distorted by the prejudices of male consciousness as the arts have been, it can be rejected as untrue in its essence, that is, untrue to the reality of the outer world as well as untrue to experience. This in turn leads to the implication that female contributions to knowledge must be different in kind as well as in quality, either because they will suffer a distortion peculiar to female consciousness which will parallel that of the male, or because they will lack that orientation characteristic of male consciousness exemplified for Miriam in the methodological dependence on logic. Richardson makes Miriam's argument quite clear; first, the education system is an indoctrination into the values of the culture, which in turn encourages a faith in scientific data, since the intellectual training appropriate to both is the internalization of the principles of logic. By logical analysis, Miriam rages, the female has been explained as 'underdeveloped man', so that the only relevance of the wonders of science for her is the department of gynaecology. Rather than accept such a truth, Miriam's implicit gesture is to dispense with education, with all of literature and even with logic itself.

Miriam's view is demonstrably Richardson's own. In her *Dental Record* column, she discusses a book by a Dr R. Murray Leslie :

> Dr Leslie hopes 'that the acquisition of intellectual knowledge may not be at the expense of certain feminine passive qualities, such as sympathy, tenderness and common sense.' - - - But the besetting sin of the average average male psychologist is very strong. His tendency is to exaggerate the angle of intellect and call it active and male, and to put the angles of feeling and wilfulness in the shade and call them feminine and 'passive' - - - - When, for instance, he castigates 'fashionable' women for going out in the frost dressed in fur coats and openwork stockings he should not forget the part played in the comedy by the corresponding male type – his perennial pre-occupation with a 'pretty ankle.'[57]

It is clear enough to Richardson, if not to Dr Leslie, that intellectual skills do not have innately male features and it is clear to her, also, that the role-playing demanded of each other by men and women is more a sign of bitter social comedy than of the fundamental structures of the psychology of women. The integrated personality, Richardson stresses, is one in which feelings, thought and will are balanced in relation to one another; it is men, she argues here, who emphasize thought at the expense of the other two factors, and it is men who claim intellect to be 'active and male'. This distinction had been explored in a previous article where she had argued that a woman is 'the synthetic principle of human life', whereas a man is 'a being whose mental tendency is to departmentalize, to analyse, to separate single things from their flowing environment and make bogeys of them'. However much he may try, a man will not be able to make a woman like himself : 'she will go on being, on the whole, rhythmic, "lunatic", swayed by the moon'.[58]

It seems to Miriam that, apart from the different values placed on intellectual skills by men and women respectively, they also seem to have different uses for knowledge. A lecture on Dante evokes a stream of impressions and reactions which are again framed by her view of the polarity between men and women : 'Most of the men present were - - - using their knowledge like a code or a weapon. But the women were really interested in it - - - - They represented something in life that was going to increase.' [59] Most men, Miriam speculates, are like her father, wanting to keep their knowledge exclusive to themselves and to use it as a weapon to crush people. The 'but' in the following sentence implies that men are not actually interested in knowledge for its own sake, as women are. Nevertheless, the women's way also leaves her with a question; a world dominated by interested women is perhaps not what she wants either. As the lecture proceeds, it begins to focus on the nature of trade and to outline socialist moral values Miriam has not considered before. Richardson, like her persona, was attracted by socialist philosophy and defended her views many times in print, notably in a protracted exchange with a regular columnist for *Crank*, an anarchist journal for which she did a number of reviews. Her first defence of socialism was in response to a criticism offered by the columnist, called 'The Odd Man', in the November 1906 issue of the journal. The main thesis Richardson offers is that in the socialist state business capacity would persist together with other forms of human genius, but that no section of the community would be able to constitute themselves as a ruling class.[60] If this view seems inconsistent with her personal affirmation of the unique quality and importance of the individual's experience, it can be better understood in the light of the counterbalancing principle which she suggests would operate in the socialist state, which would be the effort to moralize the struggle, to 'place it under the regulation of rational, ethical, and artistic ends and ideals'.[61] The 'Odd Man's' reply to this claim is that modern socialism is soulless and therefore doomed not to succeed, since moralizing the struggle depends on divine, rather than human laws. Richardson is not swayed; she sees also in socialism the possibility of independence for women from the domestic slavery of motherhood.

By endowing motherhood it would be recognized as a civil service, and by placing it on a collective basis, the mother would be made independent of the accidents which might befall her man.[62] Finally, she asserts that socialism is not a movement, but a state of mind, a shift of the idea of welfare from simple, competitive individualism to corporate good.[63] Socialism, then, might provide the means by which the male world can be modified to include women as equals.

Despite her hostility towards the power structures of the male world, Miriam is forced to face her own dependence on its economic stability; she must rely for her continued existence on her father and on her employers. Because men have wealth and power, she argues, they also have responsibility and therefore should not and must not fail. Her father's bankruptcy she finds morally indefensible and it remains a constant source of irritation and distress, as well as being a guilty secret. Her father's failure, however, is not only distressing; it forces her to be aware of her impotence as a person of any economic importance:

> Her mind revolved round the problem hopelessly. . . . Even if she went on the stage she could not make enough to pay off one of his creditors - - - - She would have to go on being a resident governess, keeping ten pounds a year for dress and paying over the rest of her salary.[64]

The almost total identification of Miriam with her father, evident here, means that she must not only respect his authority and admire his knowledge, but also that she must share his debts and take responsibility for his failure. Part of her pilgrimage towards psychological independence is the need to escape this original identification. Nevertheless, the particular nature of her father's failure makes it clear that male privilege is more than a matter of social custom; it literally controls the practical circumstances of living. Miriam's livelihood at this point depends on the restricted choice between marriage, chosen by two of her sisters, and governessing, chosen by the third. From this single, devastating experience, Richardson knew, as Miriam knows, what Woolf had to imagine in *A Room of One's Own* – that the fate of a woman with gifts and aspirations which are not necessary to her appointed social role, is entirely governed by her personal economic capacity, over which, although it is personal to her, she has so little control that she may as well have none at all. It is not until Miriam rejects both marriage and governessing by daring to attempt an independent life in London that she begins, gradually and unsystematically, to interpret the disparate elements of education, wealth, authority and power as emanations from a single source – the consciousness of the male.

Richardson's implicit claim in *Pilgrimage* is to give the reader not only an exploration of what for her is life and reality, but also an explication of how those things which appear real are not real at all, together with a rationale of why they appear to be real. Every foray into experience which Miriam Henderson undertakes is, at the point of awareness, circumscribed by language, but so often, in her case, language does not render the inexplicable any the more explicable. Her mind ranges restlessly from analysis to analysis – from personal encounter to social situation to the contemplation of intellectual systems and their embodiments – always searching for a pattern and always, simultaneously, denying (or defying) the integrity of the principles of logic upon which the formulation of such a pattern must depend. Miriam can neither enter the world of men as the female type they have invented and understand, nor can she enter it as one of their brethren. To reach the goal of her pilgrimage, Miriam must pass through the maze of her experience, but in this maze, men and their world represent a dead end. She must try alternative routes.

NOTES AND REFERENCES

1 *Pointed Roofs*, p. 28.
2 Ibid., p. 30.
3 Loc. cit.
4 Ibid., p. 31.
5 Loc. cit.
6 Ibid., p. 32.
7 Jessie Hale to Rose Odle, 27 August, 1956.
8 *Honeycomb*, p. 462.
9 *Pointed Roofs*, p. 73.
10 Ibid., p. 127.
11 Ibid., p. 128.
12 Ibid., p. 129.

13 Fromm, op. cit., p. 70.

14 *Pointed Roofs*, pp. 129-30.

15 *Deadlock*, p. 45.

16 *Dawn's Left Hand*, p. 240.

17 *Revolving Lights*, p. 303.

18 For Richardson, too, the existence of tragedy in itself denoted a male world view: 'Hence the Greek tragedies with their enclosed finalities'. DR to Peggy Kirkaldy, 25 January, 1944.

19 Fromm, op. cit., p. 136.

20 *Dawn's Left Hand*, p. 141.

21 Ibid., pp. 141-2.

22 DR to E. B. C. Jones, 12 May, 1921.

23 *Honeycomb*, pp. 463-4.

24 Ibid., p. 463.

25 See Gloria Glikin Fromm, 'Through the Novelist's Looking Glass', in *H. G. Wells: A Collection of Critical Essays*, ed. Bernard Bergonzi, Prentice-Hall, Englewood Cliffs, N.J., 1976, p. 162.

26 Bernard Bergonzi, *The Early H. G. Wells: A Study of the Scientific Romances,* Manchester University Press, 1961.

27 Ibid., p. 82.

28 Ibid., p. 168.

29 Fromm, 'Through the Novelist's Looking Glass', op. cit., p. 161.

30 *Dawn's Left Hand*, p. 223.

31 Ibid., p. 230.

32 Loc. cit.

33 Ibid., p. 231.

34 Loc. cit. Whether this account is a fair representation of what 'really happened' between Richardson and Wells is, of course, open to conjecture, as Fromm points out. See Fromm, *Dorothy Richardson*, op. cit., p. 263.

35 *Dawn's Left Hand*, p. 258.

36 The conflict has, of course, both social and personal dimensions and in each case maternalism can provide a workable resolution. The bohemianism of the Wilson world and the middle-class security of Wimpole Street represent polar opposites throughout *Pilgrimage.*

37 *Oberland*, p. 92.

38 Ibid., pp. 92-3.

39 Ibid., p. 93.

40 Loc. cit.

41 Loc. cit.

42 See 'Women in the Arts', typescript (carbon) essay discussing the problems of being a woman artist. Published in *Vanity Fair*, 24, 3, May 1925, pp. 47, 100.

43 *Honeycomb*, p.388.
44 Ibid., p. 404.
45 Ibid., pp. 422-3.
46 Ibid., p. 439.
47 Ibid., p. 380.
48 *The Tunnel*, p. 210.
49 Ibid., p. 251.
50 Loc. cit.
51 'Comments by a Layman', *The Dental Record*, XXXVI, 1, 1 January, 1916, p. 35.
52 *Honeycomb*, p. 438.
53 'Comments', op. cit., XXXVIII, 8, 1 August, 1918, pp. 350-2.
54 *The Tunnel*, p. 100.
55 Ibid., p. 122.
56 Ibid., p. 149.
57 'Comments', op. cit., XXXVIII, 1, 1 January, 1918, pp. 14-15.
58 Ibid., XXXVI, 10, 2 October, 1916, pp. 541-4.
59 *Interim*, p. 354.
60 'The Odd Man's Remarks on Socialism', *Ye Crank*, V, 1, January 1907, p. 31.
61 Ibid., p. 32.
62 'Socialism and the Odd Man', *Ye Crank and The Open Road*, V, 3, March 1907, p. 147.
63 'A Last Word to the Odd Man about Socialism', ibid., V, 4, April 1907, p. 181.
64 *Honeycomb*, pp. 424-5.

3 · *Alternatives*

I

Miriam's psychological conflict between being herself and being a woman has its extension in the outer world in terms of a conflict between isolation and marriage. Throughout *Pilgrimage* the possibilities of marriage occur always as temptations to forgo the integrity of her own identity. In *Pointed Roofs*, for example, she fantasizes about marrying a German :

> There would be a garden and German springs and summers and sunsets and strong kind arms and a shoulder. She would grow so happy. No one would recognize her as the same person. She would wear a band of turquoise-blue velvet ribbon round her hair and look at the mountains. . . . No good. She could never get out to that. Never. She could not pretend long enough. Everything would be at an end long before there was any chance of her turning into a happy German woman.
>
> Certainly with a German man she would be angry at once. She thought of the men she had seen – in the streets, in cafés and gardens, the masters in the school, photographs in the girls' albums. They had all offended her at once. Something in their bearing and manner. . . . Blind and impudent. . . .[1]

The pivot here between fantasy and awareness is the implication in 'No one would recognize her as the same person'. To marry means to become someone else, someone so unreal that a capacity for pretence greater than what Miriam feels she possesses is necessary to sustain it. Indeed, the weakness of her capacity to pretend is implicit in the prose, since the romantic image of 'sunsets and strong kind arms' is ironically sentimentalized. In reality, the mere sight of a German man is enough to provoke her anger; and the astounding generalization of such a stance is certainly more illustrative of Miriam's psychological battle-readiness than it is of German manhood.

Similarly, in *Oberland*, the romantic possibility presented by the Italian Guerini is generalized in Miriam's mind to the idea of marrying Italy:

> The life she lived with Guerini, beginning unconsciously that first evening when he had turned upon her throughout dinner his brown stare, hurrying forward during their afternoons in the snow, ending with their quarrel, begun again with the reproachful gaze he had sent across the table on the evening of her truancy, had persisted during the intervening time and was now marching off afresh on its own separate way - - - - She knew that she ought to go, that she was building up, with every moment she stayed in the room, a false relationship - - - - Even now it was a temptation. But it was the Italian background that was the real temptation. As soon as he talked of settling himself in London, he was lessened, and the temptation disappeared. Life as a single conversation in a single place, with the rest of the world going by, might seem possible when thought of in all the newness of Italy.[2]

This psychological reflex is characteristic of Miriam's more intimate encounters with men. The Russian Shatov is likewise credited with adding Russia to Miriam's mental map of Europe, and his Jewishness, seen by Miriam as an embodiment of Jewish culture, becomes a further rationalization for her refusal to marry him. By generalizing nationality in this way, Miriam gives herself a range of reference significantly wider than the limits of individual personality to explain her consistent refusal to commit herself. What Richardson makes clear to the reader, however, is the constant underlying this reflex, which is Miriam's inability to accept the prospect of marriage. It is the anticipated role-playing Miriam resents so much and which is felt to be the obstacle to relationship. And it is the role-playing which Miriam feels must attack the integrity of the self and therefore must attack and distort reality.

In interesting contrast to Miriam stands Fräulein Pfaff, whose jealousy and prudery has quite other sources. The kind of reaction she had to Miriam's meeting with the Pastor is elicited in more detail in a later incident with the French teacher, who has been discovered talking about men. Richardson conveys admirably Miriam's sense of shock:

> *'Männer – geschichten.'* Fräulein's voice rang out down the table. She bent forward so that the light from both the windows behind her fell sharply across her grey-clad shoulders and along the top of her head. There was no condemnation, Miriam felt, in those broad grey shoulders – they were innocent. But the head shining and flat, the wide parting, the sleekness of the hair falling thinly and flatly away from it – angry, dreadful skull. She writhed away from it. She would not look any more - - - -
>
> Fräulein whispered low.
>
> 'Here, in my school, here standing round this table are those who talk – of men.
>
> 'Young girls . . . who talk . . . of men' - - - -
>
> 'Is there, can there be in the world anything that is more base, more vile, more impure? Is there? Is there?' [3]

Miriam is revolted by this display of the Fräulein's repressed passions, a revulsion that becomes compounded by embarrassment, anger and finally rejection :

> 'Eh-h', she sneered. 'I know, *I* know who are the culprits. I have always known.' She gasped. 'It shall cease – these talks – this vile talk of men - - - - The school shall be clean . . . from pupil to pupil . . . from room to room. . . . Every day . . . every hour. . . Shameless!' she screamed - - - -
>
> Mechanically Miriam went downstairs with the rest of the party. With the full force of her nerves she resisted the echoes of Fräulein's onslaught - - - - The essential was that she would be dismissed, as Mademoiselle had been dismissed.[4]

Miriam knows she will have to go, that she cannot acquiesce in the Fräulein's frenzied purity any more than she can acquiesce in the social expectations of role-playing. When she does resign, the Fräulein makes no attempt to keep her.

Despite Miriam's inability to pursue a romantic ideal of marriage, and despite, equally, her inability to identify with the opposing polarity of the Fräulein's repressive spinsterhood, she finds no relief in the more temperate world of female companionship, which seems always to her to have the implicit goal of marriage as the basis of interchange. The conformity demanded of women, by women, is something Miriam not only rebels against, but which enrages her. She notices, for instance, a great difference between the styles of English and German girls who play the piano. The English style seems insipid and mechanical, the German affective. She spends a long time methodically practising herself, waiting for the inspiration to play as the Germans do :

> she began to understand the fury that had seized her when her mother and a woman here and there had taken for granted one should 'play when asked' and coldly treated her refusal as showing lack of courtesy. 'Ah !' she said aloud, as this realization came, 'Women.' [5]

Conformity of this kind inhibits the spontaneity and individuality of the artist and encourages the femininity which to Miriam is characterized by smugness and 'smiling' : 'Millie was smug. Millie would smile when she was a little older – and she would go respectfully to church all her life - - - -' [6]

Miriam's life at school reinforces her conviction that she is different from the 'smilers'. In a later incident, having taken the students swimming, Miriam becomes aware of the paradoxical nature of her feelings; however much she despises the mass of women who conform, they are the ones who are successful in social and domestic terms. The gossip indulged in by Gertrude, one of her pupils, irritates and repels her, but it represents a normality which she recognizes to be what men like :

> 'Old Lahmann's back from Geneva,' came the harsh panting voice.
>
> 'Pastor Lahmann?' repeated Miriam.
>
> 'None other, madame.'
>
> 'Have you seen him?' went on Miriam dimly, wishing that she might be released.
>
> 'Scots wha hae, no ! But I saw Lily's frills.'
>
> The billows of gold hair in the gallery were being piled up by two little hands – white and plump like Eve's, but with quick clever irritating movements - - - - They were all the same. Men liked creatures like that. She could imagine that girl married.[7]

What Miriam wants is to be her 'self' and to have this self accepted, to live in true relation to her real moments. The outer world, however, seems to her only to recognize a self through the roles it is able to play, and for Miriam, the requirement to behave as a feminine woman is devastating. In *Backwater*, still as a resident teacher, she is shown reading and reflecting at night, during the last weeks of the summer term, trying to rediscover her real self :

> It was not perhaps a 'good' self, but it was herself, her own familiar secretly happy and rejoicing self – not dead.[8]

But the sight of her flesh, her own hands lying on the coverlet, depresses her. Always at such points, Richardson reminds the reader of the essential disjunction Miriam suffers between her mind and her body :

> - - - they oppressed her by their size and their lack of feminine expressiveness - - - - But they were her strength. They came between her and the world of women.[9]

And reflecting further on the awfulness of women leads her to the conclusion :

> I'm some sort of bad unsimple woman. Oh, damn, damn, she sighed. I don't know. Her hands seemed to mock her, barring her way.[10]

This image is an important focus for Miriam's conflict, carrying the double weight of literal and metaphorical meanings. She is aware that she has her life in her own hands, but she is aware also that her hands express the duality of her nature : that her kind of femininity is out of phase with what the world expects but that it is equally something she cannot deny. She cannot deny that she is a woman, so she concludes that she must be a 'bad' one and that her own hands, her own actions prevent her from being any other kind.

The books she reads and the responses they elicit serve to heighten the uncertainty which characterizes her sense of femininity. During the time she spends as a teacher, reading offers an escape from the role of a single, professional woman which she seems to have chosen but which she cannot integrate into her self-image. This kind of therapeutic reading, especially of novels, elicits none of the scorn or frustration which otherwise frames her judgements of novels. The first and very obvious reason for this is her choice of women novelists who do not project to Miriam any of the usual male images of what women are like, or what they ought to be like. Secondly, and more fundamentally, these women novelists do not belong to the tradition; Miriam does not turn to Jane Austen, Emily Brontë or George Eliot, but to Ouida[11] and Rosa Nouchette Carey.[12] These writers were popular sentimental novelists of the 1890s, whose writing presents no intellectual challenge whatever. Their special appeal for Miriam lies elsewhere, in their depiction either of flamboyant women who could live dangerously, flout convention, yet still be admired for some quintessential femininity, as in Ouida's *Moths*, or of women who could find perfect serenity in 'happy marriages and heaven'.[13] Escapist reading of this kind allows Miriam a dream-world in which 'it had seemed quite possible that life might suddenly develop into the thing the writer described'.[14] This is a world which can render her virtuous :

> From somewhere would come an adoring man who believed in heaven and eternal life. One would grow very good - - - -[15]

Her reverie of having 'good' femininity conferred on her by an unthreatening, 'adoring' man is broken, however, by the insistent murmuring of reality, which cannot be quelled even by this most peaceful of fantasies. And the reality which threatens is the reality of 'women' :

> Those awful, awful women, she murmured to herself stirring in bed. I never thought of all the *awful* women there would be in such a life. I only thought of myself and the house and the garden and the man. What an escape! Good God in heaven what an escape! Far better to be alone and suffering and miserable here in the school alive. . . .[16]

It is the knowledge that identification as a woman is not conferred only by men, however 'adoring', but also by women, which destroys for Miriam the possibility of contemplating domestic bliss. In Rosa Nouchette Carey's world, she concludes, she would have to be a 'bad' woman, unsocialized, disreputable and probably miserable. She turns, then, desperately, from the 'mocking happy books' [17] to Ouida's 'bad' books, which become 'the centre of her life'. Her conversion to a world in which conventions can be defied is as intense as a religious conversion; indeed, it is a substitute for religion :

> She ceased to read her Bible and to pray. Ouida, Ouida, she would muse with the book at last in her hands. I want bad things – strong, bad things. . . .[18]

Of the sentimental stereotypes presented to her by escapist fiction, Miriam identifies more easily with the 'bad' unconventional woman. Even in her fantasy life, the rewards of socialized femininity are not sufficient to seduce her.

Later, in yet another residential teaching position, this time in a country house, she is again torn between her natural sympathies and the feminine posture she is expected to adopt :

> - - - the men with whom she was linked - - - and the women on the sofa, suddenly grown monstrous in their opposition of clothes and kindliness and the fuss of distracting personal insincerities of voice and speech - - - shouting aloud to her that she was a fool to be drawn into talking to men seriously on their own level, a fool to parade about as if she really enjoyed their silly game. 'I hate women and they've got to know it,' she retorted with all her strength - - -[19]

The activity with which she expresses her rebellion is to smoke a cigarette in front of both men and women :

> - - - Miriam discharged a double stream of smoke violently through her nostrils – breaking out at last a public defiance of the freemasonry of women. 'I suppose I'm a new woman – I've said I am now, anyhow,' she reflected, wondering in the background of her determination how she would reconcile the role with her work as a children's governess.[20]

When an action as simple and harmless as lighting a cigarette produces such an intensity of reaction and is seen as such a socially daring thing to do, it is not surprising that a person of intelligence and sensitivity such as Miriam should spend a lot of time and energy trying to break out of the role strictures which society has provided for her. *The Tunnel* records Miriam's first experience of life in London as a dental secretary, an important part of which is visiting her friends, Jan and Mag, who share a flat. Her friends are also trying to break out of the trappings of their expected role. Just as Miriam's smoking was daring and rebellious, their daring deed is to learn how to cycle, and the freedom it allows them is something they relish conveying to Miriam :

> 'We went out – last night – after dark – and rode – round Russell Square – twice – in our knickers –'
>
> '*No*! Did you really? How simply heavenly.'
>
> 'It *was*. We came home nearly crying with rage at not being able to go about, permanently, in nothing but knickers. It would make life an *absolutely* different thing.'
>
> 'The freedom of movement.'[21]

This passage expresses, with brutal precision, the inhibition forced on young women not only by the expectations of decorum and custom, but also by the very dress they were expected to adopt. 'Freedom of movement,' Miriam breathes, with yearning.

Mr Hancock is one of the dentists in the Harley Street practice where Miriam works; she admires his dedication and professionalism and is attracted by his interest in objets d'art and his attendance at scientific lectures. But the attraction she feels brings its own kind of hopelessness. How can she communicate with such a man, any man, without behaving as women are taught to behave?

> Nice kind people would call her 'a charming girl.' . . . 'Charming girls' were taught to behave effectively, and lived in a brilliant death, dealing death all round them. Nothing could live in their presence. No natural beauty, no spectacle of art, no thought, no music. They were uneasy in the presence of these charming things, because their presence meant cessation of 'charming' behaviour – except at such moments as they could use the occasion to decorate themselves. *They had no souls.* Yet, in social life, nothing seemed to possess any power but their surface animation.[22]

The death-giving property of the traditional role is what most appals Miriam. She is not only seeking 'freedom of movement' for her own life's sake, although that is her paramount drive, but is also seeking the styles and strata of social life that will allow the sharing of real moments – that will allow the energizing and creative experiences which she has enjoyed in isolation. Because of its inherent inauthenticity, the inability of the female role to survive in the face of those things which in some way embody real moments – natural beauty, art and music, and thought– makes it anathema to Miriam on moral as well as individualistic grounds.

During her time in Mrs Bailey's lodging house, the French waiter, Mr Mendizabal, takes her in the evenings to some of the cafés in London. She luxuriates in the atmosphere with a mixed feeling of recognition and resentment:

> She could understand a life that spent all its leisure in a café- - - - It was a heaven, a man's heaven, most of the women were there with men - - - She was there with a man, a free man of the world, a continental, a cosmopolitan, a connoisseur of women.[23]

The feeling of recognition is only possible if she identifies with the men in the café. To identify with the women evokes feelings of resentment and dissatisfaction; resentment because she thinks the women who sit in cafés feel they can enter only with men, and dissatisfaction that the women should have a place only because of the behests of men.

Men, however, are the polarity towards which the female role must gravitate until the male and female intertwine in the ideal of marriage. Miriam finds the worldliness of marriage unpalatable and its far from ideal tyrannies shocking. If *Pointed Roofs* is the dawning of consciousness and *Backwater* withdrawal from the adult world, *Honeycomb* explores the enigmas of marriage as both personal and career choice. During a conversation with her employer, Mrs Corrie, and Mrs Craven, a friend of Mrs Corrie, the following exchange takes place:

> 'I don't think a man has any right to be handsome,' said Miriam desperately – she must manage to keep the topic going. These women were so terrible – they filled her with fear. She must make them take back what they had said.
>
> 'A handsome man's much handsomer than a pretty woman,' said Mrs Craven.
>
> 'It's cash, cash, cash – that's what it is,' chanted Mrs Corrie softly.
>
> 'Oh, do you?' said Miriam. 'I think a handsome man's generally so weak.'
>
> Mrs Craven stared into the fire.
>
> 'You take the one who's got the ooftish, my friend,' said Mrs Corrie.[24]

But later Miriam divorces the problem from herself:

> 'Superior women don't marry,' she said, 'sir she said, sir she said, su, per, *i*, or women' – but that meant blue-stockings.[25]

Blue-stockings are not an acceptable alternative to Miriam because they still represent a stereotype, albeit an anti-feminine one.

Most of the encounters Miriam has with men are striking in their non-resolution, and in their demonstration that an unbridgeable gap of incommunicativeness exists between Miriam and any man who wishes to know her. One such encounter takes place between Miriam and a friend of her brother-in-law, Gerald. Although she likes Mr Grove, she is awkward and uneasy with him, eventually asking him what he is going to do in life. He replies that if he had his way he would escape from the world and join a brotherhood. Miriam immediately transfers this alternative to her own life, but finds it a humiliating idea :

> 'If a woman joins an order she must confess to a man.'
> 'Yes,' he said indifferently. . . . 'I can't carry out my wish, I can't carry out my dearest wish.' [26]

Mr Grove is clearly preoccupied with his own deprivations and is not interested in Miriam's resentment at the prospect of confessing to a male priest. Nevertheless she feels a kinship with his misery :

> Neither of them were wanted in the world. No one would ever want either of them. Then why could they not want each other? He did not wish it. Salvation. He wanted salvation – for himself.[27]

The kinship Miriam feels is clearly not felt by Mr Grove, who is preoccupied with his private despair, although he acknowledges her sensitivity towards him :

> 'You have come at the right instant, and shown me wisdom. You are wonderful.'
> She recoiled. She did not really want to help him. She wanted to attract his attention to her.[28]

Even sensitive, sympathetic, likeable men seem to Miriam to be unable to respond to her for her own sake, but merely to use what she offers to alleviate their own condition, to absorb somehow a part of her into themselves. This phenomenon forces her back to the solitude of her real moments and to the sense that her moments can only be shared and expressed with someone who will feel the same way about the same things. Indeed Miriam may reprove Mr Grove for wanting salvation 'for himself', but she is surely guilty of the same egoism, since she wants 'to attract his attention to her'.

For women, however, marriage is the only security against poverty. Two of Miriam's sisters, Sarah and Harriett, marry easily; Miriam and her other sister, Eve, do not. Miriam reflects on their respective futures :

> The voices of Sarah and Harriett would go on . . . marked with fresh things. . . . Her own and Eve's would remain, separate, to grow broken and false and unrecognizable in the awful struggle for money.[29]

And security against physical attack is also ensured by marriage :

> The only way to feel quite secure at night would be to marry . . . how awful . . . either you marry and are never alone or you risk being alone and afraid . . . to marry for safety . . . perhaps some women did.[30]

Miriam's mother has been far from satisfied by marriage :

> 'Oh!' . . . Mother's polite tone, trying to be interested. That was all she'd had for years. All she'd ever had, from him - - -
>
> 'My life has been so useless,' said Mrs Henderson suddenly.[31]

This sense of uselessness precipitates Mrs Henderson's suicide, a deeply formative experience for Miriam, as her own mother's death had been, indeed, for Richardson. In middle age, Richardson revealed some of her reactions to suicide to her friend, Peggy Kirkaldy, who was similarly involved as a helpless spectator of a woman's suicide as a response to failure in relationship :

> Frightful & apparently meaningless. One can see no real motive. A lesser woman, wounded in her self-esteem might have avenged herself in this way, if she hadn't courage to shoot the man. But your description shows her gallant & fine, if she really loved the creature, could she have cast this hideous shadow over his future? - - - - I am sorry for the folks who had to shut her out & leave her in a void, & I know how you must feel, knowing you could have kept her alive if only she stayed with you. She is planted in your memory, & will recur. But those last moments may not have been so bad as you fear in going down into them from outside, as spectator.[32]

The 'hideous shadow' of her own mother's suicide cannot have failed to influence Richardson's attitudes towards marriage. The same theme comes again in *March Moonlight* in which Miriam recalls receiving a postcard from Paris where a young Russian friend, also unable to manage a personal involvement, announces her intention to kill herself. Clearly Richardson responds more to the aggressive element of suicide than she does to its expression of despair, and this is a reasonable enough response given that in the context of her life experience suicide occurred as a response to impossible relationships.

Mrs Henderson's suicide takes place while she is convalescing with Miriam at a seaside resort and it is an episode which Miriam finds too painful and searing to express, except for the most fleeting impressions and the few telling remarks her mother offers :

> The sleepless even voice reverberated again in the unbroken sleeplessness of the room. 'It's no use . . . I am cumbering the ground.' The words struck, sending a heat of anger and resentment through Miriam's shivering form.[33]

During a conversation with 'the girls', Jan and Mag, Miriam repeats her fear and distaste of the married state :

> 'I can't imagine anything more awful than what you call the sheltered life,' said Miriam with a little pain in her forehead.[34]

They go on to recount to themselves the pleasures of Sunday mornings, when they are able to do as they wish :

> 'The first cigarette anyhow, with or without the *Referee*. It's just pure absolute bliss, that first bit of Sunday morning; complete well-being and happiness.'
>
> 'While the sheltered people are flushed with breakfast-table talk –'
>
> 'Or awkward silences.'
>
> 'The deep damned silence of disillusionment.'
>
> 'And thinking about getting ready for church.'
>
> 'The men smoke.'
>
> '- - - Freedom is life. We may be slaves all day and guttersnipes all the rest of the time, but, ach Gott, we are free.' [35]

But the price to be paid for freedom is loss of status, emotional and financial security, and a sense of belonging.

Towards the end of *The Tunnel* Miriam becomes the victim of a friend of Eve's called Eleanor Dear. Eleanor Dear thinks of herself as an impoverished gentlewoman. She subjects Miriam to emotional blackmail in order to gain support, material and psychological. Eventually she blackmails a clergyman, who has been visiting her to offer comfort, with an ultimatum that he must marry her in order to vindicate them both from scandal which she assures him his visits have initiated. The clergyman, Mr Taunton, relates the conversation to Miriam :

> '- - - she broke down completely, told me that, socially speaking, it was too late to discontinue my visits; that people in the house were already talking.'
>
> 'People in *that* house!' – you little simpleton – 'Who? It is the most monstrous thing I ever heard.'
>
> 'Well – there you have the whole story. The poor girl's distress and dependence were most moving. I have a very great respect for her character and esteem for her personality – and of course I am pledged.'
>
> 'I see,' said Miriam narrowly regarding him. Do you want to be saved? – ought I to save you? – why should I save you? – it is a solution of the whole thing, and a use for your money – you won't marry her when you know how ill she is.[36]

Clearly, women like Eleanor Dear ought to be married to avoid causing an embarrassment to the social system, but Miriam is shocked by the degrading manipulations which Eleanor Dear is forced by her circumstances to employ; initially Miriam's sense of propriety is outraged but then she sees that it is the most useful solution to the problem. The underlying implication is that men who are willing may as well rescue women who need rescuing, since no one else is willing or able to do so. And it is upon this sour note that Eleanor Dear leaves the scene and *The Tunnel* ends.

Later Miriam hears that Eleanor Dear has finally, through machinations which seem to Miriam creative to the point of artistry, achieved the goal of marriage :

> Poor Eleanor, with all her English dreams; just *Rodkin.* But he was a Jew when he hesitated to marry a consumptive, and perfectly a Jew when he decided not to see the child lest he should love it; and also when he hurried down into Sussex the moment it came, to see it, with a huge armful of flowers for her. What a scene for the Bible-women's Hostel. All Eleanor. Her triumph. What other woman would have dared to engage a cubicle and go calmly down without telling them? And a week later she was in the superintendent's room and all those prim women sewing for her and hiding her and telling everybody she had rheumatic fever. And crying when she came away.
>
> She was right. She justified her actions and came through. And now she's a young married woman in a pretty villa, *near* the church, and the vicar calls and she won't walk on Southend pier because 'one meets one's

> butcher and baker and candle-stick maker.' But only because Rodkin is a child-worshipper. And she tolerates him and the child and he is a brow-beaten cowed little slave. It is tempting to tell the story. A perfect recognizable story of a scheming unscrupulous woman; making one feel virtuous and superior; but only if one simply outlined the facts, leaving out all the inside things. Knowing a story like that from the inside, knowing Eleanor, changed all 'scandalous' stories.[37]

Eleanor Dear's pursuit of the feminine ideal, a pursuit remarkable for its singlemindedness, its desperation and its perversity, haunts Miriam and becomes for her a symbol for her own repressed femininity, but a symbol whose power to seduce her away from the chosen path of self-realization fills her with fear, anxiety and scorn. If Eleanor Dear is the type of the female artist, if Eleanor Dear succeeds, through her machinations, in becoming a wife and mother, where indeed does that leave Miriam? Only Eleanor Dear's death can relieve Miriam of the threat to her own vision of this embodiment of female art:

> 'What has become of Eleanor Dear?'
>
> 'When did ye last heere of her, lassie?' The sparing, softly treading tone of his stories of his most dreadful cases: gentle judgement, without reproach.
>
> 'Oh I don't know – ages ago' – her voice was hard, frostily selfish, something for a man to fly from – 'when that heroic little Jew took her to Egypt.'
>
> 'Then ye've not heard of her death?'
>
> It was not shock or sadness that kept her silent. Immense, horrible relief in being certain now that the burden of Eleanor would never again return upon her hands. And great wonder, that Eleanor had done her dying. Somewhere, in some unknown room, she had accomplished that tremendous deed. Alone.[38]

The impossibility of accepting marriage and the conditions that go with it contributes to Miriam's sense of alienation from men generally and from those women, by far the majority, who accept the rules of the game. One of Miriam's earlier experiences of this kind of failure in herself to conform to the conventions of courtship and marriage, is the party scene in *Backwater*, during which she behaves outrageously by being unavailable to Ted, her suitor, and going off alone into the garden with his friend Max, whom she has never met before. Just when she feels Ted within her power, she abandons him:

> She must dance once more with Max. She had never really danced before. She would go to Ted at last and pass on the spirit of her dancing to him. But not yet.[39]

She goes outside to walk and talk with Max :

> He had come just at the right moment. She would keep him with her until she had to face Ted. He was like a big ship towing the little barque of her life to its harbour.[40]

Max becomes very attractive to her and is in turn attracted by her :

> 'I feel that there is no poison in you. I have not felt that before with a woman.'
>
> 'Aren't women awful?' [41]

Miriam's reply is defensive, showing her need to dissociate herself from the species of woman, from the role, from everything about women. They are interrupted by Ted, who is hurt and angered by Miriam's rejection. Max sends him off and he leaves the party, much to Miriam's surprise. When she returns to the company she finds herself 'in the presence of a tribunal'.[42] She has ignored the conventions and behaved badly, incurring the disapproval of her mother and sisters, even though what she did was to follow the natural bent of her feelings. The condemnation seems silly to Miriam, undeserved :

> People were always inventing things - - - Meg's eyes would be sad and reproachful in this quiet neatness. Terror seized her. She wouldn't see him. He had finished his work at the Institution. It was the big Norwich job next week.[43]

And that is the last mention Miriam makes of Ted.

Later, through her married sister, Harriett, Miriam meets a Mr Parrow while on holiday at Brighton. She is primarily aware of his strangeness and separateness. The sisters accompany him, together with another young man, to the station and Miriam reflects :

> Perhaps they would be able to reach the station without being obliged to speak to each other. Parrow. It was either quite a nice name or pitiful; like a child trying to say sparrow-- - -

> Nobody knew him at all well. Not a single person in the world. If he were run over and killed on the way to the station, nobody would ever have known anything about him. . . . People did die like that . . . probably most people; in a minute, alone and unknown; too late to speak.[44]

But even the thought of the ultimate loneliness of death is not sufficient to cause Miriam to break the silence and try to reach Mr Parrow. She joins him later for an outing to Crystal Palace, but is obliged to excuse herself from the fireworks they are supposed to have come to watch. She explains that she has always been frightened by the noise. Mr Parrow presses her to try the toboggan instead and eventually takes her hand :

> 'Let me go,' said her hand dragging gently at his. 'No,' said the firm enclosure, tightening, 'not yet.' What does it matter? flashed her mind. Why should I be such a prude? The hand gave her confidence.[45]

We hear no more of Mr Parrow, but the incident conveys another side of Miriam's alienation, which is her inexperience and fear. Although her verbal communication with Mr Parrow is restricted and difficult, the physical contact of his hand is reassuring to her and gives her confidence where her own speculations had not.

Miriam's relationship with the Harley Street specialist, Dr Densley, likewise reverberates with the possibility of marriage and likewise fails to meet the necessary conditions. Densley is drawn to her atypical attitudes; although she is twenty-eight,[46] he finds her a 'dear girl' (which she denies), unspoiled, and with 'a man's mind'.[47] He admires her, he is devoted to her, but she cannot feel that he recognizes her with the sufficiency necessary for mutual respect, for what she calls 'companionship'. Marriage with Densley would be easy and warm, would provide support, but it would result in a loneliness far more acute than what she bears alone. She perceives this when he comes as her guest to a Lycurgan meeting and they pass the evening as partners :

> Eyes gleamed at him as he went debonair, talking, not listening, needing no response but her radiance and abandon to his guiding arm. Solace at once; a rebuilding of strength to face this crowd- - - - Life, through all happenings, could pass like this. Happenings would be disarmed, bright strangeness rooted in an unexamined sameness. There

> would be solace for all the wounds of thought in his unconsciousness. But no companionship. For a long while nothing at all of profound experience and then, perhaps, her whole being arranged round a new centre and reality once more accessible, but in a loneliness beside which the loneliness of the single life was nothing.[48]

Densley's very kindness and ordinariness entail their incompatibility, despite that part of Miriam's nature which longs for security and anonymity. Although the earnestness and intensity of her pilgrimage always maintain their priority in her psychological orientation, she is neither capable of dependence nor proud of her solitary state. And in any case men must somehow take their place in her world, somehow be accommodated. She knows the consequences of her decision :

> Farewell to Densley is farewell to my one chance of launching into life as my people have lived it. I am left with these strangers – people without traditions, without local references, and who despise marriage, or on principle disapprove of it. And in my mind I agree. Yet affairs not ending in marriage are even more objectionable than marriage. And celibates, outside religion, although acceptable when thought of as alone, are always, socially, a little absurd. Then I must be absurd. Growing absurd. To others I am already absurd.[49]

The fact that Densley offers her a social niche is more profound than it appears at first. Miriam's awareness of her isolation strips it of glamour and prevents her from conferring on herself any significant metaphysical status. Celibates are only acceptable 'when thought of as alone', outside human company. Miriam's search is not for sanctity but for society; consequently, to deny her sexuality by rejecting marriage makes her absurd, a misfit. The force of that final 'must' is focused in ambiguity; in one sense, her destiny is sealed by the commitment she chooses, so that she knowingly embraces the position of absurdity, whereas in the other sense the consensus from outside, based on her behaviour, can reach only the conclusion that she is absurd. There is no salvation from the romantic cult of the artist, nor is there hope that the feminine principle can somehow stand gloriously alone. Yet it is not Densley in particular whom she may not marry, but everything he represents; security, ease, and all the benefits that accrue from fulfilling the sex-role expectations of society.

Richardson gave this same advice to a friend contemplating such a marriage:

> - - - supposing him willing & able to marry, do you really believe you would find lasting happiness in joining your life to his? As I see him, he needs only the home-life that is usually discoverable filling out & supporting the public life of a keen professional man. Such a man's engrossments & interests, including the speculations & scientific technicalities which are so large a part of the mental life of an investigator, his wife must either share, or leave alone & live, as do so many professional men's wives, more or less in loneliness, aware only, for their comfort, of the necessity for their man, of the serenity & quietude they provide. Very rarely, & perhaps never for very long, can an intense, emotional personal relationship flourish side by side with a real professional existence. I saw a good deal of professional ménages during my time at Harley Street & my rather narrow escape from marrying into a medical ménage was perhaps helped thereby.[50]

Richardson's personal definition of marriage is far removed from romantic identification; marriage for her meant 'unbroken companionship'.[51]

II

The conviction of a significant difference between male and female consciousness gives rise to a concomitant conviction of a difference in creative potential; during her correspondence about socialism in *Ye Crank*, Richardson remarks, in passing, that

> the art of life, the social art, the art of arts, is woman's art; I do not mean to imply that it cannot be man's too – only they are in many ways to some extent precluded, but it has never yet had full scope. . . .[52]

One of Richardson's problems in *Pilgrimage* is to explore the necessity of this dichotomy; whether it is the case that the difference in consciousness precipitates the divergence in social role conditioning and thence to different careers in practical affairs, or whether, as the bourgeois men she meets would have it, the difference in social role is caused by the inherent difference in biology and hence consciousness. To that end, it is worth considering Richardson's views on the professions open to women and the scope offered within them.

The most obvious career for women is bringing up babies. In her 'Comments' column in *The Dental Record*, Richardson discusses an argument put forward by an anonymous author of a series of pamphlets on 'The Position of Women'. This author's view is that 'the only way of putting the problem of population on a sound basis is to make motherhood an independent profession, a branch of the civil service'.[53] Richardson suggests that such a programme for liberating women 'is based on a repudiation of the idea of regarding all women as potential mothers. It includes the probable evolution of a sexless "worker" class, a female "drone", and the leaving of the business of motherhood to the elect.' The criticism Richardson offers of this prospect is generated from her refusal to accept the thesis that women must be confined and defined by their biology: 'This vision seems perfectly realizable, as long as one considers the problem of women as one with the problem of reproduction and frames one's ideal state as a sort of organised workshop of the "life-force".'

Similarly in *Pilgrimage*, Miriam insistently rejects the view that maternity is the fulfilment of feminine being:

> 'It is the same with people. Men or women. No man, or woman, can ever engage the whole of my interest who believes, as you believe and, of course, George Calvin Shaw flashing his fire-blue eyes, that my one driving force, the sole and shapely end of my existence is the formation within myself of another human being, and so on ad infinitum. You may call the proceeding by any name you like, choose whatever metaphor you prefer to describe it – and the metaphor you choose will represent you more accurately than any photograph. It may be a marvellous incidental result of being born a woman and may unify a person with life and let her into its secrets – I can believe that now, the wisdom and insight and serene independent power it might bring. But it is neither the beginning nor the end of feminine being.'[54]

The problem with this kind of definition is its assigning to an inferior role the human personality which women share with men as the chief characteristic of their common humanity. The problem, Richardson suggests, is better focused as a problem of gender rather than one of reproduction:

> The life-long union of one and one is still the secret aspiration of both men and women, and the bearing and rearing of children is incidental, a

part result, not the prime 'cause' of such a union- - - - Our aspirations- - - - The 'woman' problem is not a sex problem. It is part of the problem of the pilgrimage of humanity from Eros to Agape. We need not 'aspire' to the level of the ants and the bees.[55]

Richardson sees no reason why women should not be able to undertake technical skills, such as dentistry, which were then exclusive to men, nor why the subordinate jobs, such as dental secretary, which are exclusive to women, should be so meanly regarded and meanly paid. She writes from experience that however good the conditions might be under which dental secretaries work, the job 'does not promise a life work, it leads nowhere, it cannot be well pursued after early middle age and is sturdily condemned by the Central Bureau for the Employment of Women as a "blind-alley" profession.'[56] By contrast, mechanical dentistry does offer a future :

Women have long enjoyed the reputation of being bad mechanics. It may be that their apparent defective sense of 'form' is largely due to their parasitic relationship to life during the centuries which have seen the departure of the arts and crafts from the homestead and the reduction of housework to a tangle of de-socialised industries carried on by amateurs in isolated houses - - - - There is something in the very bearing of the average young middle-class woman of to-day, a confidence and directness that hints at an ability to handle if need be both tools and machinery without any of that 'charming' feminine ineptitude which prompted the wise man of the last generation to lock up his chisels.[57]

Furthermore, men are often deprived from exercising some of their talents. Convalescent soldiers in 1919 were producing not only the usual mats and basket-work of traditional occupational therapy, but also fine embroidery and excellently made blouses, as reported in *The Hospital* and picked up by Richardson :

How many men miss their vocation? is the final summing up of *The Hospital.* And how many women, too, one might add. All of us know of men who pursue in a more or less perfunctory manner businesses and professions in 'the world', but are at their best and happiest doing odd jobs in the house and garden- - - - And there are at least as many women whose natural bent is thwarted all the time by the exigencies of domestic life. Perhaps these types, so wrongly classified as the 'masculine' woman and the 'effeminate' man, are relatively rare; but their rarity does not justify their immolation. It is pure waste. In a socialized world where the idea of service shall have been substituted for the idea of gain, there will be a flexible adjustment of employment- - -[58]

Richardson's earliest work experience was as a teacher, a traditionally feminine profession, details about which she records in the first three volumes of *Pilgrimage.* Miriam is unfulfilled in her post with the Misses Perne because her educational philosophy is out of tune with theirs :

> 'The business of the teacher is to make the children independent, to get them to think for themselves, and that's much more important than whether they know facts,' she would say irrelevantly to the Pernes whenever the question of teaching came up- - - - Mentally she flung them [the children] out and off, made them stand upright and estranged. She could not give them personal love. She did not want to; nor to be entangled with them. They were going to grow up into North London women, most of them loudly scorning everything that was not materially profitable; these would remember her with pity – amusement. A few would escape- - - -
>
> This morning a sense of their softness and helplessness went to her heart. She had taught them so little. But she had forced them to be impersonal.[59]

Her first encounter with Mrs Corrie, who employs her as a governess, is that she is again expected to fill a traditional role in which there is no place for intelligence :

> And it was quite clear that she wanted a plain dull woman she could count on; always there, in a black dress- - - - Someone else, working for her, in her pay, would look after the children and do the hard work - - -
>
> 'Oh, I'm very fond of children', said Miriam despairingly. She stared at the familiar bars. There were the bars of the old breakfast-room grate at home, and the schoolroom bars at Banbury Park. There they were again, hard and black in the hard black grate, in the midst of all this light and warmth and fragrance. Nothing had really changed. Black and hard. Someone's grate. She was alone again.[60]

Miriam's next job is as dental secretary to a Harley Street practice. The details of the job are carefully set out in the third chapter of *The Tunnel.* However, even in the middle of a very busy, more independent job, Miriam is aware that she is in yet another trap :

> The tedium of the long series of small, precise, attention-demanding movements was aggravated by the prospect of a fresh set of implements already qualifying for another cleansing- - - - Were there any sort of

> people who could do this kind of thing patiently, without minding? - - - the evolution of dentistry was wonderful, but the more perfect it became the more and more of this sort of thing there would be . . . the more drudgery workers, at fixed salaries . . . there must be, everywhere, women doing this work for people who were not nice. They *could* not do it for the work's sake. Did some of them do it cheerfully as unto God? It was wrong to work unto man.[61]

The real problem stems from the fact that even where jobs are opened up for women, as in dentistry, there is no professional future for them :

> But the Amalgam Company probably had quite uneducated girls. Nobody ought to be asked to spend their lives calculating decimal quantities. The men who lived on these things had their drudgery done for them. They did it themselves first. Yes, but then it meant their *future.* A woman clerk never becomes a partner. There was no hope for women in business.[62]

Richardson regarded secretarial work as one of the least attractive pursuits open to women :

> An expert shorthand typist, with one language, F. or G. can today command a good salary. Free-lance typing, at home, has to compete with the innumerable bureaux who work at sweated rates. Shoals of them undertake every kind of authors manuscript at 10d & even 8d the thousand & at that rate even by working eight or ten hours per day, there is not much to be made, & materials have to come out of the total - - - - If I were in her place I think I should go for a straight housekeeping job. Veronica had a good one for a year or two running an M.P.'s flat. 'All duties' for keep & £52 a year.[63]

It is clear from Richardson's journalism, from her personal memories and from the account of her early working life in *Pilgrimage*, that all her conflicts derive from one source, which is the impossibility of reconciling her sense of self with the expected role-typical behaviours and attitudes attributed by her society to women. Her intelligence finds no real outlet in the professions open to her. Her social life is in turn frustrating, embarrassing and fragmentary – she finds it impossible to communicate with men, because they cannot see her for herself, or with women, because she cannot identify with them. The insights she gains during moments of heightened perception remain personal and unshared. She is limited to a sparse material existence by her inability, as a single woman, to earn more than a pittance. All these various and disparate experiences lead her to radical positions; to socialism, because it seems to offer the prospect of a society in which women like herself would be freer to develop their particular excellences; to solitude, because the social fabric around her offers her no possible function; to feminism, because, above all, it allows the possibility of a female consciousness which can counter-balance the male reality principle. Science she rejects as a system derived from the analytic structure of the male mind. She rejects it as a basis for social philosophy, because its planning power excludes the vital female principle of synthetic experience, just as she rejects the conclusions it reaches by analysis, for instance the Darwinian view that a woman's function is entirely dictated by her biology.

III

Clearly Miriam suffers a disjunction between mind and body which obstructs her ability to integrate her romantic attachments to men with the sexual commitment of marriage. It is clear too that her commitment to the pursuit and expression of her individual female consciousness obstructs her ability to act within the modes of sexual behaviour defined by the feminine role and characteristics of the means of livelihood available to women. This is a point of impasse which Richardson shows Miriam trying to break through along two distinct paths. The first involves the extension of her romantic attachments to women; the second involves the extension of her artistic manipulative powers to the materials of life itself.

In Miriam's mind, attachments to women necessarily avoid role expectations and the compromising of independence which she is convinced are characteristics of marriage. They also avoid, equally necessarily, the expected creative fulfilment of the female, that of maternity.

Ulrica Hesse is a student at Fräulein Pfaff's school. Miriam's first meeting with the girl is intense and overpowering :

> - - - a girl with a smooth pure oval of pale face standing wrapped in dark furs, gazing about her with eyes for which Miriam had no word,

liquid – limpid – great-saucers, no – pools . . . great round deeps - - - -

The girl's thin fingers had come out of her furs and fastened convulsively – like cold, throbbing claws on to the breadth of Miriam's hand - - - -

'Lehrerin!' breathed the girl. Something flinched behind her great eyes. The fingers relaxed, and Miriam, feeling within her a beginning of response, had gone upstairs.[64]

It is typical of Miriam to need to escape from the immediacy of relationship when no distortions of role-playing or fanaticism have impaired the reality of response. One of the paradoxes of her nature is that the drive towards truth is counter-balanced by a need to modify it or escape from it; the feelings responding must be rationalized by the mind appraising. For Miriam, the drive towards truth is not initially a drive towards experience. Ulrica arouses a romantic passion in Miriam which is unmatched by her response to men :

It was Ulrica, Ulrica . . . Ulrica . . . Ulrica sitting up at breakfast with her lovely head and her great eyes – her thin fingers peeling an egg - - - Ulrica peeling an egg and she, afterwards, like a mad thing had gone into the *saal* and talked to Millie in a vulgar, familiar way, no doubt.[65]

Miriam's adoration is not only aesthetic; she is like a young gallant who wishes physically to protect the heroine :

- - - Miriam wished that the eyes could be raised, when the reading ceased, to hers and that she could go and put her hands about the beautiful head, scarcely touching it and say, 'It is all right. I will stay with you always.' [66]

She wants to feed upon[67] the sight of Ulrica, to have her just to look at.[68] This protective, possessive response is threatened during one of her few exchanges with the girl. They are talking at night after a thunderstorm which Ulrica likens to her confirmation :

'I weeped so ! All day I have weeped! The all whole day! And my mozzer she console me I shall not weep. And I weep. Ach! It was of most beautifullest.'

Miriam felt as if she were being robbed. . . .This was Ulrica. . . .[69]

It is the girl's mother, after all, who has the protector's place. Again the intensity is too much for Miriam; her controls intervene and she terminates the conversation. At the end of the novel, when Miriam is preparing to return to England, we are told simply that she did not look at Ulrica.[70] The pain of separation must be endured alone.

Miriam's response is clear but the relationship is not put to the test, since Ulrica is never approached. Miriam makes no attempt to engage with her ideal or to explore the nature of her response. Her encounter with Amabel, the young drama student whom she meets at her club, is, by contrast, uninhibited from the start, owing to Amabel's own impulsiveness. Their first meeting is characterized by Miriam's feeling that 'she had embarked in sunlight upon an unknown quest'.[71] Amabel immediately tells Miriam of her affair with a man, which she feels usually creates a barrier between herself and English women, who are all 'pewre'. But the barrier of the male does not obtrude between them :

> Her hands came forward, one before the other outstretched, very gently approaching, and while Miriam read in the girl's eyes the reflection of her own motionless yielding, the hands moved apart and it was the lovely face that touched her first, suddenly and softly dropped upon her knees that were now gently clasped on either side by the small hands.
>
> Alone with the strange burden, confronting empty space, Miriam supposed she ought to stroke the hair, but was withheld, held, unbreathing, in a quietude of well-being that was careless of her own demand for some outward response. She felt complete as she was, brooding apart in an intensity of being that flowed refreshingly through all her limbs and went from her in a radiance that seemed to exist for herself alone and could not be apparent to the hidden girl.[72]

The prose here has a very different quality from the passages exploring Miriam's relationships with men; the flow of language is smooth and confident, the querulous note having modulated to affirmation. Richardson implicitly assures the reader that this time Miriam knew what she was feeling. The posture is dangerously difficult to describe; one woman kneeling to another is in itself suggestive of the ludicrous. But what is especially interesting about the encounter is its stasis. Miriam feels both held and withheld, at a midpoint where her emotions neither ebb nor flow and where Amabel's gesture needs no response. This contrasts sharply with the erotic arousal Miriam feels in response to Shatov's gesture, which 'thrills' her, or Wilson's letter, which makes her heart beat. With Amabel, the body is no hindrance; it does not assume a life of its own. The intimacy felt between the two women is unconstrained, not because sexuality is denied, but because it has no identifiable aspects. It could, and would, be argued by Freudians, for instance, that all physically intimate gestures display libidinous drives, so that the intimacies of this encounter and those subsequent to it, can only be interpreted as repressed lesbian desires. The terminology, however, is irrelevant, first because neither Miriam nor Amabel is aware of specifically sexual feelings in one another, and, secondly, because the qualitatively different tone of this passage, compared with the parting from Shatov, for instance, renders the qualitative difference in Miriam's responses inescapable. Later, as a reinforcement of her gesture, Amabel scrawls a message on Miriam's mirror for Miriam to find when she returns home; the message simply says 'I love you.' [73]

What so moves Miriam is the sense that at last she has access to another individual and the other to herself. She feels no demands made upon her energies, no invasion of her personal territory, no need to assume a role, with all the correlative feelings of solicitude, frustration and resentment, no need to explain herself. Amabel writes her a letter, which, unlike Wilson's letter, does not provoke the judgement that it is out of place :

> 'Forgive – I watched you – in your little English clothes – go across the square – oh, my lady – my little – you terrified my heart – I held it out to you – my terrified heart – in my two hands –'
>
> Real. Reality vibrating behind this effort to drive feeling through words. The girl's reality appealing to her own, seeing and feeling it ahead of her own seeings or feelings that yet responded, acknowledged as she emerged from her reading, in herself and the girl, with them when they were together. Somehow between them in the mysterious interplay of their two beings, the reality she had known for so long alone, brought out into life.[74]

The interplay between two beings, if it is to be 'real', must assume the aspects of Miriam's inner dialogue to the point where her inner life is not discontinuous with her life in the world; such a demand is nothing less than the demand that the perceiving consciousness itself, in its act of perceiving, should become a social event, capable of being entirely known and shared by another, with equal reciprocity.[75] What seems to make this possible, according to Miriam, is that Amabel presents herself in a way that makes Miriam forget herself, her own 'seeings or feelings', in the first instant. The release given by this experience is an important indication of the deeper motivation implicit in the prose of *Pilgrimage* : through her very commitment to the veracity of the individual consciousness, Richardson discovers an ambiguity. The care with which she strives to describe the particularities of experience, the puritan intensity of her commitment to her own sense of integrity, her struggle for complete independence, all constitute only a technical mastery of 'reality', however detailed, without the validation of relationship. What is particularly feminist here is that Amabel must recognize and accept Miriam entirely at her own valuation, *in order to make that valuation generalizable* : in order, that is, to demonstrate Miriam's conviction that the mutuality of consciousness she yearns for is a feminine need and a feminine capability, not just a demand specific to herself. That is why the prose very carefully insists to the reader that Amabel's attitude towards Miriam is exactly like Miriam's attitude towards Amabel, even though Richardson's technique proscribes any direct statements from sources of consciousness outside Miriam's.

What is also crucial about Miriam's need for romantic attachments to members of her own sex is that although sexuality should not be expressed, it must not be denied. Although Miriam does not understand Fräulein Pfaff's jealousy as a symptom of the frustration of her spinster's life, she is nevertheless unable to tolerate it and must reject the demands that such a jealousy seeks to place upon her. Similarly, Selina Holland, another professional woman and also a spinster, incurs Miriam's rejection with an expression of frustration which shows her deeper jealousy. Miss Holland would have liked a romantic attachment to Miriam, but the atmosphere is soured by Miriam's affection for her men friends. The relationship finally breaks down under the pressure of Miss Holland's jealousy when Miriam fails to fulfil Miss Holland's expectation :

> 'Had it been made to a *man*, your promise would at once have been carried out.'
>
> Miriam forgot her anger in amazement at the spectacle of a châtelaine with a volcanic temper and a spiteful tongue- - - -
>
> For herself, the little idyll in the rooms was at an end- - - -
>
> She and Miss Holland were separated now, utterly.[76]

Eleanor Dear, yet another ageing spinster, terrifies Miriam with demands and dependence; and Miriam reluctantly agrees that, for Eleanor, this emotional tyranny will only be dissipated in marriage.

Miriam herself, when contemplating an affair with Hypo Wilson, concludes that there is something odd and unacceptable about celibacy:

> And celibates, outside religion, though acceptable when thought of as alone, are always, socially, a little absurd. Then I must be absurd. Growing absurd. To others, I am already absurd- - - - Marriage, or sooner or later absurdity. Free-love is better than absurdity. . . .[77]

Amabel, unlike these others, does not threaten Miriam with the denial of sexuality, especially since she confides openly about her lovers.

It is central both to Richardson's technique and to her world-view that the individual is a true microcosm of society and that therefore the experience of the individual is representative of the state of the group. This view underlines her assessments of social theory:

> Murry, like Aldous Huxley, is old enough to have grown up under the shadow of a misapplied Darwinism & still, to some extent, shares the pathetic Wellsian illusion of the possibility of a simultaneously unanimous humanity. But Murry's 'socialism' is less naïve, & far less unimaginative than that of Wells. He realises, as did Buckle nearly a century ago, & later Kirkup ('Social Efficiency') that while each individual starts at scratch, with all the potentialities of his remotest forbears, & while humanity does not per se, progress, yet the man born today enters (particularly, in certain respects, in England, the first determined antagonist of absolutisms) a society which, in the matter of conscience is a deposit of centuries & will be either ahead of, or behind, himself. But he goes, I feel, astray in concluding thence that the corporation known as society is now, & increasingly to become, the unit of being rather than the single individual - - - - his anticipation of Utopia *once war is abolished*, is as pathetically naïve and unimaginative as that of Wells & Co.[78]

The model of society which Richardson implicitly suggests is one in which the stance of the individual is matched by the stance of another individual equal in level of insight and intuition to the self. Therefore, prescriptive generalizations which do not take account of such differential degrees of attainment are doomed to be unworkable and are, she suggests, naïve. In an unequal match there is not only a division between the two individuals, but there also occurs an inner division in the consciousness of the individual. In the love scene with

Wilson, for example, the reader is aware not only of Miriam's alienation from Wilson, but also of her inner alienation between body and mind. With Amabel, the contrast is marked; not only is Miriam's inner consciousness integrated, but she appears to Amabel as she appears to herself. Their empathy is enhanced by its deliberate exclusiveness of everyone else :

> Amabel downstairs at dinner, ignoring everyone but me, both of us using the social occasion to heighten our sense of being together, making it impossible for any one to break into the circle where we sit surrounded and alone. So strongly enclosed that not one of those with whom at other times she talked and flirted could mistake the centre of her interest. Bad manners. But how resist the enchantment? Why should all these people resent our silence in our magic enclosure? [79]

Unlike Miriam, Amabel is capable of flirting and coquetry, which serves to increase Miriam's pride that Amabel ignores everyone but herself. The weak comment 'bad manners' is the feeblest rebuke of their self-conscious exclusiveness, since Miriam clearly feels that the enchantment is its own justification. The seeming ingenuousness of Miriam's asking why the others should resent their mutual absorption, overlays Miriam's sense of outrage; how can these other people dare to criticize an experience whose power approaches magic? At this point the tone is becoming strident, betraying Miriam's unwilling awareness that social demands also have their reality and cannot be used to strengthen the perimeters of the 'magic enclosure' without the discomfiture following upon self-indulgence. The empathy between Miriam and Amabel may be intact, but the social context of their relationship is yet to be understood.

If the social meaning of their relationship is unclear, its existential meaning is not. It is, significantly, in the conversation with Wilson immediately following their first sexual encounter that Miriam admits the priority of her love for Amabel. She tells Wilson that she is 'perpetually preoccupied' with Amabel, who is 'treasure' beyond his or anyone's 'power of diagnosis'.[80] This claim provokes Wilson's interest; he wants to know more. Miriam sketches Amabel's background and antecedents, although she judges her very desire to convey to Wilson the quality of the relationship, to be 'a kind of treachery' to Amabel.[81] Yet she must make the attempt because of Amabel's overwhelming importance to her :

> There was in the whole of her previous experience, that with all its restrictions of poverty and circumstance had seemed to him so rich and varied and in many respects so enviable, nothing that could compare with what Amabel had brought. Nothing could be better. No sharing, not even the shared being of a man and a woman, which she sometimes envied and sometimes deplored, could be deeper or more wonderful than this being together, alternating between awareness of the beloved person and delight in every aspect, every word and movement, and a solitude distinguishable from the deepest, coolest, most renewing moments of lonely solitude only in the enhancement it reaped by being shared.[82]

Miriam's direct juxtaposition of the erotic relationship between a man and a woman with the 'being together' of herself and Amabel leaves her in no doubt about which has pre-eminence for her. The distinguishing difference is, of course, the direct sexual expression central to the one and irrelevant to the other. Part of the foundation for this judgement is her personal ambivalence towards the sexual act, which she 'sometimes envied and sometimes deplored'. Also lying behind her judgement is her feminist repudiation of man's unequal regard for himself, on the one hand, and for women, on the other.[83] What Miriam is grappling with here is the problem of understanding what love is like when its origins proceed from the feminine context and the extent to which it can illuminate the feminine principle. Miriam's love for Amabel is not directly nor overtly sexual; that distinguishes it from the love between men and women. Nor, however, is it of secondary importance : it is, surprisingly, greater in importance. Miriam does not deny the power of sex, nor is she frigid, nor is she unsought by men, nor does she reject her own desire to find a mate. Why, then, is the relationship with Amabel so paramount? Two possibilities occur : first, that the love between Miriam and Amabel fulfils a specifically feminine need which neither enhances nor diminishes the need for an erotic relationship with a man, but which stands outside it, and, secondly, that the quality of relationship Miriam describes occurs only between members of the same sex, so that its masculine equivalent would by analogy fulfil a specifically masculine need. When women love one another, according to the psychiatrist Charlotte Wolff, 'it is not homosexuality but homoemotionality which is the centre and very essence' [84] of their love. It is this constant state of emotional consummation which Miriam feels Wilson may not understand, whether because he is a man, or because he is the kind of person he is, she is not sure. The usual assumption about such a relationship, Miriam knows as well as the reader does, is that its lack of sexuality makes it merely sentimental and therefore insignificant. There are men, however, who agree with Richardson about the different quality of same-sex love, who agree with Miriam in the estimation of its significance and who assert, as she implies, that sexuality in this context is not denied but is felt to be irrelevant. C. S. Lewis, for instance, in his theory of friendship, agrees with Richardson that shared solitude is its distinguishing characteristic:

> Lovers seek for privacy. Friends find this solitude about them, this barrier between them and the herd, whether they want it or not.[85]

Friendship, he argues, is the least natural of the types of love, having no foundation in biological necessity; its provenance is a relation at the 'highest level of individuality'.[86] He argues, further, that its restriction to members of the same sex is a direct result of differential sex-role typing:

> In one respect our society is unfortunate. A world where men and women never have common work or a common education can probably get along comfortably enough. In it men turn to each other, and only to each other, for Friendship, and they enjoy it very much. I hope the women enjoy their feminine friends equally.[87]

Miriam's capacity to love Amabel is an extremely crucial stage in the liberation of her consciousness and provides her, as nothing else has done, with an emotional context within which, because she feels fully known and accepted, she can acquire the confidence to discriminate between her confusing ambivalence towards men and marriage. Her love for Amabel and her relationships with men are not alternatives for her; she needs the one in order to resolve the other.

Within a short time, Miriam's identification with Amabel reaches such a pitch that it elicits Miriam's primary memory, her first instant of consciousness, which thus equates Amabel with the origin of perception and sensation:

> - - - I said without thinking: 'This is the birthday of the world,' and, while she flew to fling herself down at my knees, I was back in the moment of seeing for the first time those flowerbeds and banks of flowers blazing in the morning sunlight, that smelt of the flowers and was one with them and me and the big bees crossing the path, low, on a

level with my face. And I told her of it, and that it must have been somewhere near my third birthday, and her falling tears of joy and sympathy promised that never again should there be in my blood an unconquerable fever.[88]

In Richardson's value-system, these moments of special insight and integration always retained the position of highest priority. In 1948, the year of her husband's death, she wrote to John Cowper Powys :

'Tout passe, tout lasse, tout casse' *No*, Mr neatly logical Frenchman, & the wistfuller poets of all nations. Youthful confusion of brevity with disappearance. For these moments *announce,* even as they pass, their immortality. Pass into consciousness, never into nothingness. Are dividends paid out from invested capital, on which we may live when everything *seems* taken away.[89]

That Miriam tells Amabel her 'bee memory' is proof therefore, of the empathy she feels; but it is also a reinforcing of the validity of her experience which nothing can ever modify against her volition. Amabel's highly charged response, 'tears of joy and empathy', guarantees for Miriam what she has always suspected : that the psychological dangers of intense feeling retreat when the isolation of the individual consciousness is breached, although the intensity itself is not diminished. Miriam has, in this strange way, validated her unwillingness to compromise her sense of herself, by eliciting Amabel's capacity to recognize and accept her in her own terms.

This is the high point of the relationship; afterwards it admits flaws. Miriam begins to find the emotional drain exhausting : 'Separation from Amabel used to bring both regret and relief. Relief from the incessant applause-demanding drama, regret for failure to emerge unwearied.' [90]

By contrast, Miriam's friendship with Jean is mellower, more relaxed, fulfilling. This relationship is the motivation for *March Moonlight,* the final novel in the *Pilgrimage* sequence, written in fragments over a number of years, subsequent to the 1938 Dent Collected Edition of *Pilgrimage*, and only published posthumously. In the first section of *March Moonlight*, Miriam is staying with her sister Sally, convalescing after influenza. The novel opens with Miriam reading a letter from Jean, who calls her 'Dick'. It becomes clear that Miriam had arranged for Jean and Miss Hancock (the daughter of her former employer, Mr Hancock, the Harley Street dentist) to share a holiday in

Oberland, the place most intensively associated with renewal for Miriam, and the subject of the novel which bears its name. Intimations of cycle and renewal are therefore implicit in both time and space dimensions of *March Moonlight.* Technically, the reading of the letter, as with all letters, takes in two periods of time : the one in which it was written and the one in which it is read. For Miriam there is a third : the time previous in which Jean and herself were together, reminiscences provoked by reading the letter :

> The moment we found ourselves together, time stood still - - - our intermittent silences, rather than tension-creating searches for fresh material were fragments of a shared eternity - - -[91]

Jean's ability to accept what comes without resentment and her lack of possessiveness enhance Miriam's final awakening. The reminiscences of Miriam's relationship with Jean frame *March Moonlight.* Through Jean, Miriam learns that self-knowledge and self-acceptance need not, indeed cannot, be purchased in isolation. Jean allows her the freedom of her individuality without withdrawing from her and without needing to keep their companionship exclusive, as it is Miriam's instinct to do :

> Renewed every morning, it reached perfection during our afternoons in solitary possession of the balcony. Silent, or endlessly talking. One of the prices of this perfection she taught me: to accept incursions without invasion or resentment. ('Hadst thou stayed, I must have fled.') Jean knows that *nothing* can be clutched or held. Were we ever more fully together than during that evening when we were impelled, after the snowstorm, to escape and creep out into the moonlight? At the very door we were caught by Miss Lonsdale emerging from her hall-bedroom. I could have slain her as she stood, schoolgirlishly hopping while she announced her intention of joining us. And, as we wandered about, for her lyrical outcries, Jean, responding, made her happy.[92]

Jean, in a letter to Miriam, admits the power of their friendship – 'I am silent before the wonder of it' [93] – but Miriam knows that such things cannot be said face to face, only written or lived.[94] This constraint is not only relational : it is also symbolic. The direct expression of their bond would entail a commitment which must become exclusive – Miriam knows enough about the power of language to realize that. And, too, she has experienced the erosion of her relationship with Amabel precisely because in that relationship no constraints were placed upon their confrontations, so that Miriam eventually succumbed to the strain of searching 'for fresh material'. What is unsaid can remain indefinitely potent; here, finally, the reader is shown Miriam demonstrating in experience the ambivalence towards language which has characterized her search for fulfilment from the beginning. Richardson's reverence for silence is as determined in *March Moonlight* as it was in *Pointed Roofs*, betraying her temperamental affinity to the mystic, rather than to the novelist. And yet, even here, we can detect that her retreat from the commitment entailed by language is, in part, her still unsure searching for the authentic nature of the feminine. She feels that the secrets of understanding are to be discovered in relationship rather than in interaction between herself and the world, the particular and the general. The delineation of identity needs reinforcement from another person :

> Jean. Jean. Jean. My clue to the nature of reality. To know that you exist, is enough- - - -
>
> With Jean, for me, friendship reaches its centre. All future friendships will group themselves round that occupied place, drawing thence their sustenance.[95]

Jean internalized, introjected, has become the arbiter of Miriam's shifting perceptions and senses of herself. The two women do not meet in *March Moonlight*; the rest of this short novel recapitulates other important characters, Amabel and Shatov in particular, who are by now married and have a child. *March Moonlight* also introduces the young painter, Mr Noble, whose original, Alan Odle, Richardson married in 1917 : thus she brings the chronological end of the novel to the point where, in reality, she had begun to write it.

The central claim Jean has on Miriam's consciousness is a far cry from Miriam's earlier exasperation with women : her contempt for the socially idle, her disdain for the husband-hunters, her guilt for the lot of women like her mother and Eleanor Dear, who lose their grip on life in their struggle to hold their own in a man's world, her discomfort with militant women who become absurd, in her eyes, by aping men. Where, amongst all the women she knew, did she fit? How was the feminine principle to be located and examined? By loving Ulrica, Amabel and Jean, the roots of femininity have been uncovered and her feminist impulse has been sustained. In relationships with other women, the male world could be excluded and a space found in which women's feelings, independent of men's image of them, could be generated and developed. Miriam's love for Jean is therefore one of the crucial resolutions of her quest, since it affirms her female identity.

NOTES AND REFERENCES

1 *Pointed Roofs*, p. 167.
2 *Oberland*, pp. 122-3.
3 *Pointed Roofs*, pp. 177-8.
4 Ibid., p. 179.
5 Ibid., p. 58.
6 Ibid., p. 74.
7 Ibid., p. 103.
8 *Backwater*, p. 282.
9 Ibid., p. 283.
10 Ibid., p. 284.
11 Ouida was the pseudonym of Marie Louise de la Ramée (1839-1908), a self-educated, single woman who became a 'society' novelist. She achieved notoriety with her representation of rebellion against moral conventions. *Moths*, her most famous book, was published in 1880.
12 Rosa Nouchette Carey (1840-1909) was also self-educated and unmarried. She was a friend of Mrs Henry Wood. She prided herself on having taken only one character from life.
13 *Backwater*, p. 284.
14 Ibid., pp. 283-4.
15 Ibid., p. 284.
16 Loc. cit.
17 Ibid., p. 285.
18 Ibid., p. 286.
19 *Honeycomb*, pp. 435-6.
20 Ibid., p. 436.
21 *The Tunnel*, p. 148. In 1943 Richardson wrote to her friend Peggy Kirkaldy: 'But not only did we play tennis and rounders in those perilous garments, we also rowed and sculled and punted in them, to say nothing of skating and later, cycling. And cycling it was that brought that first breath of release by substituting, for one of our petticoats, *knickers*, but only of course, for the brazen few.' DR to Peggy Kirkaldy, 9 June, 1943.

22 *The Tunnel*, pp. 174-5. Mr Hancock, drawn from Richardson's employer, Mr Babcock, was, nevertheless, a genuine friend. 'While working for Dr Harry Babcock she became quite ill & seemed threatened with a nervous breakdown. Dr Babcock not only gave her a long vacation with pay, but sent her to a resort high up in the Swiss Alps. Mrs Babcock even went so far as to lend her a fur coat. Lying out in the cold sunshiny air she soon recovered her health. I am uncertain how long she stayed in Switzerland, but know it was at least one month. She often spoke to me about their great kindness which she feels she can never repay.' Jessie Hale to Rose Odle, 27 August, 1956. This convalescence provided the material for *Oberland*.

23 *Interim*, p. 394.

24 *Honeycomb*, p. 373.

25 Ibid., p. 410.

26 Ibid., p. 454.

27 Ibid., p. 455.

28 Loc. cit.

29 Ibid., p. 464.

30 Ibid., p. 466.

31 Ibid., p. 472.

32 DR to Peggy Kirkaldy, 24 March, 1937.

33 *Honeycomb*, p. 485.

34 *The Tunnel*, p. 90.

35 Ibid., pp. 91-2.

36 Ibid., p. 281.

37 *Revolving Lights*, pp. 284-5.

38 *Dawn's Left Hand*, p. 151.

39 *Backwater*, p. 218.

40 Ibid., p. 219.

41 Ibid., p. 223.

42 Ibid., p. 225.

43 Loc. cit.

44 Ibid., p. 314.

45 Ibid., p. 328. This encounter is echoed in *Oberland*, pp. 70-5, where Guerini joins Miriam on the Oberland slopes to toboggan. Like Parrow, he encourages her to dare more.

46 *The Trap*, p. 491.

47 Ibid., p. 479.

48 Ibid., p. 489.

49 Ibid., p. 495.

50 DR to Peggy Kirkaldy, 14 October, 1935.

51 DR to John Cowper Powys, 13 March, 1948.

52 'Socialism and The Odd Man', op. cit., p. 148.
53 'Comments', op. cit., XXXVI, 6, 1 June, 1916, p. 310.
54 *Clear Horizon*, p. 331.
55 'Comments', op. cit., XXXVI, 6, 1 June, 1916, p. 311.
56 Ibid., XXXVI, 10, 2 October, 1916, pp. 541-2.
57 Ibid., XXXVII, 8, 1 August, 1917, p. 376.
58 Ibid., XXXVII, 10, 1 October, 1917, pp. 485-6.
59 *Backwater*, pp. 333-5.
60 *Honeycomb*, pp. 358-9.
61 *The Tunnel*, p. 40.
62 Ibid., p. 194.
63 DR to Peggy Kirkaldy, 4 April, 1939.
64 *Pointed Roofs*, p. 34.
65 Ibid., pp. 74-5.
66 Ibid., p. 99.
67 Ibid., p. 97.
68 Loc. cit.
69 Ibid., p. 148.
70 Ibid., p. 183.
71 *Dawn's Left Hand*, p. 188.
72 Ibid., p. 190.
73 Ibid., p. 196.
74 Ibid., p. 217.
75 See *Backwater*, pp. 316-7.
76 *The Trap*, pp. 480-1.
77 Ibid., p. 495.
78 DR to DK, 19 July, 1948.
79 *Clear Horizon*, p. 286.
80 *Dawn's Left Hand*, p. 240.
81 Loc. cit.
82 Ibid., p. 242.
83 This leads her, in turn, to reject what she thinks to be men's appraisal of women: 'I am not "literary" Henry. Never was. Never shall be. The books that for you, perhaps for most men, come first, are for me secondary. Partly perhaps because they are the work of men, have the limitations, as well as the qualities of the masculine outlook. Men are practitioners, dealing with things (including "ideas") rather than with people . . . knowing almost nothing of women save in relation to themselves.' DR to Henry Savage, 11 March, 1950.
84 Charlotte Wolff, *Love Between Women*, Duckworth, 1971, p. 70.
85 C. S. Lewis, *The Four Loves*, Geoffrey Bles, 1960, p. 78.
86 Ibid., p. 72.

87 Ibid., p. 243.
88 *Dawn's Left Hand*, p. 243.
89 DR to John Cowper Powys, 28 June, 1948.
90 *March Moonlight*, p. 566.
91 Ibid., p. 567.
92 Ibid., p. 575.
93 Ibid., p. 577.
94 Ibid., p. 579.
95 Ibid., pp. 612-3.

4 · *Resolution*

I

The longest and, in many respects, the most significant relationship in Richardson's life was her friendship with Veronica Leslie-Jones, called 'Vera' and 'Babinka' in correspondence, 'Amabel' in the later volumes of *Pilgrimage*.[1] The terms of the life-relationship are carefully presented in Richardson's fictional analogue, so that the tensions between the two women mirror the inner conflict between art and femininity which Richardson suffered and which she has Miriam enact. It is therefore fascinating and, for our purposes, essential, to chart Richardson's representation of this friendship as a meaningful basis for action and, at the same time, to consider the biographical evidence underlining it which is at present available. In this way, Richardson's resolution of the conflict between art and femininity can be illuminated.

In *Dawn's Left Hand* [2] the reader is given Miriam's first encounter with Amabel:

> On her way to the door, Miriam was pulled up by the voice of a woman who had turned from a small group standing close at hand, hatless: residents. The voice had an eager, anxious, apologetic sound and gave her exit the air of royalty in procession, graciously halted to accept a petition.
>
> Turning - - - she saw only a dim outline, a pale oval of face saluting her, obliquely down-tilted above a gown glowing silky rose-red through the dusk in which the forms of the other women showed no colour. Here was 'charm', some strange grace and charm that was defying the war-

ning voice within. The figure, assuming as she confronted it a fresh attitude of graceful pleading, had now a level face whose eyes were smiling recognition, patiently-reproachfully, a much-tried adorer, who yet was making allowances, for too long an instant being forced to prompt and wait for an answering recognition. Inwardly protesting her extreme unrelatedness to this person moving so elegantly from pose to pose, yet attracted by the unaccountable glow, as if the rose-red gown shone for her in the gloom by its own light, and held by a curious intensity of being in the alien figure, Miriam waited unresponsive- - - -

Intent on escape, vaguely undertaking to be at the club again quite soon, Miriam received a gracefully-sweeping movement of thanks and withdrawal during which the girl's eyes still held her own, but with the recognizing look withdrawn, as if she were now covering a secret compact with a witness-disarming formality. With the corner of her eye, as she turned away to the open door, Miriam saw her, in the full light now switched on from the hall, move back to the styleless English group from which she had emerged, arms down, white hands a little extended as if to balance the slight swaying movement propelling her, and which the invisible feet followed rather than led.[3]

Several things are remarkable about this encounter. First it is the woman's voice, 'eager, anxious, apologetic', which affects Miriam, indeed so strongly that she is 'pulled up' by it. Here the use of the passive accentuates the sense of external psychological force which draws Miriam in spite of her own inner 'warning voice'. The scene takes place at the end of a social evening in the women's club of which Miriam is a non-resident member and of which this strange woman is clearly a resident, standing, as she does, in a 'hatless' group. As Miriam leaves, the woman turns and the quality of her voice gives Miriam the sense that she is being treated as if she were a royal person. Miriam turns in response and her first visual impression is of a 'pale oval of face', which recalls for the reader that earlier pale, oval face to which Miriam was so intensely attracted during her time at Fräulein Pfaff's school. In addition to the face, Miriam notices the rose-red gown, against which the other women appear colourless. The combination of the voice, the face and gown embodies for Miriam 'some strange grace and charm', an 'unaccountable glow', a 'curious intensity', which attracts Miriam in spite of herself. The words 'strange', 'unaccountable', 'curious' and 'alien', with their connotations of mystery, emphasize the sense that something external to Miriam's consciousness and something stronger than her own knowledge of herself, characterized by her 'warning voice', is drawing her. Miriam's rationality protests her 'extreme unrelatedness to this person', but the psychological impact is so strong that rationality recedes and it seems to Miriam that the woman's gown is shining specially for her and of itself. When Miriam meets her eyes, she finds a 'recognition' which is waiting for an 'answering recognition'.

The woman's suppliant attitude is defined by a 'down-tilted' face, a 'down-bent' head and arms held 'close to her silken form'. She is 'very young, but mannered and mature', Miriam decides. Even though they meet and speak, the impressions given by this woman remain mysterious, somehow singular. In spite of her eyes' withdrawal of the 'recognizing look', she does not merge back into the 'styleless English group' but seems to float : her white hands seem to balance the 'slight swaying movement' which propels her. She does not walk; her feet are 'invisible' and follow rather than lead her movement.

Their next encounter is similarly mysterious and again almost wordless.[4] Miriam, alone at the club at midday, begins to play the piano. Here, once more, Richardson evokes the atmosphere of *Pointed Roofs*, in which so much of Miriam's emerging conciousness is channeled through the experiences of her own piano-playing and listening to that of her students. In this case, standing in front of the piano, she becomes aware of her essential conflict between the inner 'strange centre of being' which refuses to 'accept evidence', to accommodate reality, and the 'external being' which embodies 'sanity'. It is also a conflict between consciousness and unconsciousness, between knowing and reflecting :

> Yet it was with that consciously reflecting being that she felt the unchanging presence that now joined her in the world it had restored. Everything in the room had a quiet reality, and glancing through the windows she saw how the budding trees thrilled in the sunlight.[5]

The 'yet' focuses the dichotomy of Miriam's tension : it is the unconscious which experiences reality but the consciousness which records it. The mirroring process, which is to become so characteristic of the relationship between Miriam and Amabel, begins almost immediately. Miriam hears the door click as someone comes into the room and her unconsciousness identifies so closely with the newcomer that it seems to Miriam that she herself is opening the door and coming into the room. This recalls for the reader the crucial importance of the 'bee memory', itself initiated in unconsciousness, which Miriam has always expected she must be able to share in order to relate intimately to another person, and share, not through communication, but through identification and recognition, as if she and the other person inhabit the same consciousness. Here, then, as she seems to be the other person entering the room, this process of identification is established. That the person must enter *her* room, her inner space, is itself symbolic and that Miriam is music making, not word making, further symbolizes the unconscious territory upon which the ensuing relationship is built. The newcomer, who is also herself, enters 'in triumph'. Miriam is consciously aware of her desire to sustain this 'secret world'.

The identity of the newcomer is certain :

> It was only because it could be no one else that she recognized the girl crouched on the floor at her side – looking as if she had blossomed from the air – as yesterday's figure in the rose-red gown, again producing the effect of being aware of the impression she had made, and contemplating it in the person of the one upon whom it was being directed and also, to-day, offering it as something to be judged, like a 'work of art,' detachedly, upon its merits.[6]

The suppliant attitude is further accentuated : now the 'woman' has become a 'girl', and the 'down-bent' face has become a 'figure' who is 'crouched' by Miriam's side. The sense of mystery is also sustained; the girl seems to have 'blossomed from the air' rather than to have walked in. And the merging of the two personalities is further established; the girl is aware of the impression she has made, while at the same time she seems to observe this impression from Miriam's own centre of being, just as Miriam had seemed to enter the room in the person of the newcomer. This identification is so clear and so abstracted that it seems to have the static quality of art, rather than the fluctuating quality of life, and it is indeed offered to Miriam 'like a "work of art" ' to be objectively assessed.

This time the figure is clothed in turquoise blue, not red, which is deeply satisfying to Miriam. The girl twines her beads in her fingers. Her loveliness is 'unknown', again mysterious, and already 'radiates affection'. The stasis of their encounter is enhanced by its wordlessness; each seems aware that words would interfere with their 'work of art'. The girl moves to a settee and Miriam follows :

> 'I'm not sure I should have recognized you,' said Miriam. At the sound of her own familiar voice a gulf seemed leapt. But of the one who spoke, come from afar to meet this strange girl, she knew nothing. Serenely she took the other corner of the settee, feeling as she sat down that she had embarked in sunlight upon an unknown quest.[7]

Here the mirroring and merging of the two personalities is again made explicit. It is Miriam who speaks first, but of 'the one who spoke', herself, she 'knew nothing', because it is her unconscious self, seeming to come 'from afar', which is propelled to meet this 'strange' girl.

At this point the girl kneels, looking towards the light. This is the first time Richardson has introduced 'full light', having carefully set the previous images against dim or oblique light. Here the full light correlates with a shift in psychological distance: 'Something had gone. There was thought behind the lovely silent mask, and speech on the way.' [8] The emergence of 'thought', of consciousness, allows fuller focus because it enlightens but it means also that speech is inevitable. Here Richardson's ambivalence towards language, which has been so symptomatic of the disjunction Miriam experiences between the essential reality of her own consciousness and the distorted reality of her social interaction, is carefully isolated. Nevertheless, the girl's initial use of language is startling, unconventional. She responds to Miriam's looking at her face:

> 'It's like a peach. Say it, say it.'[9]

Miriam agrees, admiring the girl's 'open appreciation of her own beauty', a beauty which is centred in the girl's eyes. Here the mirroring phenomenon is plainly stated for the first time; as Miriam looks into the girl's eyes, she finds herself gazing 'as into a mirror'. This circle of communication between the two women, and between the conscious and the unconscious, is broken by the girl's mention of a man, Basil. To Miriam it seems that 'golden light' had illuminated their communication; now they become 'distinct', that is, separated but sharply focused, in a 'dark and bitter and cold' light. Miriam resents the 'moving away from their two selves', because the girl's life with Basil, if it is important to her, will rob this 'strange meeting' of its 'chief value'. The girl notices Miriam's jealousy and asks whether it makes a difference. Miriam, lying, says not, but her attraction to the girl is so strong that her lie becomes a truth. Miriam's involvement with the girl grows so intense that the external demands of her life become indistinct:

> Towards tea-time, it was only with an effort that she could remember whither she was bound. Her current life had grown remote and unreal.[10]

The girl has returned to her place on the floor and has resumed the adoring attitude which characterized their first contact. Miriam is again aware of the mirror the girl holds up to her; she sees herself 'reflected in the perceptions of this girl' and self-knowledge compels her to admit that she does indeed possess that quality which the girl so much admires in her, but the important key for the reader is that the quality has been till now 'unconscious'. What the girl does is to reveal Miriam's inner, unconscious being to herself. This knowledge arouses in Miriam a 'patient sadness', because if the 'emerging quality' is really the 'very root of her being', then she must accept the role which ensues from it, the role 'allotted to her by the kneeling girl'. This is a crucial stage in Miriam's pilgrimage and several things are significant about it.

First, and perhaps foremost, is the realization for the reader that the preceding psychological events in Miriam's life have borne for Miriam the burden of self-definition, which has, in turn, borne the burden of attempts to interpret external form within the framework of this self-defining self-consciousness. Both the extreme individualism and the intellectualization of this position have together resulted in an alienation from the normal feminine role which, in Miriam's world, has serious consequences. She has learnt how to protect her inner self by refusing to collude with what she perceives to be society's demands upon her, but at the high cost of being unable to sustain a relationship with another human being. Her isolation is comfortable enough and even highly valued by her, but it is also sterile. When Miriam perceives the girl's perceptions of her inner self, her isolation is breached, so opening her to the possibilities of affirmation and confirmation or what is sometimes called reality-testing.[11]

The second important change for Miriam follows from the first. When self-discovery means the denial of the existing role-type, as it has for Miriam, then the possibilities for action in the external world are severely restricted. What the girl enables Miriam to discover is a role, a way of acting upon reality and within reality, in addition to observing it. Miriam has pursued, singlemindedly, the answers to philosophical questions: how to think and how to feel. The answer to the question of how to live has eluded her because it necessitates an answer to the question of how to act. She has been unable to act as a conventional woman because such action has conflicted with her discoveries of how to think and how to feel. This new encounter, so consistently described as 'strange' and 'curious', so carefully perceived within the context of 'dim light' and 'full light', has provided her with new possibilities, first of relationship, because her inner self has been 'recognized' and, secondly, of action, because a different role is offered to her.

Miriam's reactions to this knowledge are equally significant. Her 'sadness' is the awareness of commitment to this new truth about herself. And the role she perceives is one of wisdom and authority, a role, that is, with the characterizing marks of the artist. In these terms it is predictable, almost to the point of logical necessity:

> - - - it seemed almost as if this girl had come at just this moment to warn her, to give her the courage of herself as she was, isolated and virginal.[12]

The two definitive marks, 'isolated' and 'virginal', Miriam gives to her 'unconscious quality' are immensely significant, since they enhance the position of the artist, whose moral veracity is authenticated by his ability to be less corrupted than others by the demands of external reality, while at the same time obstructing the possibilities of success within a human relationship, where to be isolated and virginal is to be inexperienced and non-participatory. Here, then, is a hint of the new dilemma that Miriam, having realized her role, must face: the conflict of demands between relationship and artistic vocation. Miriam's awareness of the beginning of this conflict is psychological rather than consciously rational:

> Yet, as she stood at last taking leave of her in the centre of the twilit room, facing again her strange beauty gleaming in the space it illuminated, she was glad to be escaping back into the company of people who moved mostly along the surface levels and left her to herself.[13]

The dichotomy can indeed evoke a 'patient sadness', since Miriam's realization of a role which leaves her 'to herself', that is, an artistic role, is a realization, as Richardson's record of Miriam's consciousness shows, which could only be reached from within the context of relationship, and that in turn means that Miriam has made a commitment and has given a recognition of like kind to the girl sitting at her feet, but which she, unlike the girl, will not be able to fulfil.

In life, the girl, Veronica, and Richardson, experienced exactly this dilemma throughout the long duration of their friendship. The perceptions which Richardson fictionalized as psychological shifts of awareness were in reality consciously acted out. It is interesting, therefore , to compare the perceived reality demonstrated in *Pilgrimage* with the actual dynamic of the life relationship. Veronica habitually reproached Richardson with what seemed to her Richardson's failure to fulfil her part of the demands of their relationship. Richardson's response was, inevitably, the response of an artist. It is worth quoting one such response in full :

Dear Vera,

You sound reproachful. Imagine. All my time & strength *needed* – it used to be *given* – for my own special work. Almost *none* of it available for that work. Imagine the wear & tear of that one devastating *fact.* Again, all my time & strength *needed* for the mere business of making enough to live on, & making it, because I *can't take a regular journalistic job,* on heart-straining uncertainties, free-lancing, anything I can get & *all* of it against the grain.

Imagine the drain of something, (mutual & moral drain – for domesticity is a *state of mind* –) all the detail of it & the perpetual to & fro, between homes & the business of tenants, a whole practical life which is a *third* whole-time job. Has it ever been asked of an artist before? I doubt it. I am not complaining. But my strength is not what it was & now that London has become an increasing chorus of *claims* I begin to feel I must either cut out London or cut out visiting! It could so easily be a fourth whole-time job!

Anyway there *are* the four. With the complication that everybody, nearly enough, is apt to be reproachful. It staggers me. The absence in almost everybody of the imaginative faculty. I have friends who 'can't imagine' how I get through & still ceaselessly *pull.* You are not one of those, & you *have* imagination. So you will understand that a visit, even to one's best friends, can be a tax beyond one's strength. Especially in this heat & with the transit to London, for the very poor, what it now is. I'll hope to come on Saturday & bring Alan, but I may find I simply can't. I would like to see *you.* And the entertainment of the young people & their music is of course charming. In its particular way. Though pro-

bably I'd rather hear their talk. If the intense heat abates I'll perhaps feel more equal. At all events it seems the last *straw*. If we are able to come, we'll get along as soon as possible after tea. Getting to you about six. If we can't, I'll telephone & you'll understand.
With love
Dorothy[14]

What Richardson clearly could not allow was that commitment might permit claims to be made upon her. What is also clear in this instance is that as well as resenting the claims of relationship, she resents all claims made by reality : earning, domesticity, the business of living – everything which takes her time and strength away from her 'special work'. Nevertheless, Richardson needed relationship in order to catalyse her creativity.

At the time of Miriam's first meeting with Amabel, she is still living with Selina Holland in Woburn Place. A few days after their second encounter, Miriam returns home feeling grateful for the independence and freedom she can enjoy in her rooms. She catches sight of herself in her mirror :

> She became aware of her framed mirror on the wall behind her, reflecting, in its narrow length, her form seated in the shadowy candle-light she was so soon to leave for the cheerful blaze of gas, or the steady companionship of the reading-lamp that at Flaxmans' she had hardly used at all, and half turned to look into it and exchange over her shoulder a smile of congratulation with her reflected image.[15]

Here Richardson brilliantly manipulates the image of the mirror which, as an abstract correlative, has already become imbued with symbolic weight, as a reflector of reality, during the 'strange' encounter between Miriam and the girl. In her room, alone, Miriam turns for recognition to her own reflected image. She is again in 'dim' light – the light of a candle. And her room is her own space. She wishes to congratulate herself on her freedom. But the image given back to her is obscured :

> The glass was not clear. Across her face, that should have shown in the reflected candle-light, was some kind of cloudy blur. Holding up the candle she found lettering, large and twirly, thickly outlined as if made with chalk or moist putty, moving with a downward slope across the centre of the strip of glass. Mystified – for who in the wide world

> could have had access to her room, or achieving it, should be moved to deface her mirror in a manner suggesting it was for sale? – and disturbed by the unaccountable presence that had been silently witnessing, unpardonably mocking, it seemed to her as she pushed away the chair and stood aside to let the candle-light fall upon the strange apparition, her private rejoicings.
>
> '*I love you,*' it said.[16]

What is especially striking about this incident is the merging of unconsciousness and consciousness and of inner and external realities, achieved through Richardson's manipulation of the mirror-image. The girl's use of Miriam's 'real' mirror to convey her message transcends the barrier between inner reality – itself divided between consciousness and unconsciousness – and external reality, since the girl had herself been perceived by Miriam's unconsciousness to be a mirror. When Miriam looks for reassurance towards the reflected image of herself mirrored by an external object, she finds evidence of her other 'mirror', the girl, superimposed upon it. Further, since it is her own mirror, identified with herself, the writing on it seems from a distance to suggest that it is for sale, somehow available. The emotional message is clearly the opposite; Miriam feels she is definitely not for sale. Yet she cannot reject the meaning of the intrusion in such a simple way. The girl and the 'real' mirror both belong to the world of external reality and can both show Miriam to herself. On the other hand, Miriam's recognition of her own image belongs to the world of inner perceptions. Unconsciously, the girl has chosen as her vehicle of communication the very symbol which, for Miriam, focuses the possibility that reality is a continuum, that the barriers between consciousness and unconsciousness and between perception and actuality, can be breached. Miriam's pilgrimage towards integration can now progress, to the extent that relationship can represent the accommodation of the external world to the individual consciousness without the loss of the integrity of that consciousness. It is significant in this respect that the girl's message is written across the face of the reflected image, so that the perceiving eyes are forced to see the evidence of relationship directly before their vision. The message, that is, is both obscuring – of isolation – and revealing – of relationship. Finally, the *nature* of the message is of central significance : '"*I love you,*" it said.' The emphatic italics, the strangeness and unforeseen quality of the situation, together with the aptness of the use of the mirror, charge this conventionally erotic statement with an unusual intensity. Here, for the first time, is a direct emotional statement from the girl to Miriam but it is, again significantly, written, not spoken.

After reading the girl's message, Miriam immediately structures the situation by imagining how the girl found out where she lived, how she entered, what she may have been wearing. Again the description is characterized by words which carry connotations of the mysterious : 'shadowy', 'secretly', 'swaying and flowing'.

The next communication from the girl is also unspoken. Miriam receives a letter at work 'in a strange hand' which she recognizes at once as 'Amabel's'; only here does the reader learn the girl's name. The connotations are yet again of strangeness; the handwriting consists of 'queer' strokes, 'disjointed' curves and a 'strange' pattern of letters.[17] Miriam's need to control her excitement is very conscious and almost as urgent as the excitement itself :

> She reckoned the cost of reading the whole: the sacrifice of part of a Saturday afternoon to work that after this invasion of her unprepared consciousness might go at a dragging pace.[18]

As was the case with the previous encounters, this letter forces even further upon Miriam's consciousness the mysteriousness of this relationship. And part of the mysteriousness is again Miriam's perception that the nature and quality of the communication is somehow other than that of speech, the ordinary language mode. It seems to her 'as if' the words are spoken. The 'strangeness' itself is what protects part of her consciousness from submitting to the 'enchantment' of the letter, the connotations of 'enchantment' being carefully balanced between the sense of magic, of the power of irrationality, on the one hand, and of sentimentality on the other. The unique quality of these written words which seem 'as if' spoken is that they are, it seems to her, 'alive'. The merging of personalities is again the explanatory focus of Miriam's response; the letter 'called her directly to the girl herself, making her, and not the letter, the medium of expression.' This extraordinary statement re-enacts, because of the syntactical ambiguity of the 'making her', the process of mirroring which has so disturbed Miriam. The syntax means equally that the girl herself is the medium of expression and that Miriam, the 'her' doing the reading, is the medium of expression. Cleverly, Richardson does not give the reader the entire letter, but a fusion of Miriam's perceptions of and responses to what it contains. And yet again, between Miriam's reflections, standing alone, comes the word 'mystery'.

In contradistinction from 'mystery', however, is 'reality' which 'vibrates behind this effort to drive feeling through words' :

> 'Forgive – I watched you – in your little English clothes – go across the square – oh, my lady – my little – you terrified my heart – I hold it out to you – my terrified heart – in my two hands –' [19]

The emotional pressure propelling this passionate declaration is what Miriam calls 'the girl's reality', which appeals to her own by predicting Miriam's thoughts and feelings even before she experiences them : this capacity for identification which seems to Miriam to issue from a complete recognition of the processes of her own inner life, is the one means of access by which Miriam can engage fully with the external world. Their thoughts and feelings, passing 'somehow between them in the mysterious interplay of their two beings', enact for Miriam the experience of 'the reality she had known for so long alone', thus bringing it 'out into life'.

The existential significance of this relationship for Miriam is unique in her experience and is very powerful. Until now, her vision of the harmony of life has been relentlessly challenged by the alienation of experience, itself an analogue to the alienation within herself between the spontaneous perceptions of consciousness and the expectations of womanhood. Richardson has demonstrated the nature of both kinds of alienation by tracing Miriam's attempts variously to integrate philosophical conflicts with conflicts in relationships, but Miriam's original vision, imprinted as the sense of wholeness she experienced in the garden with the bees in front of her face, has remained isolated and unaffirmed, because unrecognized, by the external world. It is this private vision of her whole self which Amabel seems to have recognized and by recognizing, affirmed. Clearly, for the reader, it is very important for Richardson to show that this mysterious and passionate relationship is perceived and experienced without any hint of overt sexuality since, for Miriam, the commitment of the body entails, necessarily, the exclusion of consciousness, thus defeating her desire to experience her whole self as an integrated part of external reality. She has not found, nor does she believe, that a relationship between a man and a woman can be of this order, since it seems that sexuality must be the pre-eminent factor, which in turn means, for her, that she must always be conscious that it is to her womanhood that a man will relate. Therefore, the liberating relationship she has sought and seems at this point to have discovered with Amabel, can only occur with another woman. Further, it is psychologically reinforcing for the reader that Richardson's insistence on the primacy for Miriam of the mirroring of the self and its ensuing sense of recognition could only carry powerful conviction in a same-sex relationship, where the identification of personalities is correlated with the identification of bodies. It is, of course, logically apt; but it is psychologically apt because the denial of womanhood, both acquired and instinctive womanhood, is necessarily not a dynamic between two people of the same sex. The irony of this position is certainly piquant, but its potential significance for the development of an artist, perhaps especially of a female artist, is already evident, since the 'fruit' of this particular passion will clearly not be children. Equally, the conduct of such a relationship has no predictable parameters.

That her relationship with Amabel can bring Miriam out 'into life' is forcibly demonstrated by the extent to which it modifies her relationship with Hypo Wilson:

> All this she felt to-night with the strength of two. Amabel was with her, young Amabel, with her mature experience of men, who had confirmed what hitherto she had thought might be inexperience, or a personal peculiarity: her certainty that between men and women there can be no direct communication.[20]

For the first time she can feel convinced that the dissatisfaction with intimacy which she has experienced in her relationships with men is real and not fantasized, because she has her experience of recognition with Amabel with which to compare it. The 'mirror', that is, which each woman has seemed to the other, has a further power of reflection and that is the property of reflecting other details of Miriam's external life. Amabel's presence becomes so internalized that it catalyses Miriam's relationships with everyone else, especially Hypo Wilson. She has already decided to allow him to seduce her and agrees, with this decision in the back of her mind, to go to dinner with him, though she is unable to tell 'what had happened in the moment of reading' and that inability, in spite of his sympathetic attitude, leads her to conclude that 'the sacred moment was apart in her own personal and private life'. It is indeed the affirmation she has received from Amabel which gives her the power to decide, finally, to do what Hypo wants, that is, extend their relationship to sexual intimacy. There is a sense, then, in which Miriam's consciousness of Amabel pushes her into Hypo's arms. On the other hand, Miriam is far from representing the stock image of the lesbian personality which is the subject, for example, of *The Well of Loneliness*. Stephen, the heroine of that novel, displays a revulsion towards the male touch and towards male sexual desire which is taken to be the characterizing response of lesbian orientation :

> She went with him and they walked on in silence for a while, then Martin stood still, and began to talk quickly; he was saying amazing, utterly incredible things: 'Stephen, my dear – I do utterly love you.' He was holding out his arms, while she shrank back bewildered: 'I love you, I'm deeply in love with you, Stephen – look at me, don't you understand me, beloved? I want you to marry me – you do love me, don't you?' And then, as though she had suddenly struck him, he flinched: 'Good God! What's the matter, Stephen?'
>
> She was staring at him in a kind of dumb horror, staring at his eyes that were clouded by desire, while gradually over her colourless face there was spreading an expression of the deepest repulsion – terror and repulsion he saw on her face, something else too, a look as of outrage. He could not believe this thing that he saw, this insult to all he felt to be sacred; for a moment he in his turn, must stare, then he came a step nearer, still unable to believe. But at that she wheeled round and fled from him wildly, fled back to the house that had always protected; nor did she once pause in her flight to look back.[21]

By contrast, Miriam's response to male sexuality, however convoluted it may seem, is not one of revulsion. It has already been noticed that she 'thrilled' to Shatov's touch; and her response to Hypo Wilson is willing and affectionate, if not passionate. Even while she is being seduced, her contact with Amabel is present in her consciousness, enabling her to see herself as Hypo seems to see her :

> With the eyes of Amabel, and with her own eyes opened by Amabel, she saw the long honey-coloured ropes of hair framing the face that Amabel found beautiful in its 'Flemish Madonna' type, falling across her shoulders and along her body where the last foot of their length, red-gold, gleamed marvellously against the rose-tinted velvety gleaming of

> her flesh. Saw the lines and curves of her limbs, their balance and harmony. Impersonally beautiful and inspiring. To him each detail was 'pretty,' and the whole an object of desire.[22]

Here, too, the contrast of responses to herself which Miriam imputes, respectively, to Amabel and Hypo, takes its focus from the recognition of identity rather than from an implied questioning of her sexual orientation. Amabel sees Miriam as a beautiful work of art, a 'Flemish Madonna' with gleaming, red-gold hair and rose-tinted flesh and with well-proportioned limbs which display the aesthetic attributes of 'balance' and 'harmony'. The effect, also, is aesthetic for Amabel, rather than erotic; Miriam is 'impersonally' beautiful.[23] Hypo Wilson, on the other hand, does not perceive her as a work of art, but as an 'object of desire' of which each detail is merely 'pretty'. It is clear which of these responses Miriam prefers.

Immediately after their sexual encounter, Miriam takes Hypo to Donizetti's for more talk and coffee. It is Hypo who suggests that what Miriam needs and wants is to 'write a book', but that in order to do so, she would need, as other women do, a 'homeopathic dose' of life, which, he says, would be 'an infant'. Hypo interprets Miriam's frustrated creativity as a compound need to produce a baby and a book, but in his judgement the book could not be produced without the baby. The more Hypo insists that she should write a novel, the more she rebels against his admiration of the form, until, again, she takes refuge in thinking of Amabel, admitting that, at the moment, this is her perpetual preoccupation. To know Amabel is, she tells him, 'treasure, beyond your power of diagnosis. Beyond anyone's power.'[24] Her identification with Amabel now shifts to the point where she looks at Amabel through Hypo's eyes and sees 'almost everything in her escape' Hypo's perception. In response to her own fantasy, Miriam begins to explain Amabel to Hypo, which allows the reader to learn the details of Amabel's life which have hitherto remained hidden. Clearly Miriam has learned about Amabel's background, circumstances, lovers, interests and opinions during their conversation in the music room, but the reader is not informed of them until a third party, an audience, is admitted to exist. What was primarily important for Richardson to convey to the reader about Miriam was the 'strangeness' of the recognition between the two women, which, by denying the details of Amabel's life, also denied their relevance. Here, for Hypo's sake, Miriam explains that Amabel has had a secure background, has French, Welsh and Irish antecedents, has travelled, has behaved in impetuous and unorthodox ways and disappointed her family. She wants to convey, somehow, to Hypo, 'a sense of the quality pervading every moment' of Amabel's life, yet, at the same time, the very desire to convey 'seemed a kind of treachery to Amabel'.[25]

Her attempt to convey Amabel's quality to Hypo is accompanied by an interior monologue which she cannot reveal to Hypo but which informs the reader of another encounter between the two women, when they spent a day at a party, 'separated and mingling in various groups' until they were 'both filled with the same longing, to get away and lie side by side in the darkness describing and talking it all over until sleep should come without any interval of going off into the seclusion' [26] of their separate minds. At this point Miriam remembers that with Amabel she could recall and share her 'bee memory' and that that sharing had promised 'that never again should there be in my blood an unconquerable fever';[27] the 'unconquerable fever' signifies the pressure to communicate which issues from isolation. However, she continues trying to explain to Hypo something of Amabel's attitudes, but soon her sense of betrayal returns :

> He had made a remark seeming to come from far away, and inaudible because she was deafened by the shame of the realization that in a moment she would have been telling him of their silences, trying to tell him of those moments when they were suddenly intensely aware of each other and the flow of their wordless communion, making the smallest possible movements of the head now this way now that, holding each pose with their eyes wide on each other, expressionless, like birds in a thicket intently watching and listening: but without bird-anxiety.[28]

Eventually Miriam and Hypo find again a means of engaging with each other by agreeing that 'men and women are incompatible'. [29] Released, therefore, from her sense of isolation, Miriam is able to act, and thus propelled by this new version of herself, she continues her affaire with Hypo, only to find that the woman she hoped he would release in her remains imprisoned :

> But the power she felt the presented facts ought to wield, and might possibly yet attain, failed to emerge from them. Within her was something that stood apart, unpossessed. From far away below the colloquy, from where still it sheltered in the void to which it had withdrawn and

whence it had set forth alone upon its strange journeying, her spirit was making its own statement, profanely asserting the unattained being that was promising, however, faintly, to be presently the surer for this survival.[30]

With Amabel she feels free and recognized; with Hypo she feels manipulated, as if he leaves her to herself 'to demonstrate a principle: elimination of the personal'.[31]

In 1941, commenting to John Cowper Powys on his views about ecclesiastics, Richardson, consistent with her daily judgements, wrote the following:

> - - - how strange & strange & strange is your attitude, or the attitude of all the males here collected in all their variety, towards 'sex'. Each one pines for dominance, clings exultantly to the illusion of dominance, hardly seems to be able to exist without it.[32]

Dawn's Left Hand ends with this sense of gain and loss easily reconciled; the 'dawn', the beginning of Miriam's transition from isolation into 'life', or action, has come from an unexpected source, a 'left hand', with 'left' carrying, in this context, both the associations of magic and of the sinister. Amabel is Miriam's left hand. Her relationship with Hypo, alternatively, has elicited her sexuality without releasing her womanhood in the complete sense she had wanted and expected. These two relationships balance and define one another across the spectrum of Miriam's consciousness, without promise of integration. One or both of them must resolve in a way which will allow Miriam some further and more independent course of action. From the 'dawn', therefore, she must look further to the 'clear horizon' of the next chapter.

What then occurs to Miriam is an inward vision of bringing together the two opposing kinds of relationship by introducing her suitor, Michael Shatov, to Amabel. Hypo is already married and her friendship with him is of long standing; the roles Hypo and Miriam play for each other are already fixed. But Shatov's passion for her is equivalent in intensity to Amabel's. Miriam has already rejected Shatov's proposal of marriage, but she has not managed to quell her guilt at doing so; it arises in her each time he asks her for help:

> - - - with what to give to any one, or to be to any one, was she going so zestfully forward in her life, if she was failing Michael? - - - - Again and

again he had summoned her: for help in his pathetically absurd entanglements with people he attracted and entirely failed to read- - - - And each time she had hoped that on the next occasion he would himself make the necessary imaginative effort. And with each fresh telegram had had to realize afresh his amazing, persistent helplessness; and to know, in terms of real distress, that whatever hurt him must hurt her also while life lasted.[33]

The 'vision' Miriam has is very like the conception of a work of art, carrying within it both the excitement of expectation and the confidence of manipulative power:

And then, as though it had prepared itself while she was refusing to take thought, there passed before her inward vision a picture of herself performing, upon an invisible background, the rite of introduction between Michael and Amabel. It slid away. Joyously she recalled it, supplying time and place, colour and sound and living warmth. And it stood there before her, solving the mystery of her present failure to suffer on Michael's behalf, filling so completely the horizon of her immediate future that it seemed to offer, the moment it should become the reality into which she had the power of translating it, a vista ahead swept clean of all impediments. She hurried on, as if the swiftness of her steps could hasten fulfilment.[34]

Like artistic conception, the idea takes place while she is 'refusing to take thought'; it is, as it were, an inspiration. Oddly, the contrast between this 'artistic' manipulation and the usual, fully engaged, subjective conduct of this kind of conflict, is provided by a friend of Richardson's who found herself in a similar dilemma. Richardson's advice contrasts effectively with her own managing of Veronica and Benjamin Grad in life, and Miriam's managing of Amabel and Michael Shatov:

It may be as you think. We agree. And our hearts ache about equally for you & for Eve. We agree too, that the situation as it stands at present, is impossible for both of you, if not for all three - - - - Evelyn's happiness under your roof has transformed her & restored her poise. She is now a very attractive woman, to whom any man, save those who are not of her 'sort', will be drawn. Supposing B. is to be so drawn, & overwhelmingly so – which is another matter – & you, realising this, release him, will he, *then*, desire (a) to marry her, (b) to involve her in an 'affair'? Is part of her charm to be found in the fact that she is out of reach? - - - - My own feeling, when we were with you, was that you had decided, selflessly, to rejoice in the drawing together of your two friends & in the knowledge that they remain in your life. Our impression of uncertainty in regard to Eve's feelings is no doubt accountable to her personal situation. How, without treachery to you, could she encourage him? - - - - you know - - - that agonies such as you are enduring do not remain static, that they go their way changing & being modified as one is oneself. It has been said that the worst of such suffering is exactly that it *can* end.[35]

The telling judgement here is Richardson's attribution of the idea of 'selflessness' to the act of encouraging two friends to turn to one another. Equally significant is an alternative situation, in which two friends are drawn together in an 'overwhelming' way. Richardson does not explain why this would be 'another matter', but the implication is that the manipulation of a third person would be inconsequential. In her own vision, and in Miriam's, the artistic analogue occurs in the structuring of the idea as an image, in the imaginative sense, a 'vision', a 'picture' and, like the artist, Miriam is the medium and manipulator of her material, except that, in this particular 'vision', the material consists of actual people. The creation itself, again like art, is stylized, in so far as Miriam performs a 'rite' of introduction. She adds to her 'vision' the details of 'time and place, colour and sound and living warmth'. If the nature of the vision is artistic, so, too, is the nature of the problem which motivates it : the 'mystery of her present failure to suffer on Michael's behalf', which, at present, obstructs 'the horizon of her immediate future'. This obstruction must be removed so that she can find clarity. Yet the most striking feature of her vision, and the feature which most convincingly makes it an artistic analogue, is the confidence with which she feels she can indeed manipulate these people into a situation which can leave her with a 'clear horizon'. Miriam feels, that is, that she has 'the power of translating it' into reality.

The implications of her vision shock her as soon as she begins to think about it and she begins immediately to analyse her motives. Her rationality insists that she should challenge the 'subtly attractive picture' and discover its 'secret origin', in order to satisfy her moral consciousness. The analysis, however, cannot calm either her excitement or her confidence; the vision issues, somehow, from beneath or beyond her rationality :

> Something far away below any single, particular motive she could search out, had made the decision, was refusing to attend to this conscious conflict and was already regarding the event as current, even as past and accomplished. This complete, independent response, whose motives were either undiscoverable or non-existent, might be good or bad, but was irrevocable.[36]

Miriam does perform her 'rite of introduction' before a concert to which Shatov is taking her. After the three have laughed and joked together, she asks Shatov to wait downstairs for her. Upon his exit, she crosses to the window where Amabel is standing looking out :

> Reaching the window she stood at Amabel's side, looking down into the garden, and tried, by driving away every image save that of the tall tree whose small new leaves, blurred by mist, seemed rather to have condensed upon it than to have sprouted from within its sooty twigs, to turn Michael's visit into an already forgotten parenthesis in their communion.[37]

Amabel's response is certainly startling. 'Mira', she says to Miriam, 'you MUST marry him !' [38] What Miriam perceives in this injunction is a recognition of her own cruelty in deserting Shatov, together with a resolve that even if it means giving up the seclusion of their intimacy together, Shatov should not be made to suffer because of Miriam's needs :

> Saw it so clearly that she was ready, in order to secure safety and happiness for him, to sacrifice the life together here at a moment's notice. She had already sacrificed it. Judged, condemned, and set it aside. Within it, henceforth, if indeed it should continue, was isolation. Isolation with Amabel's judgment.[39]

Richardson thus makes clear for the reader, while Amabel waits for Miriam's defence of her rejection, that Miriam is quite aware of her manipulation of her friends, and, too, of the consequent moral problems issuing from it. She is aware of her 'deliberate tampering with the movement of life' [40] and that it means, first of all, separation from Amabel, for whom such depths of conscious calculation 'had no existence'. Miriam is unable, however, to decide which way of the two, Amabel's unstructured and intuitive response to life, or her own conscious manipulation of it, is right. 'There was no one alive,' Miriam thinks, 'who could decide, in this strange difference, where lay right and wrong.'[41] Amabel, unaware of Miriam's reflections, continues with an open admiration of Shatov which kindles in Miriam 'an incredible hope'. She has a vision of a future which excludes her and the words come, in her eagerness to assure it, faster than she can control. To Amabel, therefore, she suggests: 'Then marry him, my dear, yourself.'[42]

Amabel responds by dancing with glee, like a child. 'I would', she says, 'I would tomorrow!' Her first fantasy of this new projected future is that she would like his children, with their 'beady eyes'. This, too, is significant, since children, the usual fruit of erotic love, will not issue from Miriam and Amabel. Miriam's 'issue' is to be *Pilgrimage*; Amabel's, since she belongs totally to the world of unconscious life, must be children.

Michael Shatov, waiting downstairs to escort Miriam to the concert, is unaware of the approaching 'salvation' which Miriam has designed for him. Miriam, however, does not see him as a person without volition of his own, but as someone who is simply not yet aware of the like messages which will come 'from within his own consciousness'.[43] As they sit side by side through the concert, Miriam is increasingly aware of a need to confide in Shatov. She is, at this time, pregnant with Wilson's child. The 'fruitfulness' which Shatov and Amabel have separately desired for themselves, and will, Miriam is convinced, together achieve, is ironically already manifest in her own body and has, indeed, only been possible precisely because the erotic and spiritual union she has experienced with Amabel has not been characteristic of her relationship with Wilson. Here, then, the parallel possibilities of relationship and fruition converge, intersect, inform one another, and then separate again. The result is almost diagrammatic in its linearity: Miriam is a woman of divided consciousness, such that her womanhood can be engaged in a sexual relationship with a man and can, as the usual consequence follows, bear a child as the fruit of that relationship. Yet, because her womanhood is alienated from her sense of identity, she can only so engage if she is *not* experiencing an erotic and spiritual union, a sense of mirror-image reflection and recognition, with her sexual partner. This second and alternative kind of relationship is, for her, explicitly non-sexual, or, more exactly, must not be overtly sexual, which means that it may only occur with a person of her own sex, and indeed has occurred with Amabel. By contrast, Shatov's need for Miriam and, likewise, Amabel's potential needs are perceived by Miriam to be much more integrated than her own, precisely because it is Amabel, and not Miriam, who can contemplate marriage with Shatov. Hypo Wilson, in this respect, is an appropriate sexual partner for Miriam since, according to her perceptions of him, he is as unintegrated as she is. She has always been aware of the incompatibility of their consciousnesses, which has both fascinated and repelled her. He, too, is an artist, albeit of a very different temperament, so his 'fruit', like hers, lies elsewhere. The resulting basis for action, then, is ideologically anti-Romantic and culturally subversive, in that it entails, first, a separation between love and sexuality to produce, diversely, both art and children. For Miriam, and indeed for Richardson, the extent to which male creativity is expressed in the begetting of children does not seem to present to a male artist the same moral dilemma as it does for a female artist; nor does it seem that male artists suffer from the same division of consciousness. It seems to Miriam, and to Richardson, that Hypo Wilson can beget children and write his novels with an equally simple enthusiasm and an absence of conflict which is impossible for Miriam and which she diagnoses as a difference due to gender. She identifies, variously, with each of these three friends : with Wilson, because he is an artist, with Shatov, because he has a compatible temperament, and with Amabel because she can feel completely known. On the other hand, she cannot identify with Wilson's consciousness and *therefore* she can bear his child; she cannot identify with Shatov's manhood and *therefore* she cannot bear his child; and she cannot identify with Amabel's capacity to live intuitively, because it disallows the possibilities of artistic calculation. The solution, therefore, is for Miriam to bear Wilson's child and at the same time to reject the usual continuing of the sexual relationship with him as a married couple with children – this alternative would allow each of them the independent life of an artist. The solution for Shatov and Amabel, who are not artists, is for them to divert their separate erotic responses to Miriam away from her and towards each other, thus consummating their eroticism in the begetting of life. For Shatov and Amabel, because they are not artists, the acceptance of a conventional family life will not cause a conflict with the need for independence which it would cause for Miriam. The psychological conditions necessary for her to bear a child are quite other than those she projects for Shatov and Amabel and this is what she wants to explain to Shatov :

> To tell him would be to tell herself, to see herself committed, not only to the agonized breaking-up of her physical being, but to the incalculable regrouping of all the facets of her life.[44]

Shatov's response to her news that she is pregnant, which is for him 'the fact of facts',[45] is to offer to marry her 'as brother'. But what seems refuge and security to him, would be a 'permanent prison' for her.[46] It is significant that Miriam's solution becomes possible only when she is herself pregnant, as if the temporary integration of body and personality which pregnancy imposes can provide a base from which she can make the conscious divisions of experience which her friends will be party to. It is the determinism of pregnancy which is especially powerful, that being indeed the only thing in her life which she has been unable 'either to impose and make it comely, or to check its outrageous advance.'[47] And from this new integration issues a reinforcement of her old sense of isolation, together with a new moral confidence :

> The motionless unchanging centre of her consciousness, bowed beneath the weight of incommunicable experience, announced its claims without achieving freedom from its hunger. Yet it was on behalf of those belonging to her, and not on her own behalf, that she was determined, as the life-moulded, available edge of her bent, conversational profile almost audibly announced, to sustain the ceaseless flow of events, the ceaseless exchange of unsatisfactory comments; haunted meanwhile, in the depths of her solitude, by the presence of youth mysteriously decayed, and by the gathering, upon her person, of cumbrous flesh.[48]

The moral confidence depends upon her sense of rectitude that her manipulative actions are 'on behalf of those belonging to her, and not on her own behalf' and this assurance determines her 'to sustain the ceaseless flow of events'. Having so determined, she leads the conversation with Shatov to the subject of Amabel, doing so with conscious deliberation and with 'conspiratorial eyes'.[49]

II

Ironically enough, the baby is not to be, to Hypo Wilson's genuine disappointment. He had believed Miriam to be 'booked for maternity'.[50] Now he admits that the prospect of her bearing his child had 'lifted' him up 'into a tremendous exaltation'.[51] Perhaps partly due to this pressure of expectation, it is necessary for Miriam, as it had been for Richardson, that this particular 'fruit' should not ripen.

The reviewers of *Clear Horizon* seemed to miss this important development in the 'plot'. To John Cowper Powys Richardson wrote :

> Reviews much as usual, venom or cream. More than one of those who skim & 'notice' half a dozen novels a week declare that in this book nothing happens or, if anything does, the happening is imperceptible. This fails to disturb me. But I am a wee bit dismayed in discovering that M's meditations & reactions at the meeting called (dinner included) by Hypo, to make arrangements for M's immediate future (hence the dismissal of Amabel immediately after dinner) do not reveal the fact that no arrangements are needed. The revelation of Hypo's Technique in dealing with a situation he supposes to exist, her relief in having escaped the need for temporary dependence upon him, these are the inside of that comic interlude.[52]

It is psychologically consistent that with Miriam's rejection of Hypo's 'fruit' should come her rejection of their sexual involvement. That most ancient of all the characterizing marks of femininity has been tried by Miriam and found wanting. Implicit also is a rejection of sexuality itself, even without childbearing, since Richardson records no further sexual encounters in the following pages of *Pilgrimage.* Miriam's original friendship with Wilson remains important, however, and that she decides to keep and manages to keep. Miriam knows, nevertheless, that children must be born and that lovers must embrace; and she knows, further, that she must somehow have a part in those processes, despite her rejection of a direct part. With the cessation of her affair with Wilson, Miriam's search for her own part in the nature of creativity progresses one step further.

At this point, having examined Richardson's fictionalized re-enactment of these events, it is fascinating to consider 'Amabel's' assessment of the same events and, further, her commentary on Richardson's motivations. Available correspondence between Richardson and her friend is sparse : one letter and one postcard from Veronica Grad to Richardson are held by Yale. Some letters from Richardson to Veronica Grad are in private possession. But what has also survived is an important correspondence between Veronica Grad and Rose Isserliss Odle, Richardson's sister-in-law and literary executrix.[53] The correspondence belongs to the months immediately following Richardson's death, during which time Rose Odle was collecting material for Professor Leon Edel, who was considering writing Richardson's biography. Rose Odle eventually gave to Yale the letters Veronica Grad had written to her, together with an explanation of how they came to know each other. Rose Odle's letters to Veronica Grad are in private possession.*

Rose Odle found the relationship between Richardson and Veronica Grad, as reported by Veronica, 'mystifying' and 'upsetting', for which reason she was extremely reluctant to allow Veronica's letters to be read. It seemed to her to have been a 'passionate' friendship, but one in which Veronica's 'utter devotion' had been unnecessary for Richardson who, because she was a writer, had other 'resources' which had enabled her to 'shut Veronica out'. Veronica's own account of her relationship with Richardson, revealed after Richardson's death in her letters to Rose Odle, reverberates with the same sense of strangeness and of total identification which Richardson's fictionalized presentation embodies. For Veronica it was a 'queer kind of partnership', 'an odd business',[54] in which, because the two women would have liked, in some ways, 'to live the other's life',[55] they were 'lovers'. Veronica stresses that they were 'lovers' in some way she couldn't understand.[56] The identification consisted in the feeling that, although they each loved a man, that love did not encompass what they essentially were :

> & Dorothy loved Alan & I loved someone too – but it wasn't I know to either of us what *we* were – [57]

Veronica recognized in Richardson a 'tenacity of purpose in other things besides her writing' which she describes as 'queer'.[58] Thirty years of her own life, she writes, were 'so much Dorothy's too', not as a writer but as a person,[59] and the identification remained so total that it was striking even to an outsider, the healer William MacMillan :[60]

> First I loved her – unquestionably – whole mindedly – later on I loved her for the love I had had for her – I remember Mac (the healer) telling me that the business of Dorothy & me was quite the most astonishing example of enduring & unrequited love he had ever heard or read of – He went further; when Dorothy had her attack of shingles & four days later I had it too he saw some connection between these two events – I

* This correspondence is reprinted in the Appendix.

> had it in its worst form – nearly died, & was in hospital for nine weeks – & still suffer from its after effects – This I do not pretend to understand but I am ready to believe that he knew what he was talking about.[61]

The effort to understand the strange and elusive quality of their identification leads her to speak of them as 'twins' [62] or 'two halves' of a whole,[63] each complementing the other, especially, she says, in that Richardson was 'a complete egoist', whereas she was 'born without any glimmer of how to be one'.[64]

This interpretation of their complementary personalities has an important place in an understanding of Richardson's manipulative intentions. In the first place, Veronica Grad was quite aware that, despite their mutual feeling of identification, it was necessary for Richardson that Veronica should allow herself to be manipulated. Veronica Grad accepts that the fictionalized account in *Pilgrimage* differs only in two details: Richardson's suggestion that Veronica and Benjamin should marry took place in reality after Veronica's lover had died, when she and Richardson spent the night together in the same bed:

> The night the man *I* loved died v. suddenly – we slept in the same bed & I wept & wept & towards morning – both of us exhausted Dorothy suddenly said 'Vera, *now* you can marry Benjamin' & I remember saying 'Yes' – because what I had really said when in the book she makes me say – 'I would I would & have his beadyeyed children' I had added 'but not while Philip is alive' – It was half in jest but she knew I would for *her* – if she asked me & she did, & I did, & Benjamin knew why I married him ...[65]

Veronica had agreed to marry Benjamin only after her own lover was dead. Benjamin, in his turn, also knew why Veronica agreed to the marriage. This leads Veronica to affirm that because she and Benjamin had knowingly colluded in Richardson's plan, Richardson was right to think of their children as her own:

> & so you see in a way she was quite right in feeling David was hers in a way he was – Benjamin loved Dorothy, but he wanted to marry anyway & above all he wanted a son – I never pretended – to be in love with my husband but in the end he grew v. jealous of Dorothy & me – & then our lives seperated [*sic*] because she went to live at 32....[66]

Indeed, the final image in *Pilgrimage* is that of Madonna and boy-child, which embodies Miriam's eventual acceptance of her own maternal longings, but the striking difference from the traditional image is that the child she holds is not her own – it is the child of Amabel (Veronica) and Michael (Benjamin). When Miriam reflects on her relationship with Amabel, she insists that it has remained 'untouched', either by Amabel's marriage or the birth of the child :

> Something of the inexpressible quality of our relationship revealed itself in that moment she did not share, the moment of finding the baby Paul lying asleep in his long robe in the sitting-room, gathering him up, and being astonished to feel, as soon as he lay folded, still asleep, against my body, the complete stilling of every one of my competing urgencies. Freedom. Often I had held babes in my arms: Harriett's, Sally's, and many others. But never with that sense of perfect serenity.[67]

Richardson endorses Miriam's claim here that the fruit of the union of her friends is her own fruit, created by her initiative and will and returning to her a sense of fulfilment. The Grads actually had two children, the second being a daughter; but it was the son who was so important for Richardson in reality and no daughter of Amabel and Michael is mentioned in *Pilgrimage*. This is ultimately the only way in which Richardson could satisfactorily integrate, both in life and art, the claims of the male sex; in both her marriage and in her relationship with Veronica's son, the principal psychological dynamic demonstrated is her maternal affection. In what seems a semi-conscious way only, she affirmed, in other contexts, this conviction that maternal affection was especially appropriate to the accommodation of the male sex :

> Doesn't it make you feel *complete*, holding a sleeping infant close? But wait till you hold a *boy* infant, belonging to a sister or someone very dear by choice rather than by the fact of common blood. The difference is complete & startling. You hold so much less and so much more. You have the world in your arms. But if the childless can so experience, what of mothers? [68]

This psychological solution is an essential key to an understanding of how Richardson finally held together the conflicting goals of her femininity and her vocation. By initiating a marriage between two people she loved and who loved her, she created and, indeed, manipulated her material for the purposes of artistic production and for the possibility of children she could call her own.

Rose Odle, in reply to Veronica's account of how she came to marry Benjamin Grad, adds an interesting endorsement to Veronica's interpretation of this side of Richardson's personality :

> I *do* understand about the relationship. The day I left Hillside after I had been nursing her, I knew if I did not go then, I would never get away.[69]

This generalizing observation suggests the implications of Richardson's manipulative power which, in Rose's experience as well as in Veronica's, was correlated with a capacity for detachment astonishing in its severity to both women :

> I appreciate your experiences of D's 'not being involved'.
>
> They spent a week as our guests every summer. In 1932, when my life broke up (I had 18 wretched and difficult years, & a family to support alone for most of that time), I tried to tell D something. 'I don't want to know.'
>
> I neither wrote nor heard from either of them till 1948, when I wrote first after Alan's death – which I saw announced in the Times.[70]

Veronica, however, does not excuse Richardson's manipulations on the grounds of Art. To her, the novels of *Pilgrimage* are 'as damming [*sic*] a picture of personality as were ever written',[71] because, in Veronica's judgement, Richardson behaved towards real people exactly as an artist must towards his or her creations – that is, she observed, manipulated and analysed, but she did not sympathize or become 'involved'. It is clear from Richardson's account in *Pilgrimage* that for her such attitudes were justifiable.

But although her sense of rectitude may have been uncompromising, her intellectual formulations about the status of art were not :

> Let us by all means confess our faith. In this case faith in Art as an ultimate, a way of salvation opposed, though not necessarily contradictory, to other ways of salvation, Religion, Ethics, Science rather existing independently and though aware of them regarding them only as making for the same bourne by different routes. . . . Art by all means. Let us live and die in and for it. But when we condemn the inartistic let us beware of assuming aesthetic excellence as always and everywhere

and for everyone the standard measure. If we feel we must condemn popular art let us know where we are, know that we are refusing an alternative measure and interpretation of the intercommunications we reject.[72]

For Veronica Grad, however, Richardson's sense of rectitude was mistaken and indefensible :

> I have at last seen her as she really was – I loved her but Dorothy never for one moment 'loved' anyone but herself. Not even Alan – not anyway as I see love – Dorothy never paid any prices. She took an avid interest in other people their lives, their misfortunes, their successes, but she never – looking back I see – gave either sympathy or help – or let herself become in any way involved – I am not thinking only of myself. I call to mind a dozen examples of utter self-protective ruthlessness – Her own sisters – Florence Daniel – Jane Wells – Lissie Beresford – Benjamin – my own children. Maybe it was all worth it as a sacrifice to her 'Art' I can't judge of that – You think she loved David, she did in a way. I think she *thought* she did. I even am able to believe she thought she loved me – but first everyone was 'copy' material not only for books but for stimulation for Dorothy – You know she was rather like a vivisectionist in her attitude to us all – but, I cant [*sic*] see myself that the handful of pioneer books makes it any less ugly –[73]

Richardson was not invulnerable to judgements of this kind, and her own detachment was compounded, in daily life, by her husband's even more stringent exclusivity. Comments written to John Cowper Powys after Alan Odle's death are revealing in this regard :

> There are many variants of the phrase 'Trevone will never be the same again.' Amazed, he would have been. For though down here in these last years he had grown to his full height & not long ago had told me he no longer felt that those not actively engaged in Art or Literature were negligible, outside the pale, he still would rather go the long way round rather than encounter & be obliged to find something to say. And they were aware of him, of the quality of his being. This lifts from me a sometimes half guilty sense that our life was too much a 'solitude à deux' even 'égoisme à deux'.[74]

At the end of Veronica's letter, quoted above, she again accuses Richardson of having a 'completely uninvolved interest in other peoples [*sic*] tragic lives'. Whether or not an understanding of Richardson's creative drive leads to an endorsement of Veronica's moral condemnation depends on the value-system thought pertinent to the conduct of personal relationships. Many, including Rose Odle, would agree with her. Nevertheless, 'uninvolved' is hardly an apt description of Richardson's role; on the contrary, she is implicated in the lives closest to her to an extraordinary degree. Veronica and Benjamin Grad, and others in less radical ways, could, from Richardson's standpoint, be seen to have surrendered their autonomy and to have allowed themselves to become her 'material'. That she may not have been sympathetic or compassionate in the ways usually expected is a charge against her personal behaviour and its affect, a charge, further, which has been levelled against many other writers. It may be that Rose was right in implying that Richardson needed to protect her creative energy from being expended in relationship rather than in writing, which is where she chose to direct it. Whether or not the 'handful of pioneer books' excuses Richardson's egoism or even whether it is deemed that they should, depends on which relationship between art and life is considered an appropriate context within which such a judgement can be formulated. Richardson's own view of that kind of egoism, which may indeed be taken to be a rationalization of her own conduct, was that it held the seeds of virtue as well as of vice :

> For the essential characteristic of women is egoism. Let it at once be admitted that this is a masculine discovery. It has been offered as the worst that can be said of the sex as a whole. It is both the worst and the best. Egoism is at once the root of shameless selfishness and the ultimate dwelling place of charity.[75]

Questions of whether egoism is justified by art, and if so, which kinds of egoism and which kinds of art, belong more properly to the domains of ethics and philosophical aesthetics. What can be said here, and with confidence, is that Richardson's contribution to literature is not only significant for its technical innovation but also for its challenge to the traditionally defined divisions between art and life.

III

In a letter to Rose Odle, Richardson, significantly after her husband's death, outlined some of the ideological precepts which eventually allowed her a sufficient degree of integration between the complex and warring elements of her experience. Responding to a comment about men presumably made by Rose Odle, Richardson has the following to say:

> Agreed, too, that most Englishmen dislike women. Know nothing about them, or, at any rate, less than any other males in the world. Hence clubs & pubs. The English pub is alone in being, primarily, a row of boys of all ages at a bar, showing off. That of course is a bit harsh & insufficient. Volumes would be required to investigate & reveal the underlying factors. Vast numbers of Englishmen are so to say spiritually homosexual. Our history, our time of being innocently piratical, then enormously, at the cost of the natives in our vast possessions, wealthy & 'properous' so that our culture died, giving place to civilisation (!), is partly responsible. For it made millions of women unemployed, vacuous, buyers of commercialised commodities, philistine utterly; sponges, in fact. Now, in our poverty, we have a better chance. The whole question, as between men & women, is complex to the limit of the term. Difficult to know whether one wants men to become more womanly or women more manly. Personally, I have shared, with few exceptions, the masculine dislike & suspicion of women, have avoided & evaded them &, as it happened, lived almost entirely amongst males. Of late, i.e. since 1939, this attitude has been revising itself. A subtle change, fully shared by Alan. Down here, during the war, we associated almost entirely with women, a new experience for both of us, with grass widows chiefly &, when their men came back, were little less than astonished by the incompatibilities of the two, the abysmal 'unawareness' of the male, his sometimes rather engaging childishness & self-conceit. There are of course exceptions. But on the whole we are inclined to agree, with Shaw, that men are, all their lives, nursery infants, & with Forster, as revealed in *Howard's End*, that the characteristic quality of woman-at-her-best is pity. This of course presupposes that most men are extravert & most women introvert. But there are such infinite gradations. And not only artists, but many others in the multitude are bi-sexual. The Odle men, with all their sensibility, are I think, on the whole, despisers of women, while realising their dependence on them. It was our mutual dislike of the sex-as-a-whole that first drew Alan & me together. In the end, down here, his sensitive nature, capacity (truly feminine) for imaginative sympathy & vicarious living cured him of his blindness towards Philistia, & gave both of us a fresh outlook on women. Lovers, they are, of course, in a way rarely possible, given their grand & fruitful preoccupation with things, to men, whose picture of 'the Absolute' is male entirely, as is that of the Churches, who all moan & groan & obsequiously supplicate an incense-loving divinity. Mary Baker Eddy's picture is essentially feminine. Is that not why the Christian Science churches

grow & spread & are hated, unexamined, by all clerics?[76]

Here, in compressed, conversational form, are stated the elements which finally made Richardson something of a recluse: the divisive nature of society which she diagnosed as 'homosexual', the anachronistic role allotted to women, the irrelevance of orthodox religion, the anomalous 'bi-sexuality' of the artist. Revealingly, she attributes her initial attraction to Alan Odle to their mutual dislike of women as a social group and her adjustment to an individual man in the intimate relationship of marriage she achieved, was possibly only able to achieve, because of his 'truly feminine' nature. To this end her personal pilgrimage led. And under these psychological conditions she was able to practise her art. They were, however, even by her own admission, hardly ideal conditions. In response to a request from the journalist Louise Theis (formerly Morgan) she explained what for her were ideal conditions of work:

> Ideally, everything that favours collaboration between the conscious and the unconscious.
>
> The best conditions in my experience are winter solitude and inaccessibility. I mean solitude. Servantless, visitorless and, save for a single agent, tradesmanless. Such conditions fell to my lot just once. Deliberately to seek them might be fatal.
>
> Short of this, the avoidance of anything that breaks the momentum of the unconscious once it is set going.[77]

These general conditions would be endorsed by most writers; what is slightly provocative is the implication that literary creativity is the giving of free range to the process of unconscious association, but in Richardson's special case, since for her real experience takes place outside the usual conventions of the temporal continuum, what she means by 'unconsciousness' bears particular reference to the accessibility of her experiential material. Further, she specifies conditions of work applicable to a woman writer:

> Ideal conditions are more easily obtained by men than by women. However provided with service, space, leisure, a woman will not entirely escape transient preoccupations: with the welfare of her entourage, both animate and inanimate.
>
> These preoccupations, plus solicitude, are asset as well as tax, of course. They are nevertheless the main reason why nothing short of a

> dehumanised solitude will serve the woman at work. And they are, also of course, the secret of the relatively small amount of first-class 'art' produced by women not only in the very domestic past, but at any time. All they produce is in the teeth of demands from which most men, for good or ill, are free.[78]

Like the accommodation achieved in her personal life, this accommodation of her personality to the demands of art, is a compromise. In each case the fact of her femininity is the obstacle which obstructs her capacity for integration. In each case, too, the fact of her femininity is experienced as alienating. The key issue, for Richardson, is that a woman, by her very nature, must be engaged in and by the ordinary demands of daily living, and that she cannot, except at the cost of 'dehumanization', be detached from them, although she recognizes that detachment is a pre-condition for the practice of art :

> Art demands what, to women, current civilization won't give. There is for a Dostoyevsky writing against time on the corner of a crowded kitchen table a greater possibility of detachment than for a woman artist no matter how placed. Neither motherhood nor the more continuously exacting and indefinitely expansive responsibilities of even the simplest housekeeping can so effectively hamper her as the human demand, besieging her wherever she is, for an inclusive awareness, from which men, for good or ill, are exempt.[79]

The conclusion to be drawn from these two accommodations, or compromises, is obvious enough. If an adequate life-style and adequate working conditions can only be achieved at such considerable psychological cost, then the kind of art which will result may betray, both in its style and its content, the unease of its evolution. This is particularly true in the case of *Pilgrimage* precisely because Richardson chose the raw material of her own life as her subject.

It may certainly be objected that Richardson's diagnosis of the female artistic temperament and the evils besetting it is not sufficient evidence to demand a reappraisal of the traditional canons of literary aesthetics. Her views must, on the other hand, be considered of primary importance in evaluations of her own work, since they not only influenced, but indeed directed, both her life and work. Fromm suggests that Richardson did not achieve greatness because she could not choose between art and life[80] to the extent of submitting to the division between them and then choosing art and leaving life behind.

That is a possible, but ultimately unhelpful, interpretation – unhelpful in that it pays insufficient tribute to the unique way in which Richardson struggled to unify the divisions in her personal universe and to make coherent the experiential reality she perceived. Her greatness, if indeed greatness is a relevant term, lies elsewhere; she is one of the very few to attempt the very complex task of explicating a feminist world-view at the same time as developing a feminist aesthetic in a work of imaginative literature. The attempt may be thought misguided, even offensive, but that *Pilgrimage* enacts such an attempt is fundamental to its stature.

NOTES AND REFERENCES

1 In later life Richardson even used the name 'Amabel' to refer to the living person.
2 Originally entitled *Amabel.* See Fromm, *Dorothy Richardson,* op. cit., p. 212.
3 *Dawn's Left Hand*, pp. 174-5.
4 Ibid., pp. 186-7.
5 Loc. cit.
6 Ibid., p. 187.
7 Ibid., p. 188.
8 Loc. cit.
9 Loc. cit.
10 Ibid., p. 191.
11 This is one among many affirmations of twentieth-century phenomenalism. See, for example, W. H. Auden, *Secondary Worlds*, Faber & Faber, 1968, p. 144.
12 *Dawn's Left Hand*, p. 192.
13 Loc. cit.
14 DR to VG [no date]. In private possession.
15 *Dawn's Left Hand*, p. 196.
16 Loc. cit.
17 Ibid., p. 214.
18 Ibid., pp. 214-5.
19 Ibid., p. 217.
20 Ibid., p. 223.
21 Radclyffe Hall, *The Well of Loneliness*, Jonathan Cape, 1928, chapter 11.

22 *Dawn's Left Hand*, p. 231.

23 Interestingly, Miriam's assessment of Amabel's response to her is borne out by Veronica Grad's memory of her actual response to the young Dorothy Richardson: '. . . no one but me now can remember how *pretty* Dorothy was when I first met her – Slender & pink & white & her hair pure gold brushed back in wings each side of her face. . . . When at night she let her hair into two long plaits she was so heart-breakingly sweet I adored her. . . . I still remember how she looked her glasses off & her hair in plaits & her schoolgirl nightgown. . . .' VG to Rose Odle, Appendix, Letter 2.

24 *Dawn's Left Hand*, p. 240.

25 Ibid., p. 242.

26 Ibid., p. 243.

27 Loc. cit.

28 Ibid., p. 245.

29 Ibid., p. 246.

30 Ibid., p. 258.

31 Ibid., p. 263.

32 DR to John Cowper Powys, 29 October, 1941.

33 *Clear Horizon*, p. 284.

34 Ibid., p. 285.

35 DR to Peggy Kirkaldy, 12 August, 1936.

36 *Clear Horizon*, p. 286.

37 Ibid., p. 290.

38 Ibid., p. 291.

39 Loc. cit.

40 Ibid., p. 292.

41 Loc. cit.

42 Ibid., p. 293.

43 Ibid., p. 295.

44 Ibid., p. 300.

45 Ibid., p. 302.

46 Ibid., p. 303.

47 Ibid., p. 305.

48 Loc. cit.

49 Ibid., p. 308.

50 Ibid., p. 324.

51 Ibid., p. 325.

52 DR to John Cowper Powys, 19 November, 1935.

53 Richardson's literary estate, originally to have been executed by Owen Wadsworth, was eventually left to Rose Odle. See DR to Rose Odle, 13 February, 1951.

54 Appendix, Letter 1.
55 Loc. cit.
56 Loc. cit.
57 Loc. cit.
58 Appendix, Letter 2.
59 Appendix, Letter 9.
60 William J. MacMillan was a religious healer and author of several books, the best known of which was *The Reluctant Healer* (1952). For a time, Veronica Grad was his secretary-housekeeper and friend. Richardson also knew him and admired both the man and his work.
61 Appendix, Letter 9.
62 Appendix, Letter 13.
63 Loc. cit.
64 Loc. cit.
65 Appendix, Letter 2.
66 Loc. cit.
67 *March Moonlight*, p. 658.
68 DR to Peggy Kirkaldy, 2 March [no year; 1933?]
69 Appendix, Letter 3.
70 Appendix, Letter 10.
71 Appendix, Letter 9.
72 'The Thoroughly Popular Film', 'Continuous Performance' IX, *Close Up*, 2, April 1928, pp. 44-50.
73 Appendix, Letter 9.
74 DR to John Cowper Powys, 13 March, 1948.
75 'Women and the Future', op. cit.
76 DR to Rose Odle, 27 November, 1949.
77 DR to Louise Theis, 5 October, 1931.
78 Loc. cit.
79 'Women in the Arts', published in *Vanity Fair*, May 1925. This argument is developed from a previous article, also for *Vanity Fair* (April, 1924), in which she claimed 'It is because she is so completely *there* that she draws men like a magnet.'
80 Fromm, *Dorothy Richardson*, op. cit., p. 395.

APPENDIX

Correspondence between Veronica Grad and Rose Isserlis Odle

This correspondence is collected here for the first time. Veronica Grad's letters to Rose Odle are held by the Beinecke Rare Books and Manuscript Library, Yale University. They were lodged there with considerable misgiving by Rose Odle, as is clear from the explanatory note she appended to them. Rose Odle's letters to Veronica Grad are in private hands.

Many of the letters are undated. They are ordered in what appears to be their correct sequence, although it is clear that some letters are missing.

ROSE ODLE'S NOTE, SENT WITH VERONICA GRAD'S LETTERS

April 2nd. 1968.
Upper Landour, 11, Sunningvale Avenue, Biggin Hill, Kent, England.

These letters reached me after the death of Dorothy M. Richardson author of 13 novels that make up 'Pilgrimage'.

They were written by Veronica Grad, the 'Amabel' of the novels, widow of Benjamin Grad, 'Michael Shatov' of the novels.

D.M.R. left instructions that the following were to be informed of her death:

Rose Odle (sister-in-law)
Phillip Batchelor (nephew)
Bryher – the historical novelist who was a great friend and to whose help and encouragement Dorothy owed so much.
David Grad, son of Veronica and Benjamin.

Permission to quote from these letters must be obtained from [Veronica Grad's executors].

I bequeath these letters to the University of Yale, asking that they shall not be made available to the public, except by my special request, until after my death, and with permission [of my executors].

Origin

On Monday, June 17th, 1957 at 7 a.m. a telephone call from Phillip Batchelor told me of Dorothy Richardson's death. I had last seen her the Friday before, when she was barely conscious and did not know me, and was not surprised.

At eight o'clock, the same morning, I received another call: a woman's voice, in great distress, accused Dorothy of having ruined her life, and continued in this strain for several minutes.

The owner rang again the next day, saying her long friendship had brought her so much happiness that everything had been worthwhile, and she talked on, alternately blaming and eulogising D., in a mystifying, and to me, upsetting way.

The next day, she rang again, asking, 'could she have D.'s wedding ring? The Odles had been hard up: Benjamin and Veronica had bought the ring and given them a cheque.

I consulted Phillip Batchelor, and we rang up the Nursing Home, but her body had been taken away by an undertaker, to go, as instructed by Dorothy, to a hospital. Neither the undertaker nor the matron of the Home, had noticed the ring. The hospital no longer had the body, it had gone to a research laboratory. Here finally we traced it, with the ring still on the finger, and it was posted to me. I sent it to Veronica Grad, and received another long call, thanking me, with a more coherent account of the passionate friendship, also a request. Might she call, with her son? They came, the mother of 72, the son 49.

I had expected to see an excitable, perhaps hysterical woman, but she was rather quiet, leaving David to do the talking. Her face was thin and lined, with good bones, and the tall slim figure, in severely elegant costume, a quick, expressive look in her eyes, all this was attractive and suggested great beauty in her youth. . . .

I told them biographers had asked me for details about her [Dorothy's] early life, but that I could give them little not to be found in the novels, and that Mrs Grad was the nearest to a contemporary I had met who could help.

David said roughly, 'Why should people want to know'? and clamped down firmly on any possible remarks by his mother, who signed to me, putting a finger to her lips.

Vera, as she asked me to call her, did help, however, coming twice to see me, speaking freely, and writing these letters. She was, as would be expected of a friend of D.'s, perceptive and intelligent. I liked her very much. As you will see by the letters, the shock of death had made her take stock of herself, leave no longer any bitterness, but memory of a relationship that had enriched her life.

As we sat in the garden, on a day of sunshine, looking across at the hills, an air of joyousness came over her, I could see the laughing Amabel of the novels.

My own impression of the friendship that in 30 years had been so close that they seemed to live their own and each other's lives, could not go on so. Dorothy, a creative writer, had resources that shut Veronica out. Montaigne said, 'Help people with your shoulder, not with your liver and your guts.

The utter devotion of Veronica had become a burden.

[*Handwritten note*] I did not probe for any information about personal relationships – V. wanted to give it – & talked to me. I was enquiring for factual information – I had so little to go on re D's early life.

LETTER 1

VG to RO *undated* [*1957*]

Dear Rose,

Your note with the ring came this morning. Thank you very much for all the trouble you've taken.

It's fantastic – you've often I'm sure seen Dorothy's hand as she talked stretched out with a cigarette with it on her finger – It always made a vivid picture to me that somehow holds all the other endless pictures and today in an odd way my hand has looked to me like Dorothys – as if she were still close – I'm not being morbid but I'm not a brainy person & I can't work things out – but I do know that even after she married Alan we still were part of each other – even in these last years after we both had shingles & I had to go on being active & she gave up it was still a queer kind of partnership that briefly she recognized when I visited her & now I've a bit lost.

Once down at Hillside we were talking & I said – 'You know Dorothy I suppose I've always been a bit jealous of you of your life' & she said 'But Vera, *I've* always been jealous of you!' – We weren't really – we both had a deep admiration for the thing each other was in some ways we both would have liked to live the others life – We were in some way I don't understand more 'lovers' than we ever could be to any man – & Dorothy loved Alan & I loved someone too – but it wasn't I know to either of us what *we* were – Its been an odd business & while I'm so glad shes away at last for her – I feel sort of cheated because I've got to go on living still – oh I expect it sounds crazy or silly – but I think perhaps you *may* understand I'm glad Edel will do the book I think Dorothy would *like* a book done, but I'm glad *not* Kay Dick – Affectionately

Vera

[*Note in margin of first page*] Again please do come one of these days to T[unbridge] W[ells] –

Letter 2
VG to RO *undated* [*1957*]

I wrote this just before your letter came so I send it —
at 2 Lansdown Road
Tunbridge Wells

Dear Rose,

I feel I just must write to say 'thank you' for being so perfectly sweet to me when we came to see you the other day – and for the trouble you have taken for me – I've meant to each evening & never got round to it, you see I am still really working – After David's wife left him a series of housekeepers had done their worst – Its true they have to be both housekeeper & shop assistant & its not easy to get any one who can do both, its not like running a grocery store – So I took over – I live nearby & go in every day at nine & run the house & shop (David is out all day attending sales & I leave him an evening meal ready & get back here about 7 pm. generally too tired to do anything but flop – The whole house is a 'show room' & its pretty hard work keeping it up to scratch – Hence the delay –

While we were talking I kept thinking that no one but me now can remember how *pretty* Dorothy was when I first met her – Slender & pink & white & her hair pure gold brushed back in wings each side of her face – the dentists insisted on her wearing black – She wore little cheap black frocks with lace collars but for 'going out' she had a period frock – 'moyen age' – When at night she let her hair into two long plaits she was so heartbreakingly sweet I adored her – fragile, overworked underfed – & nearly always gaie I mean *alive* – but always so tired. Her vitality was so low that just my superabundance of it often was just more than she could take altho' she drew from it too – Sometimes in the evening I'd be full of my days doings at the RADA or a love affair, anything – & she say 'Not tonight Vera – I'm too *tired*' Then I'd just put her to bed like a child – I still remember how she looked her glasses off & her hair in plaits & her schoolgirl nightgown.

It is of that period I missed all the pictures that and a bit before I knew her – Perhaps she destroyed them herself – 'unsophisticated' was the word for Dorothy at the time I first knew her – In almost every way we were exact opposites and yet even then she had a 'hard core' – of course her amazing brain – a queer tenacity of purpose in other things besides her writing.

The night the man *I* loved died suddenly – we slept in the same bed & I wept & wept & towards morning – both of us exhausted Dorothy suddenly said 'Vera, *now* you can marry Benjamin' & I remember saying 'Yes' – because what I had really said when in the book she makes me say – 'I would I would & have his beadyeyed children' I had added 'but not while

Philip is alive' – It was half in jest but she knew I would for *her* – if she asked me & she did, & I did, & Benjamin knew why I married him & so you see in a way she was quite right in feeling David was hers in a way he was – Benjamin loved Dorothy, but he wanted to marry anyway & above all he wanted a son – I never pretended – to be in love with my husband – but in the end he grew v. jealous of Dorothy & me – & then our lives seperated [*sic*] because she went to live at 32 – & met Alan – & Alan didn't like me very much anyway altho' I did him – I didn't mean to write all this but you were so sweet to me on Wed: Burn it won't you?

Affectionately Veronica

[*Note in margin*] Don't forget you've *promised* to come and see us – We'd both David & me like it so much.

LETTER 3
RO to VG *undated* [*1957*]

Upper Landour
11 Sunningvale Avenue
Biggin Hill
Kent
Biggin Hill 0370

Dear Vera,

Thank you so much for your letter. I'm so sorry to bother you about a receipt but would you mind just dropping a *card* or note saying you had received it, which I can forward to her nephew? Until probate he feels he has to account to her executors (Coutts) for possessions

I find the description of Dorothy young fascinating.

Now can you add anything of interest re the Dorothy Wells affair. ANYTHING. (so long as not libellous!) I lunched at Brown's Hotel with a Professor Ray from Illinois University who is doing a book on Wells with the permission of the Wells family.

I think he was disappointed that I had no letters from Wells in the mss. But I promised to get into touch with anyone who knew D. at the time.

So if you can do let me have such soon.

I *do* understand about the relationship. The day I left Hillside after I had been nursing her, I knew if I did not go then, I would never get away.

Now I want permission from you to copy out & have typed the description of the young Dorothy, & IF any BBC Memorial (v. doubtful) comes off to quote it. No one else I know has anything of the kind.

Yes my dear, I really will come. I wish I lived nearer & would give you a hand with the shop. It is a great deal to do. I cannot write more – still have seven letters to write this morning. And don't worry about the letter – I won't keep it, except for description as above. We *will* keep in touch.

With love

Rose

LETTER 4
VG to RO *undated* [*1957*]

2 Lansdown Road
Tunbridge Wells

My dear Rose,

I am so sorry I haven't answered your letter before, it must have seemed rude of me, but I didn't mean to be. Please forgive me. –

Partly you see, you started me 'remembering' & I came to the conclusion that I just can't remember bits unless I remember it all – I have no gift of speech & as Dorothy used sometimes to tell me my vocabulary is limited in the extreme but – mostly for David's sake I think I'm going to have a shot (it mayn't come off) of getting all this exceedingly odd life of mine down on paper But in the meanwhile if you like I'll do from when I met Dorothy to when we parted company first and you can sort out what you like.

I *do* know (& it fits in) a gt deal about Dorothy & HG – but I am quite sure nothing that you would think *proper* to pass on – but I've a feeling that it would do *me* good anyway to see how it looks to me – in perspective – I think I owe you an apology for when David and I came to see you – I know you saw me check him when you mentioned Mac – I realized you knew nothing of the saga of Dorothy & me & Mac – it went on for several years – You see, Mac had a clinic in St Johns Wood two minutes from 32 – & I lived with him & was his sec: Receptionist & ran his 'home life' & it was a very close association – & oddly repetitive of the grouping of me and Dorothy & my husband – It wasn't that I wanted to keep anything from you – but I just felt it was not the moment somehow –

His sudden death almost at the same time as my husbands took it out of me rather – Its been such a lot of deaths recently – for a couple of days, Gilbert Murray's bowled me over completely too – Now I'm, after all, so old myself it seems unreasonable that I've got to watch everyone else go first or be compelled to realize that I am comparatively young –

Dear Rose, unless reincarnation is the answer, it does all seem too futile for words – but I imagine that that *is* the answer & I don't like it much –

Looking forward to seeing you in Aug –

Yours v Sincerely

Vera

But my name really is Veronica did you know? –

LETTER 5
RO to VG

24.8.57

Upper Landour
11, Sunningvale Avenue
Biggin Hill
Kent
Biggin Hill 0370

24. VIII. 57

Dear Vera,

I enclose copies of 2 letters from Leon Edel. He is one of the most famous critics of to-day. Now we can stop worrying about any inferior writers. Needless to say, I am cooperating in every way. In fact I have a bump on my index finger due to the at least 100 letters written since June 17.

Now is spite of what he says about reminiscences I *am* asking people for such (I include copies of some that may interest you) because D's contemporaries are not young, nor am I and [*sic*], & we may all be in that silent & private place where none of us may be contacted later!

Now my dear, don't worry about any vulgarising: that is impossible with a man like Edel. Would you be kind enough to do a little vignette of the young Dorothy? You did do something of the kind in an earlier letter – something that can be used to build up a picture of her? And anything you like to write that will not cause you grief in the writing. I, & I don't exaggerate in saying: posterity will be grateful.

Secondly: if you have any letters of Dorothy's they have a value. Later I am offering mine to Yale University. I have already had suggestions from New York & Illinois Universities – but I know Bryher & Hilda Aldington have bequeathed theirs to Yale, & I think it would be good to have them together. Will you think it over? I won't be sending mine till later. They house them in a special room, always available to students, & they pay for them. *Thirdly* Do you know anything about Bernice Elliot? There are some old letters from her in America.

My letter in the Times has put me in touch with E.B.C. Lucas (formerly Jones – author of Quiet Interior) and Mrs Ruth Pollard. These with Peggy Kirkalday [*sic*] and Pauline Marrian, J.C. Powys – make up letters so far – hundreds – that I am having typed with 3 carbon copies. If you have any letters you *could* lend (the letters are your property, the copyrights mine) I should be very grateful.

I have been very tired: reading through hundreds of letters, on top of chores, garden, visitors etc. But after advertising, I have now a woman, a retired nurse, living in the bottom bungalow, who in return for no rent, is looking after me & seeing to chores. I really felt almost unable to carry on after this busy period since D. died. I've also done three BBC scripts – (I shall be on the air on Wed 28th at 4.45 – see R. Times). Now I hope to hear from you – please return carbons.

Trust me re editing of anything you send in, & we can trust Edel. I saw an agent Mark Paterson, who had contacted me earlier, yesterday & he thinks it worth while to try a collection of stories for U.S.A. I am more doubtful but am getting them together & getting them typed. To date have spent £15 – 10 on typing & £5 on photo of latter! No joke! Wouldn't mind getting a bit back from the States.

Now I do hope to see you before I go back to town in October. Meanwhile to hear from you.

Yours affectionately & greetings to David,
Rose

[*Written above the address on the first page*] Do you know why she called Alan Sergeant?

LETTER 6
RO to VG

29.9.57

Upper Landour, 11 Sunningvale Avenue,
Biggin Hill, Kent Biggin Hill 0370
(If no answer from 0370 try 0913 (i.e. lower Bungalow)

Dear Vera,

How are you?

I have had hundreds of letters in, but no one knows anything of the *young* D.M.R. I have been asked to do a talk on her to a little club I belong to in Kensington on Oct 11th. I shall be here only till about Mid-October, & till then, be Thursday & Friday until Sat. a.m. every week end in town. Is there any possibility of your coming over before – I do so much want your help & would anyway like to see you very much. If you & David can manage I can always do lunch, & as you suggest he could pick you up later. It will be April 1958 before I shall be here again!

So have a think & let me know.

Do hope you are keeping well & not overtired. I've had a bout of pleurisy, & one of Asian flu. But survived!

With love
Rose

LETTER 7
RO to VG *23.11.57*

14 Westbourne Grove Terrace
London, W.2
Bayswater 4666

23. XI. 57

Dear Vera,

How are you? Could you get here. I am here until Dec. 31. Now I have some money in hand for expenses for all this D.M.R. business from a friend of hers. Would you let me pay for your train – & taxi to & from Ch.X & give you lunch – if you will spare me a day here?

You are the only one of Ds friends who knew her when she was young. I shall be 70 in Feb. & I leave England for some months on Dec. 31st. I do want to get all the material for Edel's biography (Did you see the wonderful notices – a whole 1st page in Times Lit. Sup – for his last book 'Literary Biography') – sent before I leave. He is a great man – the best living biographer one could have; the soul of kindness & discretion. And really, I have not, apart from the letters, much biog. matter to give him.

Do try, it would be a last act of goodness to Dorothy. You know in a letter to the Powys' she wrote, reluctant as she was to meet them, thinking authors were better unknown to readers as persons in their lifetime – she yet wrote 'But let truth be served.'

I have had in some hundreds of letters – & some I think you would enjoy.

I send Edel the scripts (have sent 8 pkts so far including photostats) & have the carbons here.

This room – a 'little everywhere' is rather a lark, & fun to see. I've made a flat in a room 10 x 12 feet. I'd love you to see it. And just opposite, if I don't feel like cooking, I can take you to a realy [*sic*] well cooked meal. Have a day out, & come! Only hope you are keeping fit enough for such.
My regards to David.

With Love
Rose (Odle)

Plan enclosed

Tell taxi-man Westbourne Grove Terrace is 3rd turning after Queen's Cinema in Westbourne Grove.

[*sketch plan follows*]

14 is last house on left *Ring bottom bell* twice
I believe Wednesday or Sunday are good days for you – and for me.

Drop a line.

With love
Rose.

Letter 8
RO to VG *3.12.57*

14 Westbourne Grove Terrace
London, W.2
Bayswater 4666

3. XII. 57

Dear Vera,

Are you alright? I did write asking if you could spend a day here. I do hope you were not offended by my offer of expenses – but my dear I have been subsidised *just for this purpose* – everything in connection with the biography. Philip Batchelor her nephew inherited the estate (quite a bit, as it turned out) but the friend who helped Dorothy so much in her later years, is helping me to deal with all this literary executive expense. (No light matter – I have sent 8 parcels of letters & photostats so far to Leon Edel in America) I would love to see you before I go to Lisbon on the 31st December. But if it is quite impossible, could you write a few lines about D. as a *young* woman. No one I have met so far knew her as such. Also do you know the identities of 'Jan' & 'Mag' in the Tunnel – & have you remembered who Winifred Ray was? I am sorry to bother you but feeling very exhausted myself, do want to get everything possible sent to Leon Edel before I go away. I can't get out at all in this cold, and until I get into warmer climate am a prisoner. I just collapse in cold.

Are you alright? I know you are not strong. Would David care to do a few lines – impressions – I could send? Now I don't want to worry you, so if this is harassing, or wearying, let it go. But drop a line how you are & how things are with you. If I may, I hope to call on you in the spring. With love Rose Odle

[*Note in margin*] Greetings to David – Such lovely references to him in her letters.

Letter 9
VG to RO *undated*

Dear Rose, I am really sorry to have caused you to write a second letter because of my delay in answering – forgive – No of course I wasnt 'offended' but I have been having a difficult time & the days flew & I didnt realize & as with you the truly dreadful weather didnt help – But I *have* been thinking & I believe am now clear in my own mind – I do not think I can do anything less than write the whole story as I see it – I am not, and never have been, interested in Dorothy's writings as literature – But

Dorothy herself her *life* more. I remember & look at it from the objective point of view that I *can* now take is interesting & it is *my* life, my husband's & childrens – and Rose the picture that emerges is not very pleasing. Dorothy may have been a literary pioneer but what I see is that her books (which I only vaguely remember & haven't read since they were first published) are as damming [*sic*] a picture of personality as were ever written – I have at last seen her as she really was – I loved her but Dorothy never for one moment 'loved' anyone but herself. Not even Alan – not anyway as I see love – Dorothy never paid any prices. She took an avid interest in other people their lives, their misfortunes, their successes, but she never – looking back I see – gave either sympathy or help – or let herself become in any way involved – I am not thinking only of myself. I call to mind a dozen examples of utter self-protective ruthlessness – Her own sisters – Florence Daniel – Jane Wells – Lissie Beresford – Benjamin – my own children. Maybe it was all worth it as a sacrifice to her 'Art' I can't judge of that – You think she loved David, she did in a way. I think she *thought* she did. I even am able to believe she thought she loved me – but first everyone was 'copy' material not only for books but for stimulation for Dorothy – You know she was rather like a vivisectionist in her attitude to us all – but, I cant see myself that the handful of pioneer books makes it any less ugly – The picture Dorothy built up of her marriage to Alan was one of devotion & sacrifice. Alans life was prolonged, he was a Reformed Character. Dorothy mothered & took care of him. Now – my picture is different it always was this is no sudden verdict – Alan was always referred to as 'Dorothy's husband' – Prince Consort in fact. Years ago Mac & I realized that what her marriage did for Dorothy was to open up all sorts of possibilities – enable her to meet all manner of people that to many of them – (I could give names but I wont) she was 'Alan Odles wife' that lots of them frequented 32 quite as much for Alan as for Dorothy – that Alan, who did truly love & admire her & who was certainly quite as talented as she was & quite as cultured – provided her with a background & a setting and an atmosphere that were beyond price to her – & at a price of self effacement & devotion that is very rare – We all make pictures of ourselves – Dorothy was no exception – but most of us I think in time, anyway in bits, see through our self deception As far as I know Dorothy never did, or of her pictures of other people – Everyone was neatly labeled & there we stayed – We might grow & change & develop – but it didn't fit into Dorothy's picture & wasnt so – It is not my idea to put any of this into what I propose to write – all I want to do is write what happened *as* it happened & certainly without any emotional feelings – It will take time & as yet I don't see how I am going to *get* the time. Its *my* life I want to write but as quite thirty years of it was so much Dorothy's its hers (as a person not an authoress) too. If I can do it, I'll let you or someone say like Richard Church? read it & decide whether its any good or not to anyone –

At the moment, I don't see my way – but if I *am* to do it, I will, and if I do it ought to be done by the time you get back to England – I have talked to David about it & he agrees with me about this – & he appears to think that in spite of my age I can do it, & he is usually my most critical judge –

I accept cleverer peoples judgement that Dorothy's work justifies all this interest in her – but I myself can't see it – First I loved her – unquestioningly – whole mindedly – later on I loved her for the love I had had for her – I remember Mac (the healer) telling me that the business of Dorothy & me was quite the most astonishing story example of enduring and unrequited love he had ever heard or read of – He went further; when Dorothy had her attack of shingles & four days later I had it too he saw some connection between these two events – I had it in its worst form – nearly died, & was in hospital for nine weeks – & still suffer from its after affects – This I do not pretend to understand but I am ready to believe that he knew what he was talking about. After Alan died he went down to Dorothy & came back & and asked me to go – which I did – she was in a pretty bad way & he had not been able to break through & he thought I might & partially I did – but as you know from then on – Dorothy never did any more real work – Lacking Alan –

Much affection & I hope you'll have a lovely time in Lisbon –
Yours really affectionately
Vera

Oh yes – I knew those two girls one was a German girl – from a Prussian officer sort of family – they both had jobs sort of sec: work. Their relationship was much like D's & mine only less so. J. was the intellectual one. M – a pretty fluffy – I don't remember their names. I suppose I'll have to read the books again. I've been trying to remember that girl who married Benjamins friend the one that died of T.B. then later she isnt in the books there was that Russian girl who killed herself in the YWCA at St [*continued in margin*] Johns Wood – two more examples of Dorothys completely uninvolved interest in other peoples tragic lives – There were so many young girls who 'fell for' Dorothy – I don't mean that in any not nice way – I wish for your help I could think of anyone still alive who knew D before her marriage.

Letter 10
RO to VG

undated

My dear,

I feel what it costs you to write. But if you can throw off the past by putting it down, it may be well worth while. I appreciate your experiences of D's 'not being involved'.

They spent a week as our guests every summer. In 1932, when my life broke up (I had 18 wretched and difficult years, & a family to support alone for most of that time), I tried to tell D something. 'I don't want to know.'

I neither wrote nor heard from either of them till 1948, when I wrote first after Alan's death – which I saw announced in the Times.

When she had shingles Miss Simmons & Owen begged me to come, & I was nursing her, & posted the card she wrote to you

The Russian girl's last card to D is here – Vera Sokolov.

Now I hope to see you when I get back – & have a long talk – but before then there is one thing I cannot discover – & Philip Batchelor (who has done pretty well out of the estate – he is her heir) does not know, & that is *where* (& if) they married? Do you know. There are no marriage lines in her belongings.

So if you do, will you drop a line in the enclosed? I am sending main biog. details to Edel (who is the soul of discretion and kindly – has written a brilliant little book on 'Literary Biography' – just out).

I hope Christmas will bring you a rest, & the writing if you do it, ease of mind. Greet David for me, & keep a good heart until we meet again. I shall be back at the end of February. I will write from Lisbon. Yours sincerely & affectionately
Rose

[*Note in margin*] Thank you for information re Jan & Mag. V useful.

LETTER 11
VG to RO *undated*

Dear Rose, yes I knew *you'd* know that what I wrote was true – thank you for your letter – I am at the moment in bed with flue [*sic*] – getting better – Oh yes – they were married at night – Alan had just been exempted from Mil. Service he had to go before a tribunal & was so obviously fragile & useless from a *Mil.* point of view that they exempted him. They were married from 32 Q. Ter. at a Reg: Office – they had no money at all & just amalgamated their two rooms which ajoined [*sic*] each other – I had two small children & we decided that (I mean Dorothy & I did) B & I would not go over, but Benjamin gave her as large a cheque as we could manage & when she said they couldn't afford a ring I paid for it – they must have been married I think in a nearby Reg. office – unless it was at St Pancras T. Hall but surely one can get marriage certificates like birth ones can't one? – It was earlyish in the first war – Soon after that they went to Cornwall. Alan not expected to live long & D completely shattered by war conditions in London – we were living in Stamford Hill – Benjamin was in the Home Guard doing sentry duty most nights at Blackwall Tunnel. It was just then I discovered what Dorothy had known all along that Benjamin had been in a lunatic asylum in Basle at the age of 20 – for over a year & had not told me anything about it before I married him. It was an old story. Don't think I am in the least bitter I'm not – I simply see it all more of a fascinating study in psycology [*sic*] both of her & me –

Love & best wishes Vera

Letter 12
RO to VG *2.6.58*

Upper Landour
11, Sunningvale Avenue
Biggin Hill
Kent
Biggin Hill 0370

2. VI. 58

Dear Vera

How are you ? I hope better than you were. I came back from Tangier to Spring, as I thought – & arrived for snow, cold, rain & what have you. Now I hate to bother you, I feel you want to leave all the D.M.R. business alone – but just two things I have been asked for :

'Winifred Ray' – you said you & David knew, but could not recall. Can you now?

And who was Selina Holland? If you cannot recollect the names, can you give any details?

To save you time & energy I enclose an addressed card.

The country is very lovely here, and I am keeping my lower bungalow *unlet* for ever I hope (after a very unpleasant experience with an ex-nurse) & free for family & friends. So if you ever want a couple of days 'off' – there's a good bed, c. hot water, all cons – you make your own breakfast – get up when you like – join me for other meals – otherwise – liberty. Its just that [it] is so lovely here, & so restful – I like giving people who are very occupied – a little break – counting my blessings in having the place.

Kindest regards to yourself & David. If you can bear it, hope to see you & him here sometime – any day you feel like a run.

Yours sincerely
Rose Odle

[*Note in margin*] Peggy Kirkaldy died on 29th – Did you know her?

LETTER 13
VG to RO *undated*

2 Lansdowne Road

Dear Rose, Forgive that I haven't answered you sooner – I was away for three days with my daughter – *Do* I remember S. Holland! Her real name was Moffatt. If she is still alive she must be over 90 – She was an evening class teacher for the L.C.C. – she must have been round about forty. *Very* proper – & spinsterish – Dorothy met her because she was also a member of the Arachne Club where I was a resident – They were both, I don't know how you say – outside members – I imagine for them both it was somewhere where they could invite people – It was for Dorothy – It was for Miss M. also exceedingly dashing. Miss Moffatt deceived by Dorothys being a dentists sec. & her modest apperance [*sic*] suggested their sharing – to Miss M's horror Dorothy blossomed out, as to her, everything undesirable – I suppose she was forced to be very mean, her economies *were* a sort of pride to her – She was always *angry* in her outlooks – She made her own blouses – she always wore a neat blouse & skirt, she was a big woman – If you saw her setting off to her job in the evening – shed tell you 'Ive broken the back of that blouse I've been making' meaning she'd got over the worst of the job, nearly finished – she set her teeth at everything & battled on – She was worried about me – did – with much embarassment [*sic*] & from a real sense of duty – her best to warn me of D's lack of moral sense. What got her down was D having an affair 'with a married man' – She had curious morals really – when I told her that sofar [*sic*] from being myself a well brought up ('*obviously* a gentlewoman, how your parents came to *allow* you to go in for the theatrical profession! !') I was at 20, only living at the Club to be near my lover thirty years my senior she advised me to give it all up & she would help me to emigrate & find a husband 'who would never know' – she didn't seem to be so shocked by me as by Dorothy – *I* had obviously been 'led astray by an elderly roué' – She was disgusting & mean & ugly from D's point of view but she was rather a dear too. D left Endsliegh [*sic*] Street to go & share with her & when it didn't work went back to Endsliegh Street & I left the Club & went there too – But Rose *why* do you want to know who people were what poss: interest can it be to anyone? And you know, my dear you've got me all wrong too – I have no desire to forget anything – I have not been harrowed by my recollections of Dorothy. Most of my mememories [*sic*] are painful – but one doesn't do any good by 'forgetting all about it' – *So* you lose all you've learnt in life. Dorothys death jerked me into making a real effort to *understand* to arrive at a true assessment of cause & affect [*sic*] & consequences – gain & loss – very much like – a bank statement 'reconcilliation' [*sic*] Bookkeeping I've found fascinating & I've found this sort of spiritual bookkeeping fascinating too – painful but worth it all the time – I am not in the accepted sense religious or a Christian – but I was born with a religious temperament just as other people are born musical etc. & the other one of the odd ways in which D & I were twins – no two halves, was that while D was & according to J.C.P. quite rightly a complete egoist – & he may be right at that, too, I was born without any glimmer of how to be one. My besetting sin of unselfishness has done more harm than I can begin to tell you to many people. You can't imagine how 'viciously' unselfish I am – not by trying or because I think it a virtue but because I can't *help* it – There is of course another name for it – as any analyst knows –

My dear – your invitation is most kind – but when ever I do get away I go to Rachel – & that v. seldom –

Oh – Winifred Ray – I don't like to be certain, but I know she was quite young & I think she was the girl who did the automatic drawings – so does David, but why don't you ask Pauline – she'll maybe remember – Dorothy so often told me of this or that young person – she was apt to get wildly enthusiastic about – & I just didn't pay much attention – Pauline might know – but I can't imagine why she hasn't turned up among the letters she was of the later St Merryn period – during or just after the last war – Much affection – & forgive so long a letter –
Veronica

[*Note in margin*] Perhaps I ought to apologize for not being able to spell – as you perhaps notice – I personally can't see that it matters – & if I was treating you as a stranger I'd use a dic: & keep my lines straight & all that – However if you *do* mind please forgive.

Letter 14
RO to VG *8.10.58*

14 Westbourne Grove Terrace
London W2
Bayswater 4666

8.10.58

Dear Vera,

I hope your week away was a rest and a pleasant change. Now I want you to stop worrying about all this D.M.R. business.

She herself wrote in a letter to one she was reluctant to meet 'Nevertheless let truth be served.' I have made this my motto. And Edel knows what you have endured, what you felt, and what ensued. Since her life is bound to be written about, it is fortunate that a man of his calibre will do it.

I found him a pleasant, quiet modest person – nothing pompous or professional about him – very perceptive & understanding.

He stayed from 1 – to 4.30, & I stretched my mind in response to his. I said to him, 'This is a release for me; I have been living the life of another – D.M.R. for the last year, and I want to get back to my own life. Did you feel like that when working on the Henry James books?'

He answered 'No – I dare not let myself be possessed – I had to be completely detached. But then you see it was easier for me – I was not *involved*'.

Of course that was the point.

Altogether a man to be trusted.

Now I shall feel easier when I know you can let all this go from your mind. I have thought so much about you; I have handed over to E. *hundreds* of letters – paens of praise, almost adoration – that came in reply to my letter in the Times Lit. And all the time – the undercurrent in my mind, as in yours, of the tough streak in D. Mind, I think she mellowed in old age. But writers, all writers, I think are suspect – because they are so articulate – always *having* the *word*. My dear, write to me. (No living person will be named in the book) I have had a great responsibility. I have tried to do the right thing – & now I want to think you are released from black memories. Actually the book will be mostly critical; it is the literary values that concern E; but what can be known of events, it is only fair that he should know.

Bless you,
With love,

Rose

LETTER 15
VG to RO *undated* [*16 October, 1958*]

F.E.W. Florence E Worland – Tolstoyan soc: (Florence Daniel) Editress of 'Healthy Life' – 'The Crank' comes in to the party Dor: gave at the Club the first night we met for the first time remember? –
J.H.B. Harry Badcock [*sic*] her dentist employer
Winifred Ray This is awful both David & I clearly remember a period when we were always hearing from D about 'Winifred' & we just *cant* remember *what*! I am tempted to attach her name to various personalities that I listened to without much interest. D & I kept saying 'was she the one who?'
I may click but I mayn't
[*Note in margin*] if I do I'll tell you. She's a later period than mine –
Love Vera

[*On front of postcard*] Florence & Charlie Daniel Dorothy & me a whole chapter of my life – Florence died of cancer – Charlie was always thought of as single lad. *You* know 'David' – They had one son whom they called Henry George in memory. – Flor: & I remained friends till her death but she & D: parted company long before.
I'll write a letter one of these days.
Love V.

BIBLIOGRAPHY

Much of the material used for this study consists of unpublished correspondence and papers to which access is difficult. Some of this, however, is reproduced in the *Supplement* to *Feminist Consciousness: A Study of the Work of Dorothy Miller Richardson,* D.Phil. thesis, by Gillian E. Hanscombe, lodged in the Bodleian Library, Oxford. The letters to E. B. C. Jones and S. S. Koteliansky are held by the manuscript department of the British Library. The bulk of the correspondence and unpublished papers cited in this text is held by the Beinecke Rare Book and Manuscript Library, Yale University.

A UNPUBLISHED PAPERS OF DOROTHY MILLER RICHARDSON CITED IN THIS TEXT

'Literary Essays' (autograph manuscript draft of an essay on her development as a writer; 2 pp.).

'Sussex Period' (autograph manuscript notes on her artistic development and the feminist movement; 8 pp.).

B PUBLISHED WRITINGS OF DOROTHY MILLER RICHARDSON

1 *Autobiography*

'Beginnings: A Brief Sketch', in *Ten Contemporaries: Notes Toward Their Definitive Bibliography*, Second series, ed. John Gawsworth, Joiner & Steele, London, 1933.

'Data for Spanish Publisher', ed. Joseph Prescott, *London Magazine*, 6, June 1959, pp.14-19.

2 *Non-Fiction and Prefaces*

The Quakers Past and Present, Constable, London; Dodge, New York, 1914.

Gleanings from the Works of George Fox, Headley, London, 1914.

John Austen and the Inseparables, William Jackson, London, 1930.

Black, E. L., *Why Do They Like It?* Educational Documents I, Paris, 1927, pp. ix-x.

Dumas, F. Ribadeau, *These Moderns: Some Parisian Close-Ups*, trans. Frederic Whyte, Humphrey Toulmin, London, 1932, pp. 5-10.

3 *Pilgrimage*

FIRST EDITIONS

Pointed Roofs, Introduction by J.D. Beresford, Duckworth, London, 1915.

Backwater, Duckworth, London, 1916.

Honeycomb, Duckworth, London, 1917.

The Tunnel, Duckworth, London, February 1919.

Interim, Duckworth, London, December 1919.

Deadlock, Duckworth, London, 1921.

Revolving Lights, Duckworth, London, 1923.

The Trap, Duckworth, London, 1925.

Oberland, Duckworth, London, 1927.

Dawn's Left Hand, Duckworth, London, 1931.

Clear Horizon, J.M. Dent & The Cresset Press, London, 1935.

COLLECTED EDITIONS

Pilgrimage, including *Dimple Hill*, 4 vols., J.M. Dent & The Cresset Press, London; Alfred A. Knopf, New York, 1938.

Pilgrimage, including *March Moonlight*, Introduction by Walter Allen, 4 vols., J.M. Dent & Sons, London; Alfred A. Knopf, New York, 1967.

Pilgrimage, Introduction by Walter Allen, 4 vols., Popular Library, New York, 1967.

Pilgrimage, Introduction by Gillian E. Hanscombe, 4 vols., Virago, London, 1979.

TRANSLATIONS

Pointed Roofs, ed. with Introduction and notes by Junzaburo Nishiwaki, Kenkyusha, Tokyo, 1934.

Toits Pointus, trans. Marcelle Sibon, Mercure de France, Paris, 1965.

4 *Periodical Publications*

The periodical publications have not to date been collected or reissued. They are listed here according to the periodicals in which they were published. The periodicals are themselves listed in alphabetical order and the items within each periodical are listed chronologically. For a bibliography arranged according to type of item (review, short story, etc.), listed chronologically, see Fromm, *Dorothy Richardson*, op. cit., pp. 426-433, which incorporates her earlier bibliography, together with Joseph Prescott's 'A Preliminary Checklist of the Periodical Publications of Dorothy M. Richardson' (1958).

ADELPHI

'About Punctuation' (essay), I, 11, April 1924, pp.990-6.

'The Parting of Wordsworth and Coleridge: A Footnote' (essay), I, 12, May 1924, pp.1107-9.

'A Note on George Fox' (essay), II, 2, July 1924, pp.148-50.

'Brothers Rabbit and Rat' (essay), II, 3, August 1924, pp.247-9.

'Disaster' (poem), II, 4, September 1924, p.277.

'A Sculptor of Dreams' (review), II, 5, October 1924, pp.422-7.

'What's in a Name?' (essay), II, 7, December 1924, pp.606-9.

'The Status of Illustrative Art' (essay), III, 1, June 1925, pp.54-7.

Theobald, R. (pseudonym), 'Why Words?' (essay), III, 3, August 1925, pp.206-7.

Theobald, R. (pseudonym), 'Spengler and Goethe: A Footnote' (essay), IV, 5, November 1926, pp.311-2.

'Portrait of an Evangelist' (review), *New Adelphi*, I, 3, March 1928, pp.270-1.

'Das Ewig-Weibliche' (review), I, 4, June 1928, pp.364-6.

'Mr Clive Bell's Proust' (review), II, 2, December 1928-February 1929, pp.160-2.

'Leadership in Marriage' (essay), II, 4, June-August 1929, pp.345-8.

'Experiments with Handwriting' (review), II, 4, June-August 1929, p.380.

'The Return of William Wordsworth' (review), New Series, I, 3, December 1930, Review Supplement, pp.xvi-xix.

'Man Never Is . . .' (review), I, 6, March 1931, pp.521-2.

AMERICAN MERCURY

'Nor Dust Nor Moth' (poem), L. 197, May 1940, p.111.

ART AND LETTERS

'Sunday' (short story), II, 3, New Series, Summer 1919, pp.113-5.

'Christmas Eve' (short story), III, 1, Winter 1920, pp.32-5.

CLOSE-UP – FOR THE FILM GOER

'Continuous Performance', I, 1, July 1927, pp. 34-7
I, 2, August 1927, pp. 58-62
I, 3, September 1927, pp. 52-6
I, 4, October 1927, pp. 60-4
I, 5, November 1927, pp. 44-7
I, 6, December 1927, pp. 61-5
II, 1, January 1928, pp. 59-64

'A Note on Household Economy', II, 2, February 1928, pp. 58-62

'Continuous Performance', II, 3, March 1928, pp. 51-5
II, 4, April 1928, pp. 44-50
II, 5, May 1928, pp. 58-62
II, 6, June 1928, pp. 54-8
III, 1, July 1928, pp. 52-7

'Films for Children', III, 2, August 1928, pp. 21-7

'Continuous Performance', IV, 1, January 1929, pp. 51-7
IV, 6, June 1929, pp. 31-7
V, 3, September 1929, pp. 211-18
'The Censorship Petition', VI, 1, January 1930, pp. 7-11
'Continuous Performance', VII, 3, September 1930, pp. 196-202
VIII, 3, September 1931, pp. 182-5
VIII, 4, December 1931, pp. 304-8
IX, 1, March 1932, pp. 36-8
X, 2, June 1933, pp. 130-2
'Review of *Documents 33*', April-August', X, 3, September 1933, pp. 295-6

CRANK: AN UNCONVENTIONAL MAGAZINE
(later called *Ye Crank* and then *Open Road*)
(except where otherwise indicated, these items are reviews)

'Days with Walt Whitman', IV, 8, August 1906, pp.259-63.
'The Reading of *The Jungle*', IV, 9, September 1906, pp.290-3.
'Jesus in Juteopolis', IV, 10, October 1906, pp.331-2.
'The Amazing Witness', IV, 10, October 1906, pp.332-4.
'In the Days of the Comet', IV, 11, November 1906, pp.372-6.
'The Odd Man's Remarks on Socialism' (essay), V, 1, January 1907, pp.30-3.
'How We Are Born', V, 1, January 1907, pp.44-7.
'Socialism and Anarchy: An Open Letter to the "Odd Man" ' (letter), V, 2, February 1907, pp.89-91.
'The Future in America', V, 2, February 1907, pp.95-9.
'Socialism and the Odd Man' (letter), V, 3, March 1907, pp.147-9.
'A Sheaf of Opinions: Lowes Dickinson's *A Modern Symposium*', V, 3, March 1907, pp.153-7.
'A Last Word to the Odd Man about Socialism' (letter), V, 4, April 1907, pp.180-2.
'A French Utopia', V, 4, April 1907, pp.209-14.
'Thearchy and Socialism' (essay), V, 5, May 1907, pp.237-9.
'Down with the Lords', V, 5, May 1907, pp.257-61.
'Notes about a Book Purporting To Be about Christianity and Socialism', V, 6, June 1907, pp.311-5.
'The Open Road' (essay), *Open Road*, New Series, I, 3, September 1907, pp.153-8.
'Nietzsche', I, 5, November 1907, pp.243-8.
'Towards the Light', I, 6, December 1907, pp.304-8.

THE DENTAL RECORD
(except where otherwise indicated, these items are essays)

'Diet and Teeth', XXXII, 8, 1 August, 1912, pp.553-6.
'The Responsibility of Dentistry', XXXIII, 10, 1 October, 1913, pp.663-5.
'Medical Austria in the Arena. The Encroaching Laity' (unsigned), XXXIV, 2, 1 February, 1914, p.143.

'Medical Austria. A Reply from "The Encroaching Laity"' (unsigned), XXXIV, 3, 2 March, 1914, pp.217-8.
'Some Thoughts Suggested by the Austro-Hungarian Problem', XXXIV, 8, 1 August, 1914, pp.519-23.
'A Plea for a Statistical Bureau', XXXV, 6, 1 June, 1915, pp.403-5.
'The Teeth of Shropshire School Children', XXXV, 9, 1 September, 1915, pp.562-4.
'Amateur Evidence in Dietetics', XXXVI, 6, 1 June, 1916, pp.300-3.
'Dental Legislation at Geneva', XXXVII, 4, 2 April, 1917, pp.161-3.
'The Forsyth Dental Infirmary for Children', XXXVII, 8, 1 August, 1917, pp.366-9.
'A Spanish Dentist Looks at Spain', XXXVIII, 8, 1 August, 1918, pp.343-5.
'Review of *Psycho-Analysis: A Brief Account of the Freudian Theory* by Barbara Low' (review), XL, 8, 2 August, 1920, pp.522-3.
'The Socialization of Dentistry', XLI, 12, 1 December, 1921, pp.611-3.
'Science and Linguistics' (unsigned), XLII, 3, 1 March, 1922, pp.149-50.

'Comments by a Layman' (an unsigned column in *The Dental Record*)

XXV, 11, 1 November, 1915, pp. 686-8
XXXV, 12, 1 December, 1915, pp. 752-4
XXXVI, 1, 1 January, 1916, pp. 33-5
XXXVI, 2, 1 February, 1916, pp. 87-9
XXXVI, 3, 1 March, 1916, pp. 140-2
XXXVI, 4, 1 April, 1916, pp. 190-2
XXXVI, 5, 1 May, 1916, pp. 247-8
XXXVI, 6, 1 June, 1916, pp. 310-12
XXXVI, 7, 1 July, 1916, pp.357-8
XXXVI, 8, 1 August, 1916, pp. 427-8
XXXVI, 10, 2 October, 1916, pp. 541-4
XXXVI, 11, 1 November, 1916, pp. 606-7
XXXVI, 12, 1 December, 1916, pp.655-7
XXXVII, 1, 1 January, 1917, pp. 19-20
XXXVII, 2, 1 February, 1917, pp. 81-2
XXXVII, 3, 1 March, 1917, pp. 119-21
XXXVII, 4, 2 April, 1917, pp. 169-71
XXXVII, 5, 1 May, 1917, pp.221-2
XXXVII, 6, 1 June, 1917, pp. 264-6
XXXVII, 7, 2 July, 1917, pp. 320-2
XXXVII, 8, 1 August, 1917, pp. 375-7
XXXVII, 9, 1 September, 1917, p. 420
XXXVII 10, 1 October, 1917, pp.483-6
XXXVII, 11, 1 November, 1917, pp. 527-9
XXXVII, 12, 1 December, 1917, pp. 577-9
XXXVIII, 1, 1 January, 1918, pp. 13-15
XXXVIII, 2, 1 February, 1918, pp.62-4
XXXVIII, 3, 1 March, 1918, pp. 110-12
XXXVIII, 4, 1 April, 1918, pp. 161-3
XXXVIII, 5, 1 May, 1918, pp. 214-5

XXXVIII, 6, 1 June, 1918, pp.262-4
XXXVIII, 8, 1 August, 1918, pp. 350-2
XXXVIII, 9, 2 September, 1918, pp. 391-2
XXXVIII, 10, 1 October, 1918, pp. 427-9
XXXVIII, 11, 1 November, 1918, pp. 427-3
XXXVIII, 12, 1 December, 1918, pp. 509-10
XXXIX, 1, 1 January, 1919, pp. 10-11
XXXIX, 2, 1 February, 1919, pp. 57-8
XXXIX, 3, 1 March, 1919, pp. 99-101
XXXIX, 4, 1 April, 1919, pp. 136-8
XXIX, 5, 1 May, 1919, pp. 178-80
XXXIX, 6, 1 June, 1919, pp. 214-16

ENGLISH STORY
(the following items are short stories)
'Tryst', Second Series, 1941, pp.69-73.
'Excursion', Sixth Series, 1945, pp.107-12.
'A Stranger About', Ninth Series, 1949, pp.90-4

EVENING NEWS (London)
'Where is Miss Jameson's Suburbia?' (essay), 2 October, 1928, p.8.

FANFARE
'The Perforated Tank' (review) I, 2, 15 October, 1921, p.29.

FOCUS: A PERIODICAL TO THE POINT IN MATTERS OF HEALTH, WEALTH & LIFE
(the following items are essays)
'The Queen of Spring', V, 5, May 1928, pp.259-62.
'Anticipation', V, 6, June 1928, pp.322-5.
'Compensations?', VI, 1, July 1928, pp.3-7.
'Madame August', VI, 2, August 1928, pp.67-71.
'Decadence', VI, 3, September 1928, pp.131-4.
'Puritanism', VI, 4 ,October 1928, pp.195-8.
'Peace', VI, 5, November 1928, pp.259-62.
'Post Early', VI, 6, December 1928, pp.327-31.

GOLDEN HIND: A QUARTERLY MAGAZINE OF ART AND LITERATURE
'Helen' (poem), II, 7, April 1924, p.31.

LIFE AND LETTERS TODAY
'Nook on Parnassus' (short story), XIII, 2, December 1935, pp.84-8.
'C.F. Ramuz' (essay), XIV, 4, Summer 1936, pp.46-7.
'Novels' (review), XV, 6, Winter 1936, pp.188-9.
'Yeats of Bloomsbury' (essay), XXI, 20, April 1939, pp.60-6.
'Prayer' (poem in translation), XXI, 22, June 1939, p.7.
'Adventure for Readers' (review), XXII, 23, July 1939, pp.45-52.

'A Talk about Talking' (essay), XXIII, 27 [*sic*; erratum for 26], December 1939, pp.286-8.
'Needless Worry' (essay), XXIV, 30, February 1940, pp.160-3.
'Haven' (short story), XLII, 84, August 1944, pp.97-105.
'Visitor' (short story), XLVI, 97, September 1945, pp.167-72.
'Visit' (short story), XLVI, 97, September 1945, pp.173-81.
'Work in Progress' (extract from *March Moonlight*), XLIX, 104, April 1946, pp.20-44.
'Work in Progress' (extract from *March Moonlight*), XLIX, 105, May 1946, pp.99-114.
'Work in Progress' (extract from *March Moonlight*), LI, 111, November 1946, pp.79-88.
'Novels' (essay), LVI, 127, March 1948, pp.188-92.

LITTLE REVIEW

Interim serialized 1919-20, as follows:
VI, June 1919, pp.3-25.
VI, July 1919, pp.11-24.
VI, August 1919, pp.5-28.
VI, September 1919, pp.56-61.
VI, October 1919, pp.38-54.
VI, November 1919, pp.34-8.
VI, December 1919, pp.20-8.
VI, January 1920, pp.37-48.
VI, March 1920, pp.17-26.
VI, April 1920, pp.26-34.
VII, May-June 1920, pp.53-61.
'Equilibrium' (dialogue), VIII, 2, Spring 1922, p.37.
'The Man from Nowhere' (essay), X, 1 [*sic;* erratum for 2] Autumn 1924-Winter 1925, pp.32-5.

OUTLOOK

'The Russian and His Book' (unsigned), X, 4 October, 1902, pp.267-8.
'Sleigh Ride' (selection from *Oberland*), LVIII, 11 December, 1926, p.588.
'Gift' (poem), LXI, 2 June, 1928, p.678.

PLAIN TALK

'Cosmic Thinking' (review; unsigned), July 1913, p.13.
'Slavery' (review; unsigned), July 1913, pp.13-14.

THE PLOUGHSHARE

'The Reality of Feminism' (review), New Series, 2, September 1917, pp.241-6.

POETRY: A MAGAZINE OF VERSE

(the following items are poems)
'Waiting', XXIV, 3, June 1924, pp.142-4.

'Buns for Tea', XXIV, 3, June 1924, pp.144-5. Reprinted in *Yesterday and Today: A Comparative Anthology of Poetry*, ed. Louis Untermeyer, Harcourt, Brace & Co., New York, [1926], pp.152-3.

'Three Poems: Sussex; Discovery; Barbara', XXVII, 2, November 1925, pp.67-9.

'Message', XXX, 5, August 1927, p.256. Also published in *Outlook*, LIX, 1510, 8 January, 1927.

PURPOSE

'Resolution' (essay), I, 1, January-March 1929, pp.7-9.

THE QUEEN

'In the Garden' (short story), 2 July, 1924, p.11.

THE SATURDAY REVIEW

(the following items are sketches)

'A Sussex Auction' (unsigned), CV, 13 June, 1908, p.755.
'A Sussex Carrier' (unsigned), CVII, 19 June, 1909, pp.782-3.
'Hay-Time' (unsigned), CVIII, 31 July, 1909, p.132.
'A Village Competition' (unsigned), CVIII, 7 August, 1909, pp.165-6.
'Haven' (unsigned), CVIII, 9 October, 1909, pp.440-1
'The Wind' (unsigned), CVIII, 4 December, 1909, p.691.
'December' (unsigned), CVIII, 25 December, 1909, pp.785-6.
'The End of the Winter' (unsigned), CIX, 19 February, 1910, pp.234-5.
'Lodge Night' (unsigned), CX, 19 November, 1910, pp.642-3.
'Dans La Bise' (unsigned), CXI, 14 January, 1911, pp.46-7.
'Gruyères' (unsigned), CXI, 18 February, 1911, pp.208-9.
'March' (unsigned), CXI, 4 March, 1911, p.267.
'The Holiday' (unsigned), CXII, 26 August, 1911, pp.268-9.
'The Conflict' (initialled), CXII, 25 November, 1911, pp.673-4.
'Across the Year', CXII, 23 December, 1911, pp.895-6.
'Welcome', CXIII, 18 May, 1912, pp.620-1.
'Strawberries', CXIII, 22 June, 1912, pp.778-9.
'August', CXIV, 3 August, 1912, p.142.
'Peach Harvest', CXVI, 19 July, 1913, pp.78-9.
'Dusk' (unsigned), CXIII, 10 October, 1914, pp.392-3.
(Letter to the Editor)
'The Human Touch' (signed), CIX, 4 June, 1910, p.724.

SIGNATURES: WORK IN PROGRESS

Selections from *Clear Horizon*, 1, Spring 1936, n.p.

SPECTATOR

'Dark Harmony' (poem), CLXIX, 5973, 18 December, 1942, p.573.

SPHERE

'Barbara' (poem), XCV, 13 October, 1923, p.46. Reprinted in 'Three

Poems: Sussex; Discovery; Barbara' in *Poetry: A Magazine of Verse*, op. cit.

'Veterans in the Alps' (essay), XCVI, 29 March, 1924, p.354.

'Alpine Spring' (essay), XCVII, 12 April, 1924, p.44.

'Discovery' (poem), XCVIII, 2 August, 1924, p.142. Reprinted in 'Three Poems: Sussex; Discovery; Barbara' in *Poetry: A Magazine of Verse*, op. cit.

'The Role of the Background: English Visitors to the Swiss Resorts During the Winter Sports Season' (essay), XCIX, 22 November, 1924, p.226.

'Spring upon the Threshold' (poem), C, 28 March, 1925, p.350.

TRANSATLANTIC REVIEW

'The Garden' (sketch), II, 2, August 1924, pp.141-3.

VANITY FAIR (New York)

(these items are essays)

'Talent and Genius: Is Not Genius Actually Far More Common than Talent?', XXI, October 1923, pp.118, 120.

'Women and the Future: A Trembling of the Veil Before the Eternal Mystery of "La Giaconda" [*sic*]', XXII, April 1924, pp.39-40.

'Women in the Arts: Some Notes on the Eternally Conflicting Demands of Humanity and Art', XXIV, May 1925, pp.47, 100.

'Antheil of New Jersey', XXV, November 1925, pp. 136, 138.

'Talkies, Plays and Books: Thoughts on the Approaching Battle Between the Spoken Pictures, Literature and the Stage', XXXII, August 1929, p.56.

WEEKLY WESTMINSTER GAZETTE

'It Is Finished' (poem), II, 60, 7 August, 1923, p.17.

'Truth' (poem), New Series, I, 10, 5 January, 1924, p.316. Reprinted as 'Freedom' in *Modern British Poetry – A Critical Anthology*, ed. Louis Untermeyer, rev. ed., Harcourt, Brace & Co., New York, 1925, p.312.

'Death' (short story), New Series, I, 15, 9 February 1924, p.466.

WILSON BULLETIN

Letter to Dilly Tante in 'Dilly Tante Observes', VI, December 1931, p.285.

WINDOW: A QUARTERLY MAGAZINE

'Ordeal' (short story), I, 4, October 1930, pp.2-9. Reprinted in *Best British Short Stories of 1931*, ed. Edward J. O'Brien. Dodd, Mead & Co., New York, 1931.

5 *Translations*

Consumption Doomed by Dr Paul Carton, Healthy Life Booklets, Vol. 7, C.W. Daniel, London, 1913.

Some Popular Foodstuffs Exposed by Dr Paul Carton, Healthy Life Booklets, Vol. 11, C.W. Daniel, London, 1913.

Man's Best Food by Prof. Dr Gustav Krüger, C.W. Daniel, London, 1914.

The DuBarry by Karl von Schumacher, G.G. Harrap, London, 1932. [*Madame DuBarry,* Zurich, 1931.]

Mammon by Robert Neumann, Peter Davies, London, 1933. [*Die Macht*, Leipzig, 1931; Berlin, 1932.]

André Gide: His Life and His Works by Leon Pierre-Quint, Jonathan Cape, London, 1934; Knopf, New York, 1934. [*André Gide: Sa Vie, Son Oeuvre*, Paris, 1932.]

Jews in Germany by Josef Kastein (pseud. of Julius Katzenstein), Cresset Press, London, 1934.

Silent Hours by Robert de Traz, G. Bell, London, 1934. [*Les Heures de Silence*, Paris, 1934.]

C Supporting Texts

Adam International Review, XXXI, 310-11-12, 1966. (Issue devoted to the personalities and work of Proust and Richardson.)

Allen, Walter, *The English Novel* [1954], Penguin, London, 1960. (Walter Allen wrote the Introduction to the Dent Collected Edition of *Pilgrimage,* 1967.)

Alpers, Antony, *The Life of Katherine Mansfield*, The Viking Press, New York, 1980.

Alvarez, A., *The Savage God: A Study of Suicide* [1971], Penguin, London, 1974.

Appignanesi, Lisa, *Femininity and the Creative Imagination*, Vision Press, London, 1973.

Ardener, Shirley, *Perceiving Women*, Malaby Press, London, 1975.

Auden, W.H., *Secondary Worlds*, Faber & Faber, London, 1968.

Bateson, F.W., *The Scholar-Critic: An Introduction to Literary Research*, Routledge & Kegan Paul, London, 1972.

Beach, J.W., *The Twentieth Century Novel* [1932], Appleton-Century-Crofts, New York, 1960.

Beer, Patricia, *Reader, I Married Him*, Macmillan, London, 1974.

Bell, Quentin, *Virginia Woolf: A Biography*, 2 vols., Hogarth Press, London, 1973.

Benet, Mary Kathleen, *Writers in Love*, Macmillan, New York, 1977.

Bergonzi, Bernard, *The Early H.G. Wells: A Study of the Scientific Romances*, Manchester University Press, 1961.

Bergonzi, Bernard, *The Situation of The Novel* [1970], Penguin, London, 1972.

Bergonzi, Bernard (ed.), *H.G. Wells: A Collection of Critical Essays,* Prentice-Hall, Englewood Cliffs, N.J., 1976.

Bernstein, Basil, 'Social Structure, Language and Learning', in *The Psychology of Language, Thought and Instruction*, ed. John P. de Cecco, Holt, Rinehart & Winston, New York, 1969.

Bradbury, Malcolm, *The Social Context of Modern English Literature*, Blackwell, Oxford, 1971.

Brecher, Ruth and Edward, *Human Sexual Response*, André Deutsch, London, 1967.

Brittain, Vera, *Radclyffe Hall: A Case of Obscenity?*, Femina Books, 1968.

Brome, Vincent, 'A Last Meeting with Dorothy Richardson', in *London Magazine*, 6, June 1959.

Brontë, Anne, 'Preface', *The Tenant of Wildfell Hall*, July 22, 2nd. ed., 1848.

Burns, Elizabeth and Tom (eds.), *Sociology of Literature and Drama*, Penguin, London, 1973.

Chesler, Phyllis, *Women and Madness* [1972], Allen Lane, London, 1974.

Coward, Ros, 'The Making of the Feminine', *Spare Rib*, 70, May 1978.

Culler, Jonathan, *Structuralist Poetics*, Routledge & Kegan Paul, London, 1975.

Dane, Clemence, *Regiment of Women* [1917], Heinemann, London, 1966.

Eliot, T.S., 'Dante', in *Selected Essays* [1932], Faber & Faber, London, 1951.

Eliot, T.S., *Four Quartets*, Faber & Faber, London, 1944.

Ellman, Mary, *Thinking about Women*, Macmillan, London, 1968.

Ellman, Richard, and Feidelson, Charles (eds.), *The Modern Tradition: Backgrounds of Modern Literature*, Oxford University Press, New York, 1965.

Faderman, Lillian, *Surpassing the Love of Men: Romantic Friendship and Love between Women from the Renaissance to the Present*, Junction Books, London, 1981.

Ford, Ford Madox, *The March of Literature: From Confucius to Modern Times* [1938], Allen & Unwin, London, 1947.

Foster, Jeanette H., *Sex Variant Women in Literature*, Frederick Muller, London, 1958.

Fromm, Gloria Glikin, 'Through the Novelist's Looking-Glass', in *H. G. Wells: A Collection of Critical Essays*, ed. Bernard Bergonzi, Prentice-Hall, Englewood Cliffs, N.J., 1976.

Fromm, Gloria Glikin, *Dorothy Richardson: A Biography*, University of Illinois Press, Chicago. 1977.

[Fromm], Gloria Glikin, 'Dorothy M. Richardson: The Personal "Pilgrimage" ', *Proceedings of the Modern Languages Association*, 78, December 1963.

Gordon, Ian A., *Katherine Mansfield*, Longmans, Green & Co., London, 1954.

Gregory, Horace, *Dorothy Richardson: An Adventure in Self-Discovery*, Holt, Rinehart & Winston, New York, 1967.

Hall, Radclyffe, *The Well of Loneliness* [1928], Pocket Books, New York, 1964.

Hays, H.R., *The Dangerous Sex: The Myth of Feminine Evil*, Methuen, London, 1966.

Holland, Norman N., *The Dynamics of Literary Response*, Oxford University Press, New York, 1968.

Janeway, Elizabeth, *Man's World Woman's Place: A Study in Social Mythology*, Michael Joseph, London, 1972.

Kaplan, Sydney Janet, *Feminine Consciousness in the Modern British Novel*, University of Illinois Press, Chicago, 1975.

Klein, Viola, *The Feminine Character*, Routledge, London, 2nd. ed., 1946.

Kleinberg, Seymour (ed.), *The Other Persuasion*, Random House, New York, 1977.

Laurenson, Diana, and Swingewood, Alan, *The Sociology of Literature*, Paladin, London, 1972.

Leavis, F.R., 'Johnson and Augustanism', in *The Common Pursuit* [1952], Penguin, London, 1962.

Lessing, Doris, *The Golden Notebook* [1962], Panther, London, 1973.

Lewis, C.S., *The Four Loves*, Geoffrey Bles, London, 1960.

Lewis, R.W.B., *The American Adam: Innocence, Tragedy, and Tradition in the Nineteenth Century*, University of Chicago Press, Chicago and London, 1955.

Lodge, David, *Language of Fiction: Essays in Criticism and Verbal Analysis of the English Novel*, Routledge & Kegan Paul, London, 1966.

MacMillan, William J., *The Reluctant Healer*, Gollancz, London, 1952.

Marder, Herbert, *Feminism and Art: A Study of Virginia Woolf*, University of Chicago Press, Chicago, 1968.

Milgram, Stanley, 'Liberating Effects of Group Pressure', *Journal of Personality and Social Psychology*, 1, 1965.

Miller, Casey, and Swift, Kate, *Words and Women: New Language in New Times*, Gollancz, London, 1977.

Millet, Kate, *Sexual Politics* [1969], Rupert Hart-Davis, London, 1971.

Mitchell, Juliet, *Women's Estate* [1966], Pelican, London, 1971.

Mitchell, Juliet, *Psychoanalysis and Feminism*, Allen Lane, London, 1974.

M[oore], L[esley] (pseudonym of Ida Baker), *Katherine Mansfield*, Michael Joseph, London, 1971.

Murry, J. Middleton (ed.), *Journal of Katherine Mansfield*, Constable, London, 1927.

Murry, J. Middleton (ed.), *The Letters of Katherine Mansfield*, 2 vols., Constable, London, 1928.

Murry J. Middleton (ed.), *Novels and Novelists by Katherine Mansfield*, Constable, London, 1930.

Murry, J. Middleton (ed.), *Katherine Mansfield's Letters to John Middleton Murry*, Constable, London, 1951.

Oakley, Ann, *Sex, Gender and Society*, Temple Smith, London, 1972.

Ornstein, Robert E., *The Psychology of Consciousness* [1972], Penguin, London, 1975.

Paulin, Tom, 'Fugitive Spirits', review of *Dorothy Richardson* by Gloria G[likin]. Fromm, *New Statesman*, 21 July, 1978.

Popper, K. R., *The Open Society and Its Enemies, Vol. I: Plato* [1945], Routledge & Kegan Paul, London, 1962.

Powys, John Cowper, *Dorothy Richardson*, Joiner & Steele, London, 1931.

Rich, Adrienne, *Of Woman Born: Motherhood as Experience and Institution* [1976], Virago, London, 1977.

Rosaldo, Michelle Zimbalist and Lamphère, Louise (eds.), *Women, Culture and Society*, Stanford University Press, 1974.

Rosenberg, John, *Dorothy Richardson: The Genius They Forgot: A Critical Biography*, Duckworth, London, 1973.

Rosenthal, R., and Jacobson, L., *Pygmalion in the Classroom: Teacher Expectation and Pupils' Intellectual Development*, Holt, Rinehart & Winston, New York, 1968.

Rosenthal, R., *Experimenter Effects in Behavioural Research*, Appleton-Century-Crofts, New York, 1966.

Rosenthal, R., and Lawson, R., *A Longitudinal Study of the Effects of Experimenter Bias on the Operant Learning of Laboratory Rats*, Harvard University, 1961.

Rossi, Alice S. (ed.), *The Feminist Papers: From Adams to de Beauvoir*, Columbia University Press, New York, 1973.

Rule, Jane, *Lesbian Images*, Doubleday, New York, 1975.

Sacks, Karen, 'Social Bases for Sexual Equality: A Comparative View', in *Sisterhood is Powerful*, ed. Robin Morgan, Vintage, New York, 1970.

Schachter, S., and Singer, J. E., 'Cognitive, Social and Physiological Determinants of Emotional States', *Psychological Review*, 69, 1962.

Sherfey, Mary Jane, *The Nature and Evolution of Female Sexuality* [1966], Random House, New York, 1972.

Showalter, Elaine, *A Literature of Their Own: British Women Novelists from Brontë to Lessing* [1977], Virago, 1978.

Sinclair, May, 'The Novels of Dorothy Richardson', *The Egoist*, April 1918, pp. 57-9.

Spacks, Patricia Meyer, *The Female Imagination: A Literary And Psychological Investigation of Women's Writing* [1972], Allen & Unwin, London, 1976.

Spender, Dale, *Man Made Language*, Routledge & Kegan Paul, London, 1980.

Tooley, Sarah A., 'Some Women Novelists' in *The Woman at Home*, [no date; *c.*1890], pp.164-6.

Trickett, Rachel, 'The Living Dead – V: Dorothy Richardson', *London Magazine*, 6, June 1959.

Vernon, P.E. (ed.), *Creativity*, Penguin Modern Psychology Readings, Penguin, London, 1970.

Weisstein, Naomi, '"Kinde [*sic*], Kuche, Kirche" as Scientific Law: Psychology Constructs the Female', in *Sisterhood is Powerful*, ed. Robin Morgan, Vintage, New York, 1970; reprinted in *Radical Feminism*, eds. Anne Koedt, Ellen Levine and Anita Rapone, Quadrangle Books, New York, 1973.

Wells, H. G., *Experiment in Autobiography*, 2 vols., Gollancz and The Cresset Press, London, 1934.

Wells, H. G., *Selected Short Stories* [1927], Penguin, London, 1973.

Wolff, Charlotte, *Love Between Women*, Duckworth, London, 1971.

Woolf, Virginia, *Collected Essays*, 4 vols., ed, Leonard Woolf, Chatto & Windus, London, 1966.

Woolf, Virginia, *Moments of Being: Unpublished Autobiographical Writings of Virginia Woolf*, ed. Jeanne Schulkind, Sussex University Press and Chatto & Windus, London, 1976.

Woolf, Virginia, 'Romance and the Heart', *The Nation and The Athenaeum*, Literary Supplement, 19 May, 1923.

Woolf, Virginia, *A Room of One's Own*, Hogarth Press, London, 1929.

Woolf, Virginia, *A Writer's Diary: Being Extracts from the Diary of Virginia Woolf*, ed. Leonard Woolf, Hogarth Press, London, 1953.

Women and Literature Collective, The, *An Annotated Bibliography of Women Writers*, 3rd ed., The Women and Literature Collective, Cambridge, Mass., 1976.